CONSPIRING TO HEAL

CONSPIRING

to

HEAL

A LOVE STORY

VAN METAXAS

BUENA VISTA BOOKS

For Maria

•

Soul to soul
through all the years

CONTENTS

I went up to the mountain,
Because you asked me to

—PATTY GRIFFIN, "UP TO THE MOUNTAIN (MLK SONG)"

Beyond mountains there are mountains.

—HAITIAN PROVERB, QUOTED BY TRACY KIDDER IN *MOUNTAINS BEYOND MOUNTAINS*

CONSPIRING TO HEAL

introduction

◆

HOPE IS NOT OPTIONAL

I KNEW SHE WOULDN'T live forever. People with advanced colon cancer rarely do. But I'd hoped through our ingenuity and her fierce determination that she'd live to see our seven-year-old son graduate from high school. That was the plan at least—the one that motivated her every day to do whatever it took to endure the indignities of cancer and its treatment.

After my wife, Maria Grayson-Metaxas, died, thirty-one months after her diagnosis, a number of doctors told me she was an outlier, and that her reliance on cutting-edge creative oncology prolonged her life dramatically. I knew that to be the case. Even though Maria refused to hear what her prognosis was—she felt it would interfere with her will to survive—I read the medical research and knew the odds.

But as she did with most things in our thirty-year romance and marriage, Maria taught me to have faith in what I could not see, in what opened the heart, and in what was improbable. She taught me that in order to gain anything, you have to lose everything. She taught me how to love and, eventually, how to die.

We met in college, when we barely knew who we were and what we were made of. And our first flush of love inspired us to stay together, despite different backgrounds and ways of being in the

i

world, which often left us feeling disappointed, misunderstood, or hurt. Though the vicissitudes of life sometimes ground us down, they also polished us, and deepened our love and devotion. We became soul friends—or, in the words of the Irish teacher and poet, John O'Donohue, *anam cara,* two souls whose intimate bond neither time nor space can touch.

In the last weeks of Maria's life, she asked me to help her relinquish her role as wife and mother and turn to face her reunion with God. She wanted nothing less than to be fully awake and present to her own death—to use it to grow emotionally and spiritually. And she used our inestimable love for each other as a sanctuary and port of call from which to venture further and further out from her broken and bedridden body to the edge of the known universe. She got her wish: she died fully conscious and radiant, like a shimmering diamond.

AT A CRUCIAL moment in the Stars Wars movie *The Empire Strikes Back,* when Han Solo and Chewbacca are planning to avoid their capture by escaping into an asteroid belt, the droid C3PO admonishes Han: "Sir, the possibility of successfully navigating an asteroid field is 3,720 to 1."

Han snaps back, "Never tell me the odds," and then rushes the starship, the *Millennium Falcon,* headlong into the oncoming asteroids.

Maria was diagnosed with stage IV colon cancer on January 15, 2010. She never asked her oncologists what the odds were of surviving past five years, the standard benchmark for determining the severity of a cancer and the effectiveness of its treatment. On some level, she knew the odds were not in her favor, but she also knew that to improve her chances of survival she had to protect a core part of herself that believed she could beat the odds, that she could be an outlier.

Like Han Solo, she had to believe in the improbable and in her own capacity to write her own script. And that also meant not letting anyone damage the very force in her—in all of us—that's essential to healing: her spirit.

A diagnosis of a stage IV cancer means that cancer has spread from the primary tumor site, where it originated, to another organ, and is the most advanced stage. To put it in perspective, there is no stage V. Such a diagnosis can bring with it a sense of powerlessness and hopelessness, especially when a medical professional tells you that you'll never be cancer-free and will be in treatment for the rest of your life, without offering a comprehensive plan to engage your imagination, marshal all your resources, and instill hope.

From early in her treatment, Maria tried to surround herself with people who knew the difference between hope and optimism and could help her cultivate the former while grieving the absence of the latter.

"Optimism is the recognition that the odds are in your favor; hope is the faith that things will work out whatever the odds," wrote David Orr, the distinguished environmental thinker, in an essay in *Conservation Biology* called "Optimism and Hope in a Hotter Time." "Hope is a verb with its sleeves rolled up. Hopeful people are actively engaged in defying or changing the odds. Optimism leans back, puts its feet up, and wears a confident look knowing that the deck is stacked."

Stage IV cancer patients can live without optimism—they know the deck is not stacked in their favor—but they cannot live without hope. They have to roll up their sleeves, defy the odds, and take their treatment into their own hands. And that's exactly what Maria did, fiercely.

After starting cancer treatment with a traditional oncologist, she changed course in midstream and chose to pursue an integrative oncology path, which offers the very real possibility of altering the calculus of survival by actively engaging in your own treatment. Instead of being a passive recipient of chemotherapy, Maria found a team of doctors and clinicians who emboldened her to take control over every aspect of her life, from what she ate and how strenuously she exercised to taking an extensive and personalized combination of herbs, supplements, and nontoxic drugs not typically prescribed for cancer. The latter, added to a comprehensive treatment plan, strengthened her immune system and made chemotherapy itself more effective.

The full-court press added much needed time to her life, and allowed her, our son Satchi, and me to awaken more deeply to the preciousness of everyday life and to the remarkable, eternal love at the heart of our relationships.

AFTER MARIA'S DEATH, one of her doctors wrote, "Once in awhile, people enter your life and change you forever. Maria was one of those people." She changed mine, and her story just might change yours.

AUTHOR'S NOTE:

I've changed the names and identifying features of four doctors early in the book—Maria's internist, first oncologist, gastroenterologist, and surgeon—and the name of a skilled nursing facility later in the book, where my mother received physical therapy toward the end of her life. However, I have not altered conversations and have remained faithful to how events unfolded.

the

FIRST
MOVEMENT

one

♦

RECENTERING

I came home late from work that night.

I had squeezed in a new client at the end of my workday, a husband and wife who needed immediate couples therapy, and finished later than usual. Driving home to Berkeley over the San Francisco–Oakland Bay Bridge, I began to feel the anxiety I'd managed to set aside all day. The day before, Maria had had CT scans of her chest, abdomen, and pelvis to rule out gastritis, an inflammation of the stomach lining—the tentative diagnosis given to account for her anemia, weight loss, and fatigue. I hadn't heard from her during the day, and it was a quarter to nine by the time I opened the front door. I knew she'd be tired and prepping for tomorrow's colonoscopy.

She greeted me in the entryway, draped her arms around my neck, and whispered into my ear.

"Dr. Huron just called, ten minutes ago. She said I might have ovarian cancer."

She fell into my body, and we sank to the floor.

"Oh, my God. I'm so sorry."

1

"These were the hardest ten minutes of my life, waiting for you to come home from work. I didn't know how I was going to survive to put Satchi to bed without you."

We held each other tight for what seemed like an eternity, shock containing our tears, before our seven-year old son, Satchi, playing upstairs in his bedroom, called out, "Who's going to put me to bed tonight?"

"I got him," I told Maria.

I tried to compose myself, but felt shaken and disoriented, and worried that Satchi had heard us. Would he ask why we were whispering? Would he search my face for clues?

After I finished Satchi's bedtime ritual, Maria joined us on his bed. She hugged and kissed her boy, just like any other night in our household. Then she took my hand and walked me into our bedroom, where we waited quietly on the bed until we were sure Satchi was asleep.

She had fight in her voice when she began. "I can't believe Dr. Huron would call me to tell me I had cancer. It's so insensitive for her to just call and announce that out of the blue—ovarian cancer!—especially when she told us last week that she thought I had gastritis."

"I know. What an awful way to find out. I wish I were here with you when you got the call," I said, feeling both her and my own disbelief and indignation, as well as the devastation they masked. "I feel terrible that I was late tonight, that you were alone."

We rehashed the conversation, avoiding the message it so unceremoniously delivered. When my anger dissipated, I said, "But Dr. Huron knows you have a colonoscopy for tomorrow morning. Maybe she didn't want to wait until next week to get you back into her office. Maybe she only had bad choices: wait to tell us in person or call to tell you on the phone."

"You're probably right."

"What else did she say? Did she say how far along the cancer is? What the prognosis is?"

"No, she didn't say much, just that it looked like I had ovarian cancer, but I should go ahead and have the colonoscopy anyhow."

"What are we going to tell Satchi?" I asked. "I'm sure he knew something was up tonight, with us so quiet and trying not to cry."

"Probably. We don't want to scare him. But it won't be a surprise to him that Mommy's sick. He knows I've been losing a lot of weight and I'm tired all the time."

This was painfully true. Maria had become increasingly debilitated over the last six months. Down now to ninety-five pounds, she weighed what she did in middle school. After routine excursions, like walking Satchi to school, she needed to lie on the couch for hours to regain her strength. Maria's internist, Dr. Miranda Sheridan, determined that she was anemic in early December and referred her to Dr. Huron, a blood specialist in San Francisco. Because of the holidays, Maria had to wait to see her until the new year. We had no reason to believe the consultation was so important that we should have found another specialist right away.

By Christmas vacation, Maria was confined to the house and spent most of the day on the couch. It was common for her to rest when tired, but this was altogether different—and frightening. She had worked as a massage therapist for most of her adult life, started surfing in her mid-thirties, and had lived as healthfully as anyone I knew. But now that she'd lost weight and strength, she could no longer work, nor catch waves at Pacifica, her favorite local beach. Physically, she was a shadow of her former self.

"It's getting late," Maria finally said, "and we need to get up very early for my colonoscopy. Maybe we should try to go to bed."

"I doubt I can sleep. I'm full of adrenaline, like I'm in fight-or-flight mode."

"Me, too, but let's try."

In the middle of the night, I tiptoed downstairs to my computer in the living room. I learned from the Internet that cancer is classified into four categories, with stage I being the least advanced and stage IV the most severe, when cancer has spread from its original site to other organs. I also learned that ovarian cancer was referred to as a "silent killer," since it is nearly impossible to detect until it has metastasized, and then life expectancy is short in nearly all instances.

I returned to bed devastated. In the morning, I learned that Maria had also tiptoed downstairs to research her fate.

UNTIL OUR FIRST consultation with Dr. Claire Huron, right after New Year's, the word *cancer* had never crossed our minds. When Dr. Sheridan referred her to a hematologist, neither one of us knew that most hematologists are also oncologists; we had no reason to know the two are paired.

We learned that lesson when, arriving at Maria's first appointment, we saw Dr. Huron's shingle on the waiting room door: Hematology and Oncology. I noticed Maria noticing what I had just noticed, and for the very first time, I began to wonder what else might be happening in my wife's body. She'd been slightly anemic numerous times over the years, but never enough to raise concern.

A nurse collected us from the waiting room and brought us back to an examination room. Waiting to meet Dr. Huron, I noticed a picture of Venice's famed canals on the consulting room wall and said, "Shall we fly to Venice for the weekend once you get all better?"

"I'd love that," Maria responded, a smile softening the tension on her lips momentarily.

Just then, Dr. Huron opened the door, extended her hand to Maria, and sat down opposite her. Looking her over carefully, the doctor started to ask a series of well-constructed questions to determine why this ostensibly healthy forty-eight-year-old woman sitting in front of her was debilitated and unable to participate fully in her life.

Looking at Maria's blood work, she confirmed that Maria was severely anemic.

"There are three possible reasons why someone would be anemic," she said. "They're not eating well, their digestive tract is not absorbing nutrients from their food, or they're bleeding internally."

After taking an extensive history, she suspected that Maria was bleeding internally.

"Why would someone be bleeding internally?" Maria asked.

"Given your age," she answered, "It's unlikely that you have cancer, but you might have gastritis, a chronic irritation and swelling of the stomach lining." She added, "Gastritis could account for the internal bleeding and the prevailing symptom, anemia."

"Gastritis is better than cancer," I thought. Maria and I both breathed a sigh of relief.

A month earlier, Dr. Sheridan had ordered CT scans and a colonoscopy, a procedure that involves a gastroenterologist winding a very tiny camera up the rectum and through the large intestine to determine its health. As with Dr. Huron, Maria had to wait until the new year to schedule these tests. Now Dr. Huron said Maria needed to get them as soon as possible to confirm her diagnostic impressions.

I hesitated to ask the next question, since I hadn't discussed it with Maria first, but the topic was a source of marital tension, and I wanted to know. "For the past couple of years, Maria's sex drive has waned and all but disappeared. Could the anemia account for that, and will it bounce back after the anemia is reversed?"

"When you're as anemic as you are, you have very little energy for life, let alone sex," Dr. Huron said supportively. "Let's take one step at a time."

We left the oncologist's office feeling optimistic that we now had a coherent narrative to explain Maria's decline—and a plan: CT scans in one week, followed two days later by a colonoscopy, and then regrouping with Dr. Huron. We had every reason to believe that Maria would soon find out that she had severe gastritis, and that in a few months she and I would fly to Venice for a romantic weekend to celebrate her recovery. We hadn't anticipated a late-night phone call in between the scans and the scope.

FRIDAY, JANUARY 15TH

I had cancelled my morning clients several weeks before in anticipation of Maria's colonoscopy. During the two-hour procedure, I waited outside the doctor's office in the lobby of an historic San Francisco building, a 120-foot elliptical dome rising above me. I felt small, scared, and forlorn, and I prayed to God, asking for a miracle. Needing to hear a familiar voice, I called my friend Clark five times. No answer. I tried two other friends. They, too, didn't answer, and I began to feel forsaken.

When Clark finally returned my distressed voicemails—"Please call me! I need you!"—I answered my cell phone but couldn't speak. I was so relieved to hear his voice I began to sob. A woman walked into the small alcove of mailboxes where I'd retreated and handed me some Kleenex, a small act of kindness that touched me deeply. As the sobbing subsided, I told Clark about Maria's diagnosis and then started to feel cold. My body shook. Clark listened silently.

Exhausted, I walked back to the doctor's office to wait for Maria.

After the colonoscopy, Maria joined me in the waiting area. The post-procedure nurse told us Dr. Ronald Morton wanted to meet in private to discuss the results and invited us into a small side room filled with boxes and medical records and a foam sofa-sleeper hardly big enough for the two of us to sit side by side. When he arrived and sat across from us, his chair was higher than the couch. I felt like a schoolchild.

"Okay, folks. After viewing your colon, I'm certain that you have colon, and not ovarian, cancer."

Maria squeezed my hand. I felt like a life sentence had been lifted. "How can you tell the difference?" I asked.

"Well. It's hard. Ovarian and colon cancer cells look very much alike," he explained. "But after seeing the tumor, it appears to be growing from within the colon, into the colon wall. If it were ovarian cancer, it would have infiltrated through the wall, and its presentation would look different."

He stopped to take a gauge of our response, then continued, "I think a diagnosis of colon cancer can account for all of your symptoms: the bleeding, the anemia, the exhaustion."

"So what do we do from here?" Maria asked.

"A large tumor is partially obstructing your colon," he said. "A fairly simple surgery will do the trick. We can fit you in at the hospital next Tuesday."

Dr. Morton's upbeat diagnosis and treatment plan left us both confused. Something was missing.

"But why would Dr. Huron say Maria may have ovarian cancer, given your certainty that she has colon cancer?" I asked.

"I don't know," he said, "but I saw the tumor with my own eyes, and it's consistent with colon cancer."

Maybe Dr. Huron had made a mistake—after all, she had not seen the tumor with her own eyes.

"Have you seen the CT scans?" I wondered, a part of me sensing that he, not unlike the blind men who touch different parts of the elephant and draw different conclusions about the beast, had based his diagnosis on partial information. He looked surprised.

"No, I haven't seen the scans, but of course I'll call Dr. Huron right away and sort all this out, hopefully by the end of the day."

As we walked back to the car, Maria and I felt like we were on an emotional roller coaster: first the likely diagnosis of ovarian cancer; then the dramatic reprieve, a different diagnosis from Dr. Morton. But then, suddenly, everything was still up in the air—uncertain and inconclusive.

Sitting in our car, I called Clark again.

"It now seems possible that Maria has colon cancer. We hope she does; the prognosis is better." I never thought I'd hear myself say, "I hope Maria has colon cancer," but such is the strange universe you enter when a loved one is diagnosed with cancer and you start to bargain over life expectancy.

BEHIND CLOSED DOORS at home that night, Maria and I consulted with Dr. Huron on the phone. She said Maria's diagnosis was complex; the tumors in her colon were only one piece of this puzzle. She had tumors in her abdomen and pelvic area, as well as small indeterminate lesions in her liver. The pathology report might help determine what kind of cancer Maria had, though ovarian cancer and colon cancer—both a type of cancer that develops in glandular tissue called adenocarcinoma—look identical under the microscope.

Though unlikely, it was possible Maria had both colon and ovarian cancer. She would need to start chemotherapy as soon as possible and to meet with a surgeon to install a portacath, an intravenous hookup that's surgically placed under the skin below the collarbone. It serves, instead of the veins in the arm, as the access point for chemotherapy treatments. We held each other and cried. The die had been cast. There was no turning back.

Satchi, whom we'd left alone downstairs, eventually knocked on our bedroom door. We let him in. We both knew it would be better for him to be inside with us rather than listening from outside our door, alone and scared. He crawled into our arms, cried with us, and then asked, "Why are we crying?"

"Oh, honey," I told him, "We just found out that getting Mom healthy will take longer than we'd thought. This has already been so hard on you, and we're all tired, but the truth is we still have a ways to go."

Without hesitation, he asked, "Are you going to die, Mom?"

The inevitable question had arrived, earlier than either of us had anticipated. I held Maria's hand as she said, "We will all die one day, honey, but I'm going to do everything I can to live a long life."

Satchi folded into his mother's arms, and I embraced them both, the delicate cocoon protecting the vulnerable butterflies, all three of us at the mercy of forces beyond our control.

MARIA AND I met on my first day at Princeton, when I moved into a dorm room one down from hers. It may not have been love at first sight, but it was magnetic. A sophomore when we met, Maria liked to say that she repeatedly tried to get my attention—and my affections—during my first year in college, but that I, a freshman boy, was like "an errant arrow, which never hits its mark."

That wasn't entirely true. I felt a mysterious tug in her presence, but I was too scared to admit my desire. She was beautiful, with an innocence and charm about her, and intelligent. In our first conversation,

I learned that she had studied Ancient Greek and Latin in high school *and* middle school; I had barely endured eleventh-grade French. She also moved like few girls I had ever met, gracefully, as though my desire could be seen in her gait. Whenever I saw her in the hallway with her boyfriend, who was a senior (four years older than me), I felt small and inconsequential. I didn't dare test the waters only to discover that this belle from South Carolina had different designs than my own.

Years later, Maria told me that she used to hang out in the hallway hoping I would emerge from my room—and my studies—to play. When I did, we'd pass the hours sitting on the floor, talking and flirting, until a friendship developed naturally. I came to rely on how I felt in her presence: uniquely and irreplaceably accepted for myself.

A month after Maria died, I found a box of her journals tucked away in the garage. When I lifted the box from the garage floor, the bottom disintegrated and her journals tumbled to the ground. One sheet—only one, an entry from October 8, 1980, a month after we met—wafted down to my feet.

> *I've been spending more and more time with Van because I'm so comfortable with him. Nothing's been said between us, but I think we've both gotten possessive in a strange way . . . Van sees me where I am—he doesn't take shit—yet I think he knows [when I'm lonely and feeling insecure]. I'm hesitant because he's a freshman—dumb reason.*

And then on the reverse side of the page,

> *I wonder where Van will fit into things. He may be a passing stage—we don't know each other well enough for him to be on the level of [other boyfriends], but he's good material, whatever happens.*

During my freshman year, she became more than just good material, and something in me knew that she'd be a part of my destiny—how, I didn't yet know. But I also knew I needed to resist the force a little longer.

Two-and-a-half years later, in February 1983—at the beginning of Maria's last semester and on my first day back from a semester spent studying in London—we ran into each other between the iconic Nassau Hall and Cannon Green. We hugged and slipped on the ice, falling into each other's arms in the snow. Maria sparkled; her eyes revealed her desire. My own longing could've melted the snow. This time we both recognized the force of destiny and made an unspoken pact to consummate our attraction before she graduated.

But first she had to finish her senior thesis—on the image of God in radical feminist theology—and end an unhappy long-distance relationship. She turned to her friend Tom, who she'd briefly dated while I was in London (and who, thirty years later, she called to her bedside before she died), for support in resisting temptation until her thesis was bound, recorded, and turned in to the clerk of the Religion Department.

The last obstacle finally removed, I surprised her outside 1879 Hall to celebrate with champagne and a bag of Orange Milanos, her favorite cookie. That afternoon, a Friday in early April, we explored the threshold of our friendship. Then we spent her last two months at Princeton delighting in what until then we'd each only longed for in private.

Our spring love, however, and her radical thesis, brought her face to face with the limitations of her faith.

"There was no room for an image of God as Goddess in Christianity," she once said, reflecting on the personal crisis precipitated that spring. "After my thesis, I couldn't locate myself in the church anymore, and that's what I was longing to do. But I did find myself when I was with you that spring, and then that summer in Greece. I found my desire. I felt alive."

I spent the summer in Athens researching my thesis on the rise of socialism in postwar Greece. As a graduation gift to herself, Maria flew to Athens to travel the countryside with her new boyfriend, me. Monemvasia, Epidaurus, Delphi, Santorini, Mykonos: these magical places served as backdrop and inspiration for our new relationship.

In Monemvasia, we slept above a bakery and awoke, at four in the morning, to the smell of freshly baked bread. In the ancient amphitheatre in Epidaurus, we read lines from the *Oresteia* and watched the blazing Greek sun set over the mountains beyond the stage. In Delphi, we stood at the foot of the stone stairway that led to the Oracle and wondered what the future would hold for us. In a few short days, we'd go our separate ways: I back to Princeton, and she to Taizé, an ecumenical Christian monastic order and community in Burgundy, France, a pilgrimage place that for many years had inspired her.

Since her midteens, Maria had wanted to become a Christian minister, but she longed to find a way of life guided not by external authority, but by Christ's radically simple, almost revolutionary example. She experienced that at Taizé. Founded in 1940 by a young monk named Frère Roger, who himself longed to create a way of life based on Christ's teachings about peace, justice, and love, Taizé has attracted young people from all around the world with its promise of Christian reconciliation and simplicity.

At Taizé, Maria prayed and meditated in community and experimented with living in silence. Afterward, she returned to her home in Charleston, inspired to do service work there and, one day, in the third world. The main catch was what to do with this young man she had fallen in love with in Greece and now desired to be with.

"Being in love with you was easy," she remarked, "but I was tortured over being sexual with you. Brought up Christian, I was taught premarital sex was a path to hell. And yet, I was strongly influenced by the women's movement. Sex is beautiful. Our bodies are temples to be worshipped. We're the authors of our own lives. I've spent much of my adult life working out the tension between these two forces."

NOT KNOWING WHAT else to do, we followed our hearts.

During the week, Maria worked as the director of religious studies in a local church. On occasional weekends during my senior year, she or I would either drive or take the Amtrak train between Princeton and South Carolina. We exchanged books from our personal libraries—mine politics and philosophy, hers religion and spirituality—spent time with her younger sister, Anne, who was always a source of great joy for Maria, and tried to imagine a life together, in the same city, after I graduated.

But she wanted to do missionary work in Haiti, and I wanted to teach English as a second language in Greece. The desire to be together, however, was stronger than our yen to be expatriates. We agreed to move to Washington, D.C., where Maria joined a Christian service community to work with the city's poor and I pursued a career as a journalist.

Increasingly, we grew disillusioned with our work. Maria encountered a string of unethical ministers, which finished off her desire for seminary. I grew dissatisfied with investigative stories that didn't captivate my imagination. We decided to leave Washington and use a small amount of money Maria had received from her grandfather to relocate to Folly Beach, a long, narrow island twelve miles south of Charleston. There, we discovered the balance of freedom, solitude, and cheap living we needed to reevaluate what was meaningful in our lives.

I found refuge in books, reading with purpose—on depth psychology and human relationships, quantum physics, philosophy of the mind, meditation, and self-inquiry—and took long walks on the beach with Maria, peppering her with my newfound ideas about how to live my life. She pursued an interest in pottery, renting a workspace where she threw pots during the day, and studied art theory at night.

M. C. Richards' classic book *Centering in Pottery, Poetry, and the Person* became her bible. A truly liberating creativity, Maria told me, arises out of compassion, an attentive stillness, self-acceptance, and openness to creative "accidents." Her most challenging and memorable class at Princeton, a ceramics class with the renowned potter Toshiko Takaezu, taught her as much. Toshiko would throw students' creations on the ground if she felt that they hadn't come from an authentic place inside. "No ducks!" she would bark—nothing functional, nothing you can find in a store.

And that's when we started to fight.

Two highly conscientious students our whole lives, we now began to turn our attention away from the world and toward our own muses, and without the support of our community of friends, we didn't have the skills or maturity to balance our new strivings for autonomy with the need to feel secure in our relationship. My intense desire for closeness and emotional recognition, especially after long days lost in thought, threatened Maria. And her need to have her own separate center of gravity threatened me.

"I want to find me, and not what other people want me to be, including you," Maria screamed.

"I want the same thing for you," I yelled back. "But can't you come closer and find a way to tell me that allows room for me in your life?"

MARIA'S FAMILY LIVED twenty minutes from Folly Beach, in historic downtown Charleston. The proximity allowed Maria to visit her father, who was then battling tongue and throat cancer (he died two years later). Her father, Billy, didn't approve of his daughter's choices in life—or, to be more precise, he didn't want his firstborn to change. Princeton had changed her, all right. When she told him about Toshiko's class, he said, "I didn't send you to Princeton to play with mud." And when she brought me to the hospital to visit him when we first arrived on Folly Beach, he said, "Van's presence is not pleasing to me."

It was true that I didn't look the part to be dating his daughter. I was a swarthy, mop-headed, ripped-jean-wearing liberal–the child of a Greek immigrant and his Greek American wife—who'd been born in New York City and moved to Los Angeles as a teenager. I was both a Yankee and a Californian, and he was a Southerner and a John Bircher. I started with two strikes against me, even before we met and he laid eyes on me and sniffed my politics. But his displeasure had less to do with me than with the loss of control over his daughter's life. That was intolerable to him.

I didn't fully understand this then. I mostly felt misunderstood, rejected, and very angry. How could he dislike me for loving his daughter? And Maria's mom, Jane, who over the years has come to love and respect me deeply, was then caught between her own loyalty to her husband and her love for her daughter. Maria often felt like the hypotenuse of this triangle, stretched taut opposite their unyielding right angle.

Aggrieved by their united front, Maria returned to their home time and again to seek rapprochement—which was not forthcoming. Without their support, she clung to me as her substitute family. But her dependency terrified her: What if I, too, withdrew my love? Where would that leave her? Our fights became more desperate. She clamped down; I tried to pry her open. We broke up; we reunited. We spent hours, whole mornings, walking on the beach, trying to untie the knot of our craziness.

Finally, in the spring, after our winter of discontent, Maria and I had reaffirmed the love that brought us together in the first place. We drove to the Unity Church in downtown Charleston, and got married, alone, with an African American minister. Though invited, Maria's parents did not come to our private ceremony.

Eventually, the lure of Folly Beach weakened, and we decided that we no longer needed its protection. We needed the opportunity a vibrant city could provide. We cast our lot with San Francisco, a city we both loved, and drove cross-country with our cat, Lila, hopeful that we would find our callings there. Within a year, I decided to return to graduate school to become a psychotherapist, and to begin my own therapy. I was genuinely curious about the intensity of my reactions to Maria and wanted to reclaim in myself whatever hobbled me in relationship to her. I wanted to stand apart from her, strong on my own—in my own center.

For her part, Maria had learned to listen not only to clay with her hands but also to the stirrings in her heart. She decided to return to school to study massage and to explore what would become her life's ambition: to understand how the body reflects one's emotional history and trauma. Years later, she explained, "Pottery, working in the inner city, massage—they may not look connected, but, for me, they're all deeply spiritual and draw on a part of me that has to be present, still, and in my heart." As an afterthought, she added, wryly, "And if I'd gone to massage school while my dad was alive, it would've killed him."

I DIDN'T GO looking for a spiritual teacher. I didn't even think I needed one. But after I saw a flyer in our local health food store announcing the arrival of an Indian spiritual leader named Mata Amritanandamayi Devi, I felt irresistibly drawn to meet her. I stood in front of the flyer, staring at a photo of her face. If it hadn't happened to me, I wouldn't have believed it, but I suddenly felt as though a hand reached into my being and gently touched a part of me that had been dormant and dry my whole life. I longed for something I didn't even know I longed for.

Two weeks later, in June of 1992, I drove to Dominican College in San Rafael, half an hour north of San Francisco, to wait on line to meet this woman. I had just graduated from the California Institute of Integral Studies, which was strongly influenced by Indian Vedanta philosophy, but I wasn't prepared for what I saw or experienced. Even before the so-called living saint appeared, I stood amid hundreds of people, many of whom, with eyes closed and hands in prayerful position, were dressed in white cloth and chanting in Sanskrit. I could've been in a temple in Varanasi or Mathura.

My judgments took over. Who were these people? Moonies? Erstwhile Deadheads? I couldn't locate the source of my unease, but I felt superior and smug. I didn't belong here. After all, I had it all together.

Just when I was about to turn and run, she walked into the auditorium, barefoot, wearing white, and with a glorious smile on her face. I was disarmed. My mind went silent, and my heart softened as this physically diminutive woman stopped before a small crowd of people, who proceeded to garland her with colorful roses and anoint her feet with a beige paste, before waving a ritual flame in front of her. She hugged them, then walked down the aisle with outstretched arms as people reached to touch her hands.

She sat in front of the crowd, sang devotional music with her band of musicians, and then began to receive and embrace everyone in the hall, one after the other. I don't remember the actual embrace, but I do remember that something in me was activated in her presence. I felt recognized and seen at depths I hadn't experienced with anyone else before. I had no idea how this happened, but I left Dominican College feeling attached to this woman, who is affectionately called Amma the world over, and drove home to Maria with a line from the poet Kahlil Gibran repeating in my head: "I alone love the unseen in you."

Maria would have none of it. She felt threatened and didn't want to return with me to Dominican College the next night to meet this Indian woman. I thought for sure she would embrace this female image of the divine, but she'd had her fill of charismatic ministers and was not up for being disappointed and hurt again by a human masquerading as something special, something more.

"You can delude yourself into thinking she's divine," Maria said, "but I'm not buying it. You're on your own with this one."

And I was, for almost five years. As my attachment to Amma grew, so did the tension in our marriage. Whenever Amma was in town, I followed her traveling tour around the Bay Area with a friend of Maria's and mine named Prana. While driving, Prana and I would talk about her partner, Phil, and mine—and why they weren't interested in Amma and how we could get them to be. The pressure, of course, didn't help our cause. Maria forgave Prana for her exuberance, and they became the dearest of friends (Maria asked Prana to be with her at her death). But Maria felt abandoned by my relationship to Amma, as if I'd replaced her with someone more important—someone with whom she couldn't compete.

"How am I supposed to measure up to a saint?" she burst out one night, crying. "*I* used to be the most important person in your life."

"You still are," I responded honestly. "But my relationship to Amma is helping me to find myself, so there's more of me to love you."

"Yeah. Right," Maria said, stomping off.

DESPITE HER SKEPTICISM, Maria understood that I'd struggled throughout my twenties, and now early thirties, to know what I felt and needed in relationships. I preternaturally knew what others needed, but I sometimes remained a mystery to myself. That could make me insufferable in a relationship, since I wanted something but didn't feel entitled to ask for it unless I was already disappointed and angry. To top it off, when I gave, I gave magnanimously, but then I grew resentful when my partner didn't reciprocate in quite the same fashion. Maria had her hands full with me.

One day during the summer of 1993, in the middle of an argument—yes, Maria was withdrawing and I was pursuing—she said, "Why don't you grow up and start taking responsibility for yourself? You should get back into therapy."

I hated her in the moment, but she was right. She and I had participated in a number of weekend workshops designed to help us explore our early childhood experiences. We became lifelong friends with the workshop leader, Laurie, and began to chart how this terrain impacted our marriage. I got back into formal therapy and started a fourteen-year therapeutic relationship with a clinician who understood childhood and particularly early infant development. She helped me to disentangle my own history of early deprivation—I was born premature and confined to an incubator for twenty-five days—and to see how I was prone to reliving it in relationship.

The shadow of that experience had cast a very specific outline on my life.

Gradually, Maria began to see that my relationship to Amma and my ongoing therapy were changing my life, our marriage, and, unexpectedly, her too. The time I spent apart from her, at three-day retreats at Amma's ashram in San Ramon, forty-five minutes southeast of San Francisco, forced her to look at herself more carefully and at why she felt so angry when I wasn't available to her. She blessed my going to India for Christmas in 1997 to spend three weeks at Amma's ashram in Kerala, a state in the southwest corner of India with 370 miles of coast along the Arabian Sea. Later, she described what effect that time had on her:

> When you were in India, I spent the whole time crying, putting wood in the fireplace, or curled up with the cats. I got to see how catastrophically alone I felt inside myself, apart from you. And then I began to see that your relationship to Amma made you more loving and kinder and happier. I wanted more of those qualities in my life, so I decided to put my toes carefully into the Amma water and see what it felt like.

Over time, Maria began to visit Amma when she was in the Bay Area and, in December 2000 she came with me to India for the first time. Despite the vagaries and hardships of traveling there, we toured with Amma throughout northern Kerala. Our spiritual path, which had led us from Christianity to an encounter with Buddhism when we first arrived in San Francisco, had now converged in the person of Amma, who embodies selfless service, devotion to God, and compassion.

Jane Goodall, one of the world's best-known animal researchers, who in the words of biographer Dale Peterson, is "the woman who redefined man," presented Amma with the 2002 Gandhi-King Award for Nonviolence in recognition of her lifelong work in furthering the principles of nonviolence. The three previous recipients were Nelson Mandela, Kofi Annan, and Goodall herself. When introducing Amma, Goodall said, "I believe that she stands here in front of us, God's love in a human body."

OUR YOUTH SLIPPED into our forties before we were able to have a child.

From the time I was in my late twenties, I wanted to be a father. Maria was less certain about motherhood. She didn't feel ready to have another person be completely dependent on her. The thought of it frightened her. Despite her misgivings, we continued to try to get pregnant, unsuccessfully. The monthly cycle of hope followed by disappointment began to take its toll. Maria found that her body was tenser and its natural rhythms were disrupted. The more we tried to have a child, the further the possibility slipped from our grasp.

On several occasions, I told Maria that I thought we should explore fertility options. A number of our friends had done so and had healthy children to show for it. "What did we have to lose?"

"I don't want to tinker with my body," she said, as we lay on our bed one Saturday morning, the Japanese cherry tree that blooms in April outside our bedroom window in full splendor. "I'm okay with doing whatever I can do naturally to restore balance to my body, but I don't want to take drugs."

And in a memorable phrase that had a sustained impact on me, she added, "If we're destined to have a child, we will. And if we aren't, then it's a blessing not to have one."

We decided to ask Amma, when she was visiting her San Ramon ashram later in the year, for guidance. She told us "to talk more about our feelings and to accommodate each other more," adding, knowingly, that it would happen "when the timing is right."

Paradoxically, Amma's suggestion that the time for pregnancy was not yet propitious allowed us to talk more openly about our relationship and parenthood, as though it had given us a reprieve of sorts. My frustration with Maria for not wanting to pursue the high-tech fertility route lessened, and I developed a deeper appreciation for her aspirations and wisdom. We would do what we could to improve our chances of having a child, but we'd place our trust in God.

After living in San Francisco for ten years, we decided to leave the city to simplify our lives and bought a home across the bay in Berkeley, where we felt the pace of life would be more conducive to starting a family. Maria, who'd taught herself to surf a few years earlier, bought a new surfboard and a new wetsuit and hit the waves more regularly. For her fortieth birthday, I sent her to a weeklong women's surf camp in Mexico with Las Olas, whose motto is "We make girls out of women." She came home a new girl, ready to conquer the world.

We decided to try acupuncture to see if it would help our fertility. We'd heard stories from couples who had used traditional Chinese medicine to reduce stress and prepare the body for pregnancy. Its underlying philosophy also resonated with us: restore balance in natural ways so the body's own innate wisdom can heal. We discovered a father-and-son acupuncture team, Lam and Howard Kong, ninth- and tenth-generation traditional Chinese doctors, in Oakland, and they became our fertility specialists. Almost weekly, Lam would encourage Maria, "When there is harmony in the body, then you will have a child."

He was right. Within a year, her body found harmony, and she got pregnant.

FROM AS FAR back as I can remember, *family* has always meant three generations living in one place. I grew up with my *pappou,* my mother's father, living in the room next to the one my sister and I shared. We played dominoes with him, watched *Gunsmoke* and wrestling on his twelve-inch black-and-white TV, and coveted his cherry-flavored Luden's cough drops, which he dispensed liberally.

So when Maria and I moved to Berkeley and my mother and father, Stella and Manny, asked if we'd mind if they relocated to the East Bay, we jumped at the idea. After my sister Ariste's first marriage had dissolved, she and her daughter, Sabina, moved from the States to northern England to be with Ariste's new partner, Paul. Their absence made my parents anticipate a second grandchild just that much more.

Shortly after they moved from Orange County to Albany, the town next to Berkeley, my mom began to show signs of cognitive loss—nothing dramatic, but a decline nonetheless. We didn't think much of it at the time, but looking back, I can now see that it was the beginning of what her doctors would later diagnosis as dementia. By the time our son was a toddler, my mom began to need more attention. And by the time Maria was diagnosed with cancer, Dad had become a nearly full-time caregiver. Satchi's childhood memories of his grandmother would be different than mine of my *pappou,* who was involved in my life up until the last month of his life, when he died of lung cancer. I was eight years old, and I felt like I had lost a parent.

MARIA'S SLOW DECLINE was less evident than Mom's. She went to see Dr. Sheridan for regular checkups, and though there was some concern about mild anemia and sensitivity in her digestive tract, the symptoms never warranted alarm. So despite a life led trying to uncover the unseen, we were blindsided by Maria's diagnosis. I've asked myself many times if we could—or should—have seen it coming. In retrospect, the clues were scattered over the landscape of our lives, not easily detectable, but noteworthy. She'd even had mild hemorrhoid problems since giving birth to Satchi, an early warning sign for colon cancer.

But if you don't know how to connect the dots, or aren't looking in just the right direction, even the simplest outline can remain obscure. And those whose job it is to connect the dots, the doctors we place our faith in, are, like us, doing their best to interpret a world that never quite is the way it seems. We can all be humbled by the way our lives unfold.

SUNDAY, JANUARY 17TH

Two days post-diagnosis, Maria went to bed early, as did Satchi. I had not slept well in nights and was by then too tired to sleep. I paced the house, looking at family pictures on the wall: Maria and me holding our three-week-old son, beaming the joy of older parents who feel blessed to have given birth on the cusp of midlife. Satchi on a preschool outing to Tilden Park in the hills above Berkeley, looking up in unabashed delight at his mother's face, which is partially concealed as she looks away from the camera and into his eyes. The three of us on our knees in front of Amma, a photo that appeared on the front page of the *San Francisco Chronicle* and generated scores of calls from friends who were as stunned as we were.

I walked into the bedroom and gazed down at Maria's face as she slept, unable to accept that she had cancer and that it had crept undetected, like a noiseless cat burglar in the middle of the night, throughout the core of her body. How can this be? It's not possible. It's not fair—we finally have the life we've always wanted and worked for.

I had to cancel my work for the following week and the one after. I was too preoccupied and distressed to be with my clients. I couldn't provide the kind of emotional holding they deserved from their therapist; I needed that holding myself. I was scared. I didn't know if Maria, Satchi, and I had the strength to endure what I feared was ahead of us: debilitating chemotherapy treatments, the wasting away of Maria's vitality and will to live, the terrible fall from grace that comes in childhood when a parent is sick and maybe dies prematurely, single parenting, loneliness.

I was afraid to go to bed and lie awake, thinking thoughts that fueled my anxiety but I forced myself lie down next to Maria. And, as I had done for almost twenty-five years, I allowed the rhythm of her breathing—the rhythm of life—to keep me anchored.

THURSDAY, JANUARY 21ST

Maria's "baby sister," Anne, took notes at the surgeon's office. Maria had called her the morning of the colonoscopy and asked her to come. She flew in from Charleston to help us survive the earthquake that had shaken our family. As the wife of a surgeon, Anne has a facility for asking doctors informed questions. She provided ballast as we interviewed Dr. Giovanni Dipietro, the surgeon that Dr. Huron recommended we see on short notice.

"The challenge," Dr. Dipietro said, "is to determine what type of cancer you have. Every cancer is different, and its treatment follows from where it's originated—the primary tumor site—and how aggressively it's spread. Because you have tumors in your colon and in your pelvic area outside the colon, it's hard to make a definitive diagnosis. And the cancer is simply too widespread to call for surgery."

"Do you think it would be wise to prolong the start of chemotherapy to do multiple biopsies to determine if Maria has more than one kind of cancer?" Anne asked.

"I don't think so," he responded. "The tumor in Maria's colon is already so large it could cause an obstruction—and that must be avoided at all costs. I advise you to switch to a low-fiber diet to avoid an obstruction, start chemotherapy immediately, and if chemo is successful, surgery may become an option down the line."

Putting Maria's dilemma in perspective, he said, "It's common not to know the origin of a cancer," and for oncologists to have to make a credible guess about what chemotherapy protocol to pick for their patients. If their guess is right, the tumors start to shrink. If they're wrong, they try a different protocol.

Listening to him talk, I thought, Where I come from, we call this trial and error. It makes me nauseous to think that my wife will be a guinea pig in her own treatment. Picking the wrong antibiotic is one thing; choosing the wrong poison is another.

SUNDAY, JANUARY 24TH

Every day we received a flood of emails from friends with friends who've beaten cancer without chemotherapy. Their claims were remarkable.

One friend's friend ate blue-green algae. Another took megadoses of medicinal mushrooms. Several drank pH-adjusted water. Some just prayed for healing.

We weren't opposed to any of these ideas, but didn't know how to evaluate the merits of such testimonials. Jumping off the chemotherapy freight train wasn't a trivial matter. Maria's life was on the line. What kind of faith must you have to buck your doctor's advice and try a treatment that may work—and perhaps has worked for many—but for which there's only anecdotal data? What if Maria didn't do chemotherapy, and died prematurely? Would I ever be able to forgive myself for taking our "alternativeness" so seriously? And what if Maria decided to do chemotherapy and still died prematurely? Would I ever be able to forgive her (or myself) for lacking the courage to step outside the mainstream and try something radical and untested? I was tortured by these thoughts.

The Chinese have a saying: If you continue walking the path you're on, you'll get to your destination. That could be a blessing or a curse, depending on which path you choose. Maria was too tired and sick to research the many creative alternatives that I began studying. By default, I became the designated vetter. This job came with an emotional price tag: with each new claim, I found myself feeling hopeful at first, if not delusional, that I had found the cure for cancer. And then the well-trained skeptic in me began to take over, and I felt foolish for my unbridled optimism. I didn't have the medical background, or the emotional distance, to discriminate among the many options.

I wished that Maria wouldn't start chemotherapy. I wanted to believe there was a nontoxic alternative to poisoning her body in order to save her life. Chemotherapy was like waging war in order to live in peace. I feared the chemotherapy path would compromise her immune system and diminish her quality of life, and end only in death.

"SUMO MEDICINE"—THAT'S WHAT we called chemotherapy in our house. When it became clear that Maria wouldn't be a candidate for surgery, Satchi wanted to know what the doctors were going to do to destroy the cancer.

We told him that the doctors wanted to give Mom "a really, really strong medicine" to kill the cancer.

"How strong?" he asked.

"Hmmm. That's a fine question," I said, looking to Maria for help. "Well, it's a lot stronger than regular medicine. Cancer is not like, say, a cold or the flu, which you can cure in a couple of days. It's a pretty worthy opponent and can fight for a long, long time. So the doctors will have to give Mom a super-duper-charged medicine that can outlast the cancer and wear it down before going in for the kill."

"So it's not like any old medicine," he said. "It's like . . . sumo medicine. Right? Really big and really strong."

"Exactly," I said, delighted that he gave us a user-friendly name and image for chemotherapy.

We laughed at how the sumo medicine had a billowing stomach and a black loincloth, which barely covered its butt crack. We crouched down, ran toward each other, and bounced off our stomachs before falling to the floor and wrestling on the carpet, Greco-Roman style.

MONDAY, JANUARY 25TH

An email that could alter the course of Maria's treatment arrived. An old college friend, Anne, a writer and teacher of yoga and Buddhist meditation, wrote,

> I know you are undoubtedly sorting through a huge amount of information—and well-intended misinformation—as you chart a course for Maria's treatment. I don't want to unnecessarily add to the deluge, but I do want to let you know about a remarkable new cancer treatment method called immunepheresis that is being pioneered at a German clinic.

Anne had personal knowledge of immunepheresis. Her former husband, Lou, a biotech innovator, was interested in novel cancer treatments and had interviewed patients who'd received treatment at the German clinic and whose cancers had gone into remission. Apparently, an American oncologist named M. Rigdon Lentz had observed that cancer cells produce and deploy several "decoy" substances that distract the immune system from attacking and dissolving the cancer tumor itself—instead it attacks these decoys, which form a kind of cloud around the tumor.

"These decoy substances," Anne wrote, "are the same ones produced by a fetus to prevent the immune system from attacking and destroying it—in that case, of course, they serve a useful function."

Dr. Lentz's method, she explained, involves filtering the blood to remove these decoy substances. When that's done, the immune system naturally attacks and destroys the tumors, and they melt away, without the need for chemotherapy.

Intrigued, I called Anne, and she explained that immunepheresis works best if you've never had chemotherapy before. Chemotherapy attacks the immune system, while immunepheresis relies on a fully functioning immune system to do the work once the decoys are removed from the blood.

Hearing this, I felt torn. Even though we didn't know which chemotherapy Dr. Huron would pick, Maria was scheduled to start treatment in six days. Dr. Dipietro said she needed to start it or run the risk of life-threatening complications. And yet, tragically, once she started chemotherapy, she might compromise the effectiveness of a promising new treatment that could save her life.

We didn't have the time to research this new treatment, and yet I knew that we couldn't *not* research it. I hated the options that were in front us.

Maria, fortunately, was more at peace than I. "I'm a mother," she said. "I can't try a treatment that isn't well-tested. I'll do whatever I have to do to make sure I'm around for my child."

Nevertheless, she'd just found out that one of her brother's best friends, Bill Schmidt, was a medical oncologist. She asked me to get in touch with Bill before she started sumo medicine to investigate the merits of immunepheresis and to make a recommendation. Though determined to start to chemo, she was also open to an eleventh-hour about-face.

TUESDAY, JANUARY 26TH

Dr. Huron walked briskly into the "Venice" room, placed her notes on the examination room countertop, turning it into her desk, and took a deep breath. A tall, slender woman in her late fifties—with a cascade of silver hair framing her face—she was dressed in an aubergine wool skirt and a black Armani jacket, and wore a raku-glazed bead necklace.

She began by explaining that all the evidence—CT scans, tumor marker numbers, pathology report, the way the cancer had spread— now pointed toward metastatic colon cancer and not ovarian cancer.

"You don't have a classic colon cancer presentation," she observed, explaining how the tumors in Maria's abdominal and peritoneal cavity were filled with mucus, a permutation that occurs in only a small percentage of all colon cancers.

"The cancer started in the lumen of the sigmoid colon and grew into, colonized, and encased the wall of the colon, thereby closing the lumen and making it look like an apple core stuck in the pipes. Ovarian cancer would invade the colon, but not encase it. So I don't think you have two kinds of cancer." Concluding, she said, "I think you have one."

Her reasoning was convincing, if not impressive, and, in a way, relieving. "One cancer is better than two," I thought. The dread started to lift.

In detail, she described the two drug cocktails used to treat colon cancer—FOLFIRI, whose main drug is irinotecan, and FOLFOX,

whose main drug is oxaliplatin—and why, given their side effect pro-
files, she'd chosen irinotecan for Maria. Because Maria had metastatic
colon cancer, insurance would also cover Avastin, a tumor-starving
drug that works by preventing the growth of new blood vessels.

We'd thought that chemotherapy would be a one-day event, but
learned that for colon cancer it's a three-day process. After day one
of chemo in Dr. Huron's office, Maria would return home connected
to a pump and, for the next forty-six hours, continue to receive
another of the drugs in the cocktail, fluorouracil, or 5-FU, a little
bit at a time, before returning to the doctor's office on day three to
be relieved of the pump, the fanny pack in which it's placed, and the
then empty pouch of poison. To complete the ordeal, she would then
get an injection of either Neulasta, a drug that forces the marrow in
the body's large bones to accelerate production of white blood cells,
boosting the immune system, or Neupogen, a similar but shorter act-
ing drug, which does not tax the bone marrow as much.

Maria was to repeat this cycle every two weeks.

Dr. Huron then said something I knew on some level but hadn't
allowed myself to consider (the implications were too unsettling):
it was "better to start with the chemo that has fewer side effects,"
namely the irinotecan, because it's *likely to stop working*," and
then Maria would have to switch to oxaliplatin.

Reading between the lines, I realized she was saying that chemo
might not stop the cancer. The drugs would be administered sequen-
tially, like tag team wrestling—when one stopped working, the other
jumped into the ring. That raised the notion of what might follow
the second into the ring when it, too, stopped working: the first
again, or something else?

"How long will Maria need to do chemotherapy?" I asked.

"We're not going to be able to cure this cancer," she said.

The words pierced my heart. I began to feel light-headed. "We'll use this regimen as long as it's working, and as long as you're tolerating it. Then we'll have to switch to the other regimen."

I began to feel petulant. I wanted an answer to my question.

"So how long will Maria have to stay on chemotherapy?"

"Every two weeks to control things," she started. "She can have time off in the summer, but pretty much, even if she gets four weeks off, she'll have to have chemo forever."

"For the rest of her life?" I asked, stunned.

"Yes."

I was too frightened to ask what, in this context, "for the rest of her life" meant, and the doctor moved on to the next subject quickly, something about a KRAS mutation and a test to determine it. I was too distressed to focus on the new information and still preoccupied with what had preceded it: I couldn't imagine how Maria would do chemotherapy for the rest of her life—for five, ten, twenty-five years. My fantasy of a long life with Maria and the realities of this treatment plan existed in two different universes.

The first time we left the Venice room, we'd felt hopeful. This time, we were left reeling. Maria, already weak and now weakened by the news of her life sentence, held onto my arm as we walked to the car.

Driving back from Dr. Huron's office, Maria turned to me and said, "This wasn't what we had planned." I looked at her, wanting to make it all better, but I couldn't. I felt defeated. And my heart was broken.

two

◆

POOLING

Amma once said that self-doubt continues until the last moment before enlightenment, and then it disappears. Temptation, I'm sure, is no different. Over two days, I received several tempting emails from my Princeton friend Anne. Lou had contacted Dr. Lentz about Maria, and Anne forwarded his response:

> *Our responses in colon cancer appear to be influenced to a significant degree by the severity and duration of prior chemotherapy. If she is chemotherapy naïve I would expect a major response at least 50 percent of the time. We have treated four advanced ovarian cancer patients in the past and all responded. One stayed in remission for nine years and died of something unrelated.*

Anne added, dryly, "Note that 'chemotherapy naïve' means that you haven't done chemo, not that you're ignorant of it!"

I wish I were ignorant of the options and had complete faith in traditional oncology. As a soldier, it's better to go to war believing single-mindedly in your cause. But my allegiances were torn. Anne and Lou wrote,

> *It would only take a few days in Dr. Lentz's clinic in Germany to determine whether Maria is likely to be a responsive candidate for treatment. If the answer is no, she could return immediately to start chemo with no downside other than the brief delay caused by her trip. If the answer is yes—which would be indicated by immediate and dramatic signs of immune response at the site of the cancer—she could stay and pursue that treatment.*

I believed them, yet Maria knew something in her body and soul that only she could know: she sensed urgency, a slipping away of life, and she knew she couldn't endure an arduous trip to Bavaria in her condition. Chemotherapy was *the* path.

Maria and I were relying on her brother's friend Bill, the oncologist, to render a scientific and medical opinion for us. I called Bill after I read the emails. Not unexpectedly, he told me that he felt the theory behind immunepheresis—that if you could filter the blood to remove cancer cell decoys, then the immune system could more effectively target the cancer—was sound and based in solid science. However, he had reservations about whether the technology to do this was sophisticated enough to risk Maria's life in her current condition.

Only eighty to a hundred patients had tried this new treatment—and only a handful with colon cancer. From what he could tell, he thought the cancer in Maria's body had progressed so far that she needed immediate treatment, close to home, where she'd be more comfortable and benefit from the love and support of family and friends. "Bavaria is a long way from home," he added. And the cost of immunepheresis was not covered by insurance. Conceivably, we'd have to raise several hundred thousand dollars to sustain treatment (and a life in Germany) for months at a time.

Despite Dr. Lentz's openness to talk, Bill felt frustrated that he couldn't review the clinical evidence to support his claims. He hadn't published his recent work in widely read, peer-reviewed journals, Bill explained. And he appeared to be developing his treatment protocol far removed from the give-and-take of a community of scientists who could collaborate with him—and challenge him. "As a hard-nosed scientist, I can't advise you to pursue immunepheresis in the place of chemotherapy."

Perhaps it could play a role in her treatment down the road, if the integrity of her immune system was preserved. And to that endeavor, he felt, we should turn our attention.

I FELT DEPRESSED after speaking to Bill. Maria and Satchi were downstairs watching old *I Love Lucy* episodes in the living room. My mother-in-law, Jane, whom Maria asked to come to Berkeley after Anne returned to Charleston, was in the kitchen cooking a warm Southern meal—fried chicken, okra, red rice. I was grateful that Maria's sister and mom were able to drop their lives on short notice. Satchi and I needed them as much as Maria did.

With Bill's verdict, my hope for a deus ex machina was dashed; there'd be no sudden solution to the poisoning of my wife. She'd chosen the road well traveled, despite the knowledge that it might dead end abruptly one day. I walked downstairs to join them on the couch, but didn't have the heart to tell Maria just then what I'd learned. That would come later. For now, Lucy had just gotten into trouble and Ricky was reprimanding her.

THURSDAY, JANUARY 28TH

The sun rose as I waited in the Family Resource Center of the hospital where Maria was having the portacath surgery. Leaving our house at five-thirty that morning, we both felt the blessing of the cool, crisp early morning air on our faces. We felt at peace walking hand in hand in the darkness to the car and driving down nearly deserted Berkeley streets in silence to the freeway and then over the bridge into San Francisco.

The shock and aftershocks of the last two weeks were starting to settle. We no longer awakened at night in paroxysms of dread and tears, and no longer searched each other's faces looking for feelings too frightening to express in words. Even in the midst of great turmoil and struggle, we found the peaceful places that always swaddled us.

In illness, as in any catastrophe, there can be a peeling away of that which isn't essential. You remember what's important: family, loved ones, kindness, one's relationship to God. Illness can shut family members down emotionally, isolate them, and turn them into strangers, but it can also make them more transparent.

Maria and I knew instinctively that we'd need to be transparent to heal. The three of us needed each other more now than ever before; it simply wasn't a choice to add the pain of isolation to the terror of having cancer. Whether or not we chose to talk about the emotional experience of this illness, we could both feel it deep down in our bones every day when we looked at each other. We couldn't hide what we were feeling; we were simply too closely connected to sugarcoat, or prevaricate. It would be maddening to feel one thing but be told another, or nothing at all.

MARIA LOOKED RADIANT when I left her a few moments before she entered the operating room, as though she had surrendered to the first movement of the long treatment cantata set into motion by the cancer. I'd never seen her so fierce and determined, yet soft and vulnerable. She was using the opportunity presented by her illness to remove the obstacles that get in the way of giving and receiving love and opening to God's grace.

Across from me in the Family Resource Center, a young couple sat holding hands. I wondered who they were waiting for: a child, a parent, perhaps a sibling. They were young, not much older than Maria and I when we moved to Folly Beach. A doctor led them into a small room off the main waiting area. I couldn't see their faces anymore, but I could hear relief in their voices. I felt fatherly toward them, these strangers, and prayed, as the Greek poet Cavafy wrote, "that the road is long" for them and, that whatever their story, "the summer mornings are many."

I was waiting alone now. Images of a portacath under Maria's skin and its lumpy bulge on her chest intruded into my awareness. Dr. Dipietro had described it in less graphic terms—"a slight protuberance"—but I hated the transformations I knew her body would undergo as treatment progressed. The portacath merely encapsulated my distress. I began to grieve the loss of innocence we both felt when we were younger and in bloom and our bodies knew no disease but mostly pleasure. I wanted my wife's body to age naturally, gracefully, without the interference of surgery and chemotherapy.

I remembered an evening at Princeton, thirty years ago. Maria wore a purple silk blouse over a soft, diaphanous aquamarine skirt. She noticed me noticing her legs through her skirt and gave me an almost undetectable come-hither look. My heart quickened.

FRIDAY, JANUARY 29TH

I sat next to Maria in the hospital infusion room as she received two units of blood. The precious hemoglobin would continue to help her spring back from the utter exhaustion she felt toward the end of last year. Hemoglobin, the main component of red blood cells, is a protein that picks up oxygen in the lungs and delivers it to cells throughout the body, allowing them to breathe. She received three units of blood last week, and that had already made a difference in her disposition and energy level.

As I watched the bright red blood drip from the IV bag, I wondered who'd donated the blood, and if that person had any sense of how much their blood would mean to the one human life that would need it at some future time. That person's blood was going to make my wife stronger so she could be on firmer footing before starting chemotherapy and facing the hardest journey of her life. I felt deeply grateful to someone I'll never meet but who touched my life intimately—whose blood now ran in my wife's body.

MONDAY, FEBRUARY 1ST

I dreamed I was skateboarding down roller-coaster tracks with a companion who was both unpredictable and untrustworthy. Tired of the ups and downs, I jumped off, relieved to be on solid ground. My companion pursued me and convinced me to follow him to a storefront church, where the parishioners worshipped a miracle cream, purported to heal any ailment. They milled around the back room, rubbing white cream on their arms and legs and injecting the substance into their veins. Some are in wheelchairs. Some appear to be in a stupor. Those in charge tried to force me to ingest the cream, but I resisted, fighting back.

Losing strength, I finally submitted and lost consciousness. I awoke in the dream to resume the fight to free myself and called out to Amma for help. She walked through the front door and strode to my side to protect me. I clung to her body as the parishioners receded with their miracle substance.

"Oh my, you really are anxious about me getting on the chemotherapy roller coaster," Maria said, when I told her about the dream.

"I think so. And I'm worried that once you start, we'll go native and lose ourselves, and forget that these white creams might make you feel better temporarily but they won't heal you."

"Me, too. I have to start down this path, but let's keep our eyes on the prize and Amma at our side."

THREE HOURS LATER, Maria started chemotherapy. She did not have an auspicious beginning.

When the nurse pushed the second of two needles through Maria's skin to access her port, her face twisted into a long, silent pained scream. An hour earlier, I'd rubbed Lidocaine cream—a *white* cream—on Maria's skin, and then covered it with cling wrap to allow the anesthetic to numb the deeper subcutaneous tissue. However, I forgot to apply "a generous amount of cream," as Dr. Huron had instructed. I'd been stingy with the Lidocaine.

The nurse quickly injected an anti-anxiety drug through the port to calm Maria's nerves. Maria recovered quickly, but I didn't. She reached her hand out to comfort me.

Later in the morning, wearing an elegant jacket over matching pants, with a single strand of pearls around her neck, Dr. Huron walked into the infusion room and asked about the first day of the rest of Maria's life.

"Better than I anticipated," Maria said. She didn't mention the Lidocaine mishap.

Knowing that Maria and I wanted to pursue alternative treatments—acupuncture to minimize side effects, supplements to protect her immune system, and lymph therapy to drain the body of chemotherapy drugs—Dr. Huron handed me a book called *Integrative*

Oncology, a six hundred–page primer edited by Donald Abrams and Andrew Weil. She knew Abrams, the director of the Osher Center for Integrative Medicine at the University of California San Francisco, and spoke highly of his work.

When Maria fell asleep, I read chapters on the use of medicinal mushrooms, nutritional interventions, antioxidants, traditional Chinese medicine, and homeopathy. I had to restrain myself from sharing my discoveries with Maria. She was too immersed in the new experience in her body to be intellectually curious.

At some point in the afternoon, Maria took my hand and prayed that the cancer cells would be receptive to the sumo medicine and that her body would be protected from the worst of its side effects. She began to feel sad for the cancer cells and started to cry.

"They were once a part of me, but they've become dangerous intruders who are out to kill me, and now I'm out to kill them."

The battle lines had been drawn.

BEFORE LEAVING THE oncologist's office, Maria placed a small picture of Amma into the fanny pack that held the pump and the 5-FU baggy. The oncology nurse noticed Maria tucking the picture in around the pump and asked who was in the picture.

Maria hesitated. "Her name is Amma," she began. "Sometimes she's called Ammachi."

I picked up where Maria left off. "You may have heard journalists refer to her as 'the hugging saint' because she embraces everyone who comes to her." I stopped momentarily to see if the nurse wanted to hear more, or if what we'd shared already was too weird.

"Hmmm. She's a spiritual leader?" the nurse asked.

"Yes, a spiritual leader from India," I continued. "Many people consider her to be a living saint."

Maria added, "Van and I have known her for many years, and we derive great comfort and strength in our relationship with her."

At that moment, an IV beep went off in another room, and the nurse left to attend to it. When she returned, the biography moment had passed. She gave instructions to Maria about what antinausea medications to take if she began to feel nauseous at home and what to do if the baggy accidentally tore and spilled its contents, reminding us that 5-FU is a hazardous material.

I'd wanted to share more about our relationship with Amma but knew that after the short biography it would become difficult to put into words what we believed. How could I explain why Maria would place a picture of this woman, whom we've known for almost twenty years, next to the sumo medicine that we hoped would save her life?

In India, where people believe that there are God-intoxicated souls walking on the earth, it requires no explanation to say you believe that Krishna or Rama or, for that matter, Amma, is a manifestation of the divine. These avatars—gods who have taken a human body—have attained the highest level of spiritual awakening: oneness with all beings and creation. The Buddhists have no problem with this either. The first Buddha realized his own awakening was not a personal matter; if he could wake up to his true nature, any seeker could.

I was raised a Christian in the Greek Orthodox Church, and within that framework I believe that Christ is the Son of God. I've never felt uncomfortable sharing that belief. People may disagree with me, but they won't think I'm crazy for having it. My Jewish friends don't believe that Christ is the Son of God, but they believe someone *could* and very well might be the Messiah one day. Our disagreement is not in the concept but with the person who has the leading role.

Like Christ, Amma has a body, and yet she encompasses so much more than the physical. What she embodies I long for in myself. Meditating on her physical form—the act of tucking her picture into a fanny pack is a kind of prayer or meditation—directs the seeker back into her own heart. There is sumo medicine, and there is integrative medicine, and then there is divine medicine.

WEDNESDAY, FEBRUARY 3RD

Maria felt sad when her pump was removed; she'd become accustomed to its soft rhythmic sound, each double-beat whoosh dispensing poison with precision. I've heard from longtime chemotherapy patients that they grow to hate being tethered to their pump, but everything was novel and unfamiliar; we hadn't yet learned that resentment.

Even the metaphors of cancer, the most ubiquitous of which is cancer as an enemy that must be destroyed, take adjusting to. After meditating on the cancer cells proliferating in her body, Maria said, "I don't want to be at war within myself. The image of war doesn't work for me; it makes me feel like I'm a war zone, and that can't be good for my healing."

Later, while resting at home on the couch, she shared a new image that had emerged during her meditation, one that allowed her to be at once compassionate to these cells and merciless, like Mother Kali, the Hindu goddess of fierce love, who wears a garland of human heads around her neck.

"These cells used to have my signature. They were Maria-cells. Then they went haywire and started to divide quickly. With each division, they grew more and more unlike Maria-cells, until they became unrecognizable. And in the process, they've forgotten how to die." Looking sad, Maria said, "They're no longer a part of the wheel of life. They're lost souls and can't return to the source. They need my help. It's the ultimate act of compassion to help these wayward cells find their way back to nature—to help them remember how to die."

A student of human anatomy and physiology, Maria explained that a programmed sequence of events leads to the death of all cells in the human body. This process, called apoptosis, plays a crucial role in maintaining health by eliminating cells that are either too old, unnecessary, or unhealthy. Too little or too much apoptosis plays a role in many diseases, she said, cancer among them; cells that should be eliminated are not, and then become immortal, proliferating and spreading without check.

"In my new visualization, I'm Kali helping the mitochondria of these deranged cells trigger apoptosis," Maria said.

In Hinduism, Mother Kali in her compassionate form is ruthless, slaying anything that blinds us to our true nature of love—the severed heads, which represent our egos. Maria was now Kali, offering compassion to these cells by destroying them from the inside out.

FRIDAY, FEBRUARY 12TH

Having taken three weeks off to begin to grapple with our new reality, I went back to work.

At first, I couldn't imagine returning to work and hatched a plan to take six months off. Hearing my plan, my sister-in-law, Anne, said, "Many people have to deal with crises like this. They find the strength to return to work and deal with everything on their plates. So will you." Her words were strangely comforting; she could see my strength even when I couldn't. And she was right.

ILLNESS PROVIDES AN opportunity to witness one of human nature's most powerful forces, the need to attach to others when we feel shaky and to protect our loved ones when they are vulnerable.

At the outset, Maria and I decided that we needed to have another adult in our home, especially during the first weeks and early months of this new adventure. I wanted Maria to have the companionship of her family and friends, she wanted me to have practical support, and we both wanted to make sure we had a safety net in place for Satchi. We'd seen children fall through the cracks during a time of illness or significant family disruption, and we didn't want that to happen to Satchi.

To that end, we invited a steady stream of loved ones, starting with our friend Maggie and then Maria's sister and her mom to move in with us for a week at a time. After Maria's immediate family, we had her first cousin Charlotte, and then Charlotte's mom, Maria's Aunt Annie, her mother's sister from Kentucky (yes, another Anne, the third in our close circle of support). They cooked and cleaned and did our laundry, and, when I couldn't, walked Satchi to and from school. They kept Maria company during the day, and if they were crazy enough, they accepted Satchi's challenge to play soccer on the corner blacktop.

"I'm tired of playing soccer with middle-aged women, Mom," Satchi complained, half jokingly. "Can't we have some soccer players take care of us?"

With each person, we developed a strong bond, and when each of them left, we wilted a little on the inside. When Aunt Annie was leaving, Satchi told his great aunt, "I don't want you to go," and then, looking out the front window, sobbed as her airport shuttle pulled away. I wanted to cry as well.

MONDAY, FEBRUARY 15TH

When we first entered into this new strange world of doctors, hospitals, and chemotherapy, Maria and I felt at the mercy of specialists, who clearly knew more about cancer than we ever would—or could hope to. Our emotions rose and fell with their words and pronouncements.

Slowly, however, Maria and I realized that, though we knew less about cancer, we knew more than the specialists ever would about the person inside Maria's body. There are more than seven billion humans alive at this moment, but only one of them with Maria's unique fingerprint, history, and particular galaxy of hopes, dreams, and motivations. And only she could point toward *her* North Star.

AN OLD COLLEGE friend named Debbie, who herself beat cancer recently, told me that we're all programmed biologically to get past intense periods of overwhelming grief and shock. Studies, she reassured me, say this usually happens in eight weeks.

"Seriously," she added, "They've studied this. We adjust. Sometimes we adjust in healthy ways and sometimes in unhealthy ways, but as humans we can acclimate to anything. It's one of the wonders of life."

Midway through our first eight weeks, Maria had in fact gone from feeling shock to feeling empowered. We were putting together a team of specialists, here in the Bay Area but also across the country, who could be responsive to Maria's integrative vision of what healing looked like, among them Dr. Keith Block and his team at the Block Center for Integrative Cancer Treatment in Evanston, Illinois, and our local acupuncturist, Howard Kong, who, as Maria's frontline support, would provide biweekly acupuncture during each sumo medicine cycle.

We also turned to Michael Broffman of the Pine Street Clinic to help us understand how chemotherapy and integrative medicine can work hand-in-hand. Friends had urged us to consult with Broffman, whose specialty as an acupuncturist is the intersection of traditional oncology and creative, nontoxic alternative treatments that complement and even optimize chemotherapy. Unlike many alternative practitioners who flat out dismiss chemotherapy, Broffman recognizes its value, especially in instances where cancer has spread dramatically before it's been caught.

At his impressive clinic in San Anselmo, California, Maria and I learned a whole new road map for what was happening in her body throughout the fourteen-day chemo cycle, and what she could do to participate more consciously in her own treatment.

Not wasting time, Broffman explained that each two-week chemo cycle has three distinct phases, and that in order to optimize the chemotherapy—and keep her immune system strong—Maria needed to understand what was happening during each phase. The first phase (days one to three), when Maria was hooked up to her pump, he said, is the search-and-destroy part of the cycle, when the chemo indiscriminately kills cells throughout the body, both cancerous and healthy, leaving dead cells piled up everywhere. The second phase (days four to seven), was the start of detoxification, or flushing the body of the billions of dead cells that accumulated during the kill off. And the last phase (days eight to fourteen) was the strengthening or toning phase, when Maria had to build her strength and immune system back to prepare her body for the next round of chemotherapy.

The logic of each phase determines what supplements to take, and not take, and for how long. He gave us a list of supplements for Maria to consider, describing their function—those that kill cancer cells, those that boost the immune system, those that prevent new blood vessel growth in tumors, and those that either cleanse, detoxify, or have an anti-inflammatory effect on the body.

"Because chemotherapy can be exhausting, if not debilitating," Broffman continued, "many cancer patients don't have the stamina or motivation to exercise, but that's one of the most important components of cancer treatment." He recommended Maria take eight short walks a day while on chemo, explaining that exercise helps circulate the chemo drugs in the body and can add more bang for the buck. Or, more precisely, "15 percent more bang," to its objective of killing cancer cells.

Apparently, sumo chemo medicine is good at destroying fast-dividing cells but not so competent at the "search" part of search-and-destroy. Like a lazy sniper, it stays in one place and kills whatever is in front of it. That's why keeping active is so important; it moves the snipers around so they can find more cancer cells. And during the detoxification phase, it also helps the body to more efficiently flush out dead cells and toxins, which otherwise accumulate in the body and more quickly lead to serious, long-term side effects.

Maria left Broffman's office feeling empowered to approach sumo medicine as an active and discriminating partner, something she had wanted but not known how to do. Broffman gave her permission to expand the horizon of what her treatment could look like. Chemotherapy is important, but it was only one piece of an integrative puzzle that we were determined to put together.

TUESDAY, FEBRUARY 16TH

Maria looked so beautiful as she received her second round of sumo medicine, more at ease than during round one and less groggy. At one point, reclining in what looked like a first-class airline seat—what we affectionately called her "chemo-throne"—she began to tear up.

"My tears are close to the surface today. I'm in good hands. I can feel it."

I didn't ask whose hands: Dr. Huron's, the oncology nurse's, mine, our community's. We were all holding her, and God was holding us.

SIX OTHER PATIENTS, all hooked up to their particular chemotherapy cocktails, reclined on their thrones in the infusion room that day. Maria by then shared a common bond with these men and women, which only five weeks ago we could never have imagined or understood. Each person in this room was fighting to secure the healthy future that youth promises and disease steals.

The woman sitting next to us, clearly younger than Maria, turned to me and asked if Maria used ginger to manage her side effects. After her first chemo treatment for uterine cancer, she had returned home from the drugstore with four prescriptions for nausea and anxiety, much as we had two weeks earlier. Before she'd taken any pills, her mother called from China and told her about the benefits of ginger as an antidote to nausea. Immediately, she drove to a Whole Foods and bought ginger capsules.

"Since then I've not used any prescription drugs to manage my side effects," she said proudly.

Overhearing our neighbor extolling the benefits of ginger, one of the oncology nurses quickly found a journal article she had read recently in the *Journal of Clinical Oncology*, "Ginger for Chemotherapy-Related Nausea in Cancer Patients," and gave everyone on our side of the room a copy. The abstract read, "Ginger, an ancient spice, is used by practitioners worldwide to treat nausea and vomiting."

The nurse then laughed and said, "The drug companies must hate this article; they can't make any money off of ginger."

I decided I'd buy ginger pills that very day.

FRIDAY, FEBRUARY 19TH

Maria woke up feeling "a million times better" than she did the day before, when she had the sumo medicine pump disconnected. She survived the first two days of round two with minimal side effects, intermittently feeling tired and a little queasy. But on day three she felt exhausted. When she told the oncology nurses, they smiled and said, "Good, that means the drugs are working."

I read somewhere recently that the average human body has seventy-five trillion cells, and on any given day, between seventy and a hundred billion cells get replaced. Even without sumo medicine, cleaning that many cells out of the body must be a staggeringly complicated endeavor, requiring a large number of bodily systems and organs, including the liver, kidneys, lymphatic system, and skin to work in flawless harmony. With sumo medicine, the body must go into shock.

After walking Satchi to school, I came home to find Maria lying on the couch, meditative. I could tell when she was focused on her body and sending prayers to herself: she had a certain inward joy about her, as if she were caressing herself with Presence. She opened her eyes, looked up, and said, "I'm feeling so vulnerable and fragile, but, oddly, this doesn't feel like me—like Maria."

"What do you mean?"

"Well, when I tap into myself—into Maria—I feel strong and healthy."

As we sat with the paradox, we both intuited that perhaps she was sensing the cancer cells—the not-Maria cells—dying and flooding into her system, not unlike what happens when a large storm hits the Bay Area. The water treatment plants in San Francisco and the East Bay can't handle the excess runoff and they dump the combined sewage/rainwater effluent into the bay, raising $E.\ coli$ levels temporarily and causing a hazard to humans who swim in the water. Similarly, a formidable storm had just hit Maria's lymphatic system.

"The cancer cells must be feeling scared and vulnerable, being under attack. Maybe if I try to understand them, they'd be more likely to let go and stand down."

I was amazed that my wife could stay connected to the strong and healthy Maria, in whose body this battle was being waged, while keeping her heart open to the ravenous intruders. I wondered if this is what the Dalai Lama has to embrace in himself in order to transform his anger at the Chinese.

WITH THE PUMP disconnected, Maria was in detoxification mode. That night, while I should've been giving Satchi a bath, I found myself cleaning out the kitchen pantry, obsessively. I was determined to get to the bottom of a pantry-moth infestation. Midstream, I realized that Maria and I must be resonating with the new cycle of our lives: sumo medicine, detox, strengthening; followed by sumo medicine, detox, strengthening.

I found moths in the quinoa, millet, and spelt flakes. They were doing what nature tells them to do: laying eggs, multiplying, and eating their way through plastic bags and grains and spreading through our home, not unlike cancer cells. I evicted the buggers to the compost bin.

SUNDAY, FEBRUARY 21ST

The pantry moths were gone, the runoff effluent contained, the sewage treatment plants back on line. Each day, Maria got stronger and felt the difference the supplements made in her sense of vitality and resiliency. Together they boosted her body's natural defenses, enhanced healthy cell growth, and, we hoped, promoted cancer cell apoptosis. Sadly, sumo medicine (unlike, say, natural curcumin and green tea extract) targets both cells that are *pathologically* rapidly dividing—causing tumors—as well as cells that do so naturally, such as hair follicles, red and white blood cells, and digestive tract cells. This lack of discrimination accounts for the typical side effects of many sumo medicine cocktails: hair loss, mouth sores, diarrhea, neutropenia (low white blood cell count), and vulnerability to infection.

Broffman's framing of the three-phase cycle helped empower us to brainstorm about what we could do during the detoxification phase. We called one of Maria's bodywork colleagues, a lymphatic specialist named Raven~Light, and asked her to come to the house to teach me the equivalent of lymph drainage for dummies.

And when we met with Dr. Huron before round two, we told her that we were planning to do lymphatic drainage but wanted to make sure that it didn't increase the risk of spreading cancer, something we'd heard but didn't believe was true.

Startling us, she said flippantly, "Well, you can't make matters worse."

My eyes jumped to meet Maria's. I was too alarmed to say anything. What did she mean? And why was she telling us now, in this way, after we'd asked a question to empower us in Maria's treatment?

Then she added, "That's an old wives' tale; you can't spread cancer through massage."

I wished that were all she'd said.

WHEN RAVEN~LIGHT CAME to the house for my lesson, she first told us her own cancer story. Twenty years before she had been diagnosed with breast cancer on a Friday and had a mastectomy on Monday. Afterward, her oncologist told her she had twelve lymph nodes positive for cancer and gave her a fifty-fifty chance of living for five years. A second oncologist gave her a fifty-fifty chance of living for two and a half years. Crestfallen, she started chemotherapy and consulted with Broffman, who developed an integrative program for her, much as he had for Maria. Against all odds, she lived until the fall of 2012, when she died from pancreatic cancer.

"Lymphatic drainage therapy helps to drain the body of accumulated dead cells," Raven~Light taught me. "And that cleansing can help someone tolerate chemotherapy longer."

A highly sophisticated filter, the lymphatic system performs an ongoing deep cleaning in our bodies. Lymph channels (first rivulets, which then flow into lymph streams and merge, finally, into lymph rivers) recycle cell waste not picked up by the circulatory system and carry it back into the blood at the heart, via the inferior and superior vena cava. From there, the circulatory system takes over and removes the waste via the liver, kidneys, and lungs, and the body reuses the recycled spare parts to build new cells.

Once I understood the basic concepts, Raven~Light demonstrated where to place my fingertips—first on Maria's collarbone, then her neck, followed by her armpits and the crease in her groin, returning after each station to the collarbone to make sure the furthest point downstream stayed open to prevent a buildup upstream. My touch was too heavy for Maria, so Raven-Light demonstrated on my body how softly to touch each point—as much with my awareness as my fingertips, I learned.

When I got it right, Maria said, "That's it. Perfect. The lighter you touch me, the more you can sense the rhythmic pulse below the skin."

She was right. When I touched too heavily, I could only feel my own fingertips, but when I listened lightly, as though inviting a shy animal with an outstretched hand, I began to sense a barely discernible flowing presence pulsing up toward me.

"Yes," Maria said again. "You're making contact. See? You don't have to work so hard. The pulse comes to you."

I wondered how much I had missed out on in life because my touch was too heavy.

TUESDAY, FEBRUARY 23RD

The rain fell outside as Maria rested in the living room. She was starting to feel better than she had in months. For the past few years, she'd experienced a slow but persistent leak somewhere deep within herself, robbing her of subtle life energy. That had changed: her life force wasn't slipping away anymore. The leak had been plugged. I could feel her energy and presence starting to pool again, like an underground cistern filling after a long drought.

When Satchi was a baby, we read a book by a sleep expert who coined the expression "sleep begets sleep." It's also true that energy begets energy, and presence begets presence. Presence is hard to measure, but you can sense it when you look into your partner's eyes. It's an aliveness that meets your own aliveness and welcomes connection.

We were in round two of chemo; Maria had her pump removed a few days before. Her tumor marker numbers, which measure the progression of a cancer, hadn't arrived yet from the lab. We learned from the nursing staff that each kind of cancer leaves a unique fingerprint in the blood. For instance, ovarian cancer leaves a carbohydrate antigen, or CA-125, fingerprint, and colorectal cancer, a carcinoembryonic antigen, or CEA, fingerprint. The oncology nurse told us that soon we'd be learning a whole new vocabulary.

Maria quipped, "I'd rather be learning Spanish."

Unlike presence, tumor marker numbers can be measured, but it's not always clear what they mean. The problem is that a number, by itself, doesn't indicate a trend. A metastatic cancer might have lower numbers than a stage I or stage II cancer, especially if its form is self-contained, as Maria's was, like a bunch of grapes scattered throughout the lower abdomen. The only way to make meaning out of these numbers is to chart them and, over time, to follow their trend: upward and the treatment isn't working; downward and it is. Without multiple numbers, we didn't have enough data points to render a guess.

Maria hadn't wanted me to call Dr. Huron's office for the numbers, but I could barely contain my curiosity. I'd already made a chart on which to graph the second set of numbers. Since I couldn't tell what was happening in my wife's body from moment to moment as she could, I grasped for whatever anchors I could find to give me hope.

Without the numbers, I had to simply look into Maria's eyes and trust that the reservoir was filling.

FRIDAY, FEBRUARY 26TH

Broken-heartedness is the beginning of all real reception.
—Jack Hirschman

One night, after putting Satchi to bed, Maria and I sat down on the couch to talk. She was clearly troubled, but didn't know why.

Within minutes, Maria realized that an exchange with someone earlier in the week had gotten under her skin and, like a splinter, taken some days to irritate the soft tissue. She told me that a friend had told her what to him was an uplifting story, but to Maria it was a painful reminder of the uncertainty defining her life now. The bones of the story: an oncologist had told this person's friend that he had three months left to live. Against all odds, he lived, miraculously, for seven years. Telling me the story, Maria felt shattered.

"That's not enough," she cried. "I want my whole life. Seven years is not enough time. I want my seventies."

Having just tucked Satchi in, Maria added, "It's hardest when I put him to sleep. I can't bear to imagine not being with him. I want to be with that child. I want to see him become a man."

Earlier that day, returning from a walk with Maria, I checked the mailbox and discovered an unaddressed envelope. I handed it to Maria. She opened it to find a note from Satchi. He had snuck the note into the mailbox that morning, probably before going to school.

"Dear Mom," it read, "I love you."

That night, sitting next to Maria, my heart broke, too. I held her as waves of grief coursed through her body. In my arms, she yielded to her grief. I told her I was her anchor, and that I would not let her go. She sobbed more deeply.

There's no tide chart to predict when grief will come. It can flood as suddenly as it ebbs. Finally, spent, we walked upstairs and kissed Satchi on his cheek as he lay sleeping on his belly, under the curved rainbow fabric that arches over his bed.

Maria whispered, "Good night, sweet boy. *Óneira glyká*—sweet dreams. Sleep with the angels. Sleep with Amma."

three

✦

HOLDING FAST TO DREAMS

It was Maria's birthday. We spent the day at the oncologist's office, the start of round three. I'd hoped to be home in time to meet Satchi at school (he was sad when we left that morning and wanted me to pick him up after school to play kickball), but I hadn't been able to on prior sumo medicine days. After getting chemotherapy, Maria had to stay an additional hour to get an IV injection of iron sucrose, a brown, molasses-like fluid to help patients with iron deficiency anemia replenish their iron stores.

On those days, Satchi worried about his mother. He chose not to have a playdate that day, as he'd done on other sumo medicine days. Instead he came home immediately after school with Maria's Aunt Betty, her father's sister, who was visiting from Vermont, and waited for us. It was hard for him to play wholeheartedly with his friends when his mother was in the doctor's office all day battling cancer.

Driving to Dr. Huron's office, Maria had said, "I had an upsetting dream last night. I dreamed that a band of bad guys was chasing you, Satchi, and me. Not to be defeated, we fought back valiantly, sometimes the three of us together, sometimes in pairs, but never me alone—so Satchi and me, and you and me. The interesting thing is that *I* always had help." Tearing up, she added, "I feel so sad that I can't protect Satchi from the reality of having a mother who has cancer and you from having a wife who's sick. I can fight with you both on my side, but I can't spare you."

"No, we're all in this together now."

"I know, but in the dream, when the three of us were not fighting together, one of you had to face the bad guys all alone. I wonder if that's what Satchi feels on these days when you and I are together and he's in school, like he has to fight the bad guys alone. It just breaks my heart."

"Well, how does he feel about it in the dream?"

"Hmmm, funny you ask. None of us feels powerless or distressed in the dream. We're all fierce and determined."

"Fierce and determined, and maybe a little alone as well," I said, before remembering that Satchi also had a dream last night.

"Did Satchi tell you about his dream? He was hanging out with God. You and I were there, too, but unlike Satchi, we weren't on a first-name basis with God. Then God gives Satchi a bunch of pennies with red dots on them and asks him to hand them out to other children. Just then, Satchi stopped, and I said, 'Well, did you hand them out?' And he said, 'Yeah, of course, Dad, God asked me to.'"

MARIA HAD HER choice of chemo rooms. She picked the big private room, what we call the luxury condo—one chemo throne, a private TV, and a nice view—so we could be alone to celebrate her birthday. Before we met with Dr. Huron, the oncology nurse drew blood from Maria's port to determine if her blood cell counts were robust enough to begin another round of sumo medicine. A part of me hoped her counts would be low so she could be spared poison on her birthday, but I knew a low blood cell count would mean her body was not recovering well from the prior chemotherapy round, and that would be inauspicious so early in her treatment.

Dr. Huron walked into the exam room seeming a little harried, and didn't make eye contact. She sat down, reviewed Maria's last set of tumor marker numbers, and said that the numbers had started to turn and drop, not by a lot, but enough to indicate that the FOLFIRI was working.

"I think the tumors have been stunned," Dr. Huron added, "and their fast growth has been slowed. The next thing we hope to see is the tumors shrinking."

We discussed Maria's side effect profile, and then Maria asked Dr. Huron if she could delay by a week the fifth round of sumo medicine.

"We have plans to travel to Chicago during spring break for a two-day consultation at the Block Center for Integrative Cancer Treatment. And I'm wondering if it's prudent to stretch to three weeks so early in my treatment."

"Going to a three-week interval is fine," she said, "so long as it's intermittent." Some patients get tired of the two-week regimen, she explained, resent the disruption it causes, and press to scale back the chemotherapy routine. "That would not be a good idea," she added, "since metastatic colon cancer needs constant vigilance. It tends to return, even after a long dormancy."

"Well, I've heard that colon cancer, unlike ovarian cancer, takes longer to respond to chemotherapy but then can disappear and not return again," Maria said.

"That is not the case with metastatic colon cancer," she said. "There's no cure for it."

The bookshelf in the luxury condo room held a book called *After Breast Cancer*. Apparently, there is no "after" metastatic colon cancer.

"We can cure breast cancer, Hodgkin's lymphoma, even testicular cancer—the kind Lance Armstrong had—but we can't cure stage IV colon cancer. It always comes back one day, even if we manage to make the tumors disappear." Then she added, "The good news is that you're gaining weight, a pound in two weeks."

Still stunned, not about Maria's weight gain but by the doctor's prognostic certainty, I managed to joke, "You taketh with one hand and giveth with the other."

HOME AT LAST, Maria comfortable in her own bed, we talked about Dr. Huron's prognosis—that Maria's cancer cannot be cured—and the paradigm that informs it. We had no reason to doubt the cancer studies; they are certainly based on solid science and statistics. I was reminded, though, of what Mark Twain said about lies: "There are three kinds of lies: lies, damned lies, and statistics."

A little indignant, Maria said, "Those studies haven't studied *this* person. They know nothing of who I am and what's important to me—my youth, my determination, my desire to do whatever it takes."

"Not to mention your diet and exercise routine," I said, "and your attitude toward cancer, and your spiritual life, and the reason why you're here on the planet to begin with. Who really knows what your destiny is?"

In interviews with over sixteen thousand "terminal" survivors—individuals given no hope of surviving cancer—the Foundation for Cancer Research and Wellness concluded that cancer patients who get well participate intimately in the management of their own treatment. They stop treating just their illness and focus on creating wellness—for their bodies, their minds, and their spirit. Medical treatment is important, but patients who tend to survive work to heal the whole person.

One of the reasons we planned to travel two thousand miles to the Block Center in Evanston was that its practitioners believe that if patients are empowered to become nutritionally, physically, spiritually, and psychologically fit to better fight cancer, their chances of a miracle happening increase.

In his book, *Life Over Cancer*, Block, drawing on three decades of research as an integrative cancer specialist, lays out a comprehensive integrative therapy program designed to enhance conventional treatments and improve one's chances of living cancer-free. There are individuals with stage IV colon cancer who seem to live cancer-free. Science allows for outliers, but it can't account for who's selected to be one.

FRIDAY, MARCH 5TH

Maria is about the same age as her father was when he, after a lifetime of drink and tobacco, was diagnosed with cancer of the throat and tongue.

During a walk, Maria said, "For him, cancer was about ending his life; for me, it's about changing my life. I want to clear out my emotional basement so the structure of my new life is built on a solid foundation."

We all have hurt and pain in our past—there's no escaping that—but an essential ingredient of the healing process, according to the Block Center, is resolving the underlying emotional issues that serve as the architecture of our lives. So, if you drink to excess, how come? Or if you're brutally self-critical, or self-negating, how come?

The idea is not that you're responsible for creating your cancer. New Age thinkers can go too far in this direction, sometimes leaving the impression that people are to blame for their illness. But living a life out of balance, or in denial, has repercussions and can create an internal environment—through, say, a compromised immune system—that allows disease to get a foothold.

The new field of epigenetics—how your environment and your choices can influence your genes and those of your children— strongly suggests that lifestyle factors such as a rich diet, stress, and prenatal nutrition can activate the chemicals that sit atop genes and tell them when to switch on or off. These chemicals, or epigenetic marks, silence certain gene sequences and activate others, causing your body to differentiate in very specific ways, and not others. For instance, the marks switch on genes that lead to obesity or switch off genes that prevent depression.

I like to picture these epigenetic marks as sentries atop the Great Wall of China: the sentries send different signals to the villages below the wall (like prepare for battle, or prepare a feast) depending on what they see on the horizon: Hun, Mongol, or friend. So too with the epigenetic marks: the choices we make—and the choices our parents and grandparents made or had forced upon them—can affect gene expression for generations. Researchers now believe that if the marks don't work properly, they can set a sequence into motion that allows certain diseases, cancer and diabetes among them, to develop.

A romantic, I believe the power of love and prayer can set similarly powerful sequences into motion. I'm reminded of a story my friend Haran heard and repeated to me some years ago. A man was stuck in late afternoon traffic on a Bay Area freeway. Up ahead a car was totaled. He sat in his car and prayed for the person in the accident.

A year later, a woman knocked on his door and told him this story: She had died in an accident on a California freeway. As her soul left her body, she could hear the thoughts of all the drivers backed up behind her car on the freeway. People, angry at the disruption, cursed her for adding time to their rush hour commute. As she soared over the cars and their angry drivers, the connection to her body started to grow thin, like a stretched rubber band ready to pop.

Then she flew over this man's car, heard his prayers, and felt the tug of her body on her soul grow stronger. She noticed the man's license plate before returning to her body. A year later, standing on his doorstep, she told the man that she tracked him down through his license plate. She wanted to thank him for his prayers: they had saved her life.

Stories like this should be told in medical school.

MARIA BEGAN TO feel pain in the large bones of her upper body: collarbone, sternum, jaw, and the bones in her arms. Dr. Huron had prepared us for this possibility when she explained six weeks ago that the Neulasta injected to expedite the manufacture of white blood cells can produce a deep, persistent ache in the bones, the kind young children get in milder form when they go through growth spurts. Fortunately, though Neulasta stays in the body for ten days, Maria's pain lasted for only two.

To deal with the pain, Maria had me place one hand on her chest and one under her neck. After my lymph drainage experience, I took direction willingly in these matters. She instructed me to do nothing but listen with my hands. So I sat still, listened with my hands, and lost track of time. Maria stirred, opened her eyes, and said she felt 90 percent better. With the support of my hands—and presence— she'd been able to sink in below the pain, until her parasympathetic nervous system (she said) kicked in and sent waves of spaciousness into her bones.

"Just by listening you helped the bones to unwind and rest," she said gratefully. Sometimes it's better not to know what you're doing or, rather, not to think you're the one doing anything at all.

Pain returned though, not in her bones but her small intestines. She had severe, recurring gas bubbles that brought her to her knees. A good soldier, Maria tried to tough it out. She chewed on ginger. When that didn't help, she started layering on antinausea drugs. First she took Zofran, then Compazine. Finally, frightened, she called Dr. Huron. After assessing the pain, Dr. Huron tried to find a twenty-four-hour pharmacy to call in a prescription to relax the muscles of the intestines. When we couldn't find one in Berkeley, Maria asked me to rub *vibhuti*, or sacred ash, which Amma had blessed and given to us, on her lower back. Within minutes, the pain started to subside, and Maria threw up. She was then settled enough to be put to bed. She vowed never to take a Neulasta shot again. She was ready to switch to its milder version, Neupogen, which is injected in several doses over as many days.

I lay awake. After the first two rounds of sumo medicine, I'd come to expect her progress would look a certain way: linear, progressive, with quick recovery during detoxification. It looked different this time, and I was caught off guard—and scared. From week to week, I began to realize I might not know what I could count on.

MONDAY, MARCH 8TH

The gas bubbles returned. They were not nausea, nor cramps; they were like fireworks, popping painfully in her intestines. And none of the prescriptions, alone or in combinations, provided relief. Once again, *vibhuti* settled the fireworks, but Maria remained agitated.

"I've been thinking about what Dr. Huron told me the other day, that I'll never be cured. I have to tell her that what she says makes a difference to me." She began to cry, adding, "I felt touched when she stayed on the phone with me last night. But I need her to believe that it's possible that I'll make it, even if I don't. I need to feel hopeful to keep fighting."

WEDNESDAY, MARCH 10TH

The brain likes to make sense out of our experience. It doesn't like uncertainty. From birth, the amygdala scans the environment to anticipate patterns that may lead to threat, and the pleasure-reward centers of the brain try to anticipate patterns that lead to pleasure. We're programmed by evolution to try to minimize threat and maximize pleasure.

Sumo medicine throws a wrench into this process: you never know what to expect. In this regard, sumo medicine can be a great spiritual teacher; we can learn to identify all the ways in which we try to delude ourselves into believing we're in control of our lives.

When we bought our house in the North Berkeley hills, the disclosure forms indicated that it was in a "Special Studies Zone." Maria and I wondered what fauna or flora was being studied, and by whom. We innocently asked our real estate agent, expecting to hear about some species of bird native to the East Bay.

To our shock, the home we were in escrow to buy was within 200 feet of the Hayward Fault, one of several active faults dissecting the Bay Area. "Special Studies Zone" meant geologic studies, not botanical.

I spent the first few months in our new home anticipating an earthquake. I obsessed about whether to buy very expensive earthquake insurance. I studied maps from the U.S. Geological Survey and read theories about whether, when a large earthquake struck, you were safer to be right on the fault or at a distance from it. I made a deal with God. Ever pragmatic, Maria stored extra food and water under the back porch.

Twelve years later, we've learned to live with the uncertainty that sitting atop a fault bestows on its inhabitants. We know we could lose everything in ten fast seconds, but this awareness is strangely exhilarating. We know we're in God's hands. We've also retrofitted our house. As they say in parts of the Middle East, "Trust in Allah, but tether your camel."

At this point, I'd been trying to tether my camel for eight weeks. Watching Maria suffer put me in touch with my powerlessness. Surrendering to the flow of your life is not something you do once and for all—"Now I'm done. I'm surrendered." It's a process that happens to you as you let your life tumble you like a rock in a rushing river. Some days the tumbling is welcomed; some days you just want to be on the shore, watching the river pass by.

FRIDAY, MARCH 12TH

A few days later, Maria felt a strange pain along her spine. At first she thought the pain might be related to an exercise routine she was doing to help her body heal from the portacath surgery. But its persistence and recurrence at random times suggested a different cause. Maria's Western doctors were unable to account for why the soft tissue around her spine would be hurting; Dr. Huron said the pain was too far removed from chemo to be related to it.

Howard Kong, however, thought the back pain and the intestinal fireworks were due to a yin-imbalance, caused by the Neulasta. According to Eastern traditions, two forces, yin and yang, shape everything in the universe, including our health. The Chinese symbol for yin is the shady side of a hill, while the symbol for yang is the sunny side. To resist cancer, a body needs both a deep pool of yin reserves to support healing and a potent river of yang energy to mobilize fighting. A potent river without a deep pool to sustain it will eventually run dry, and a deep pool without a flowing outlet to channel it will eventually become stagnant.

In Chinese medicine, Howard explained, bone marrow is the most yin part of the body; it's where the deep pool replenishes the body with white and red blood cells. Neulasta, by prodding the bone marrow to produce white blood cells, depletes the yin energy of the body. And when yin is depleted (and yang boosted) the body's ability to cool and lubricate itself is compromised, allowing inflammation of soft tissue to persist. Not only might an inflamed gut lead to the kind of fireworks Maria had this week, but soft tissue around the spine might also be aggravated, leading to back pain. Howard was careful to say this was only a hypothesis.

"That makes sense to me," Maria said. "The first thing I noticed last week was a painful ache in my bones, as though my marrow were being taxed, and then my intestines started to have fireworks. Maybe you're right, the Neulasta taxed my yin, leading to heat and inflammation in the soft tissue of my gut."

Later, as we readied to leave after Maria's regular acupuncture treatment, Maria told Howard, "I've been struggling to feel hopeful again after meeting with my oncologist. She told me that there's no cure for metastatic colon cancer."

He responded, "It's important to remember that doctors are experts in a specific area, but outside their area of expertise they may not know how to help you. You may have to keep them away from your heart."

"'Scope of practice' and 'scope of heart' are different," I added.

"Yes," Howard said. Taking his time, carefully selecting his words, he added, "Physicians may sometimes be more concerned about being completely honest, perhaps for fear of misleading patients. They rely on statistics and probabilities, which are not the best tools for instilling hope."

As we closed the door, Howard called out after Maria, "Remember, from my perspective, it doesn't matter how much the cancer has spread, so long as we can keep your body strong . . . When the rice is strong, the weeds won't grow."

AS AN EXPERIMENT, Maria decided not to take any medication for a day while drinking a special acupuncture tea designed to regulate the heat—and rebalance the yin—in her digestive tract. The fireworks in her intestines settled, and her appetite returned with gusto. She still felt some mild irritation, but the sharp pain remitted and the pain around her spine diminished.

"I plan to see Howard right after each round of sumo medicine," Maria said. "I want to be proactive in recovering more quickly. I don't want to wait around for potentially debilitating side effects to develop; I want to forestall them rather than react to them."

EVERY NIGHT WHEN we say grace at dinner, Satchi adds, "And bless the doctors."

He learned this from his grandmother, Jane, who, when she was visiting, would say, "Dear Lord, please bless Maria's doctors that they may have the skill, knowledge, and wisdom to help her."

And now I add, "May they also have faith."

WEDNESDAY, MARCH 17TH

Maria was reading *Life Over Cancer*. She knew the chemotherapy had started to rein in the colon cancer's march of manifest destiny—and that while it was good news, tumor shrinkage as a goal would not be enough to win the battle.

Traditional oncology, Block writes, focuses almost exclusively on shrinking tumors, what he calls the "attack phase" of treatment—and likens to climbing Mount Everest. But without an integrative plan for shoring up the whole person, oncology must resort to more chemotherapy, radiation, or surgery when the tumors return, as they often do in most advanced cancers. The problem, over time, with traditional treatment is a diminishing rate of return. Not unlike bacteria that grow resistant to antibiotics, cancer cells mutate and become impervious to chemotherapy.

Cancer is not merely a tumor, Block explains, it's an underlying condition, caused by "a cascade of genetic and molecular glitches" combined with lifestyle patterns that support its spread. Tumors often reappear, Block writes,

> *with even greater resilience, if the systemic condition that nurtured them is not treated. That is why the fixation on eliminating tumors, which has dominated cancer care for well over half a century, has brought dismal results for so many patients. Yes, surgery or radiation can remove the tumor, but unless you change the environment that nurtured it in the first place, malignant cells that remain behind can simply pick up where they left off.*

At the Block Center, the most important part of treatment, what Block calls the "containment" or "growth control phase," starts after the tumors have shrunk. He likens this phase to descending from the summit of Mount Everest. In this treatment stage, the Life Over Cancer program emphasizes strengthening your anticancer biology by preparing the body—through changes in diet, fitness, and stress management—to keep residual, visible tumors and invisible metastatic cancer cells from regrouping, proliferating, and forming new tumors. "Rather than waiting passively for the results of your next scan or checkup," Block writes, "you can actively seize control of your future."

BY THEIR VERY nature, invisible, malignant cancer cells are cunning, self-protective, and highly adaptable. Practiced at guerilla warfare, they avoid detection, go into hiding, and return when the coast is clear. When they do fight, they constantly shift strategies: They can produce proteins that repair the damage caused by sumo medicine. They can produce enzymes that convert sumo drugs into less potent forms, rendering them impotent. They can send out decoys or inhibitors that confuse the immune system, which then goes after the decoys, leaving the cancer cells unscathed. And, miraculously, they can produce a protein that pumps sumo medicine out of the cancer cell as quickly as it can get in. In short, they don't give up the fight easily.

When cancer cells do retreat and seem to give up the fight, they often break away from the primary tumor site and disperse to other parts of the body, waiting for another day when the host is more vulnerable. Known as circulating tumor cells, these cells can be genetically different from the primary tumor. Traditional oncology has made cancer treatment decisions based on a "one size fits all" approach, in which everyone with a particular cancer receives the same treatment, despite genetic differences in both the primary tumor and circulating tumor cells. Tragically, these treatments may win the battle but lose the war, precisely because they may not be able to target the most pernicious cells now hiding at a distance from the primary tumor—or even within the primary tumor itself.

Recognizing this dilemma, creative oncology centers base their cancer treatments on biological and molecular testing of the tumor tissue itself, when possible, to determine what anticancer drugs and supplements work best on it, as well as sophisticated blood tests to get a snapshot of the individual's body chemistries. This chemical fingerprint guides what supplements each patient needs to strengthen his or her anticancer biology. People with the "same" cancer receive individual treatments tailored to their own bodies, not ones based on statistics from large group studies.

I emailed Broffman to let him know that we were going to the Block Center at the end of the month. I asked him if there were any new areas of inquiry that we should explore with Dr. Block.

He wrote, "Their recommendations and programs will certainly supersede the current program from Pine Street." He told us about their set of specialized blood tests and diagnostics, as well as their very sophisticated line of complementary nutritional supplements, and encouraged us to explore any creative, nonstandard interventions and clinical trials that are relatively nontoxic, which, he emphasized, "can be employed *after* the chemotherapy is completed."

Reading Broffman's email, Maria and I did a double take; that was the first time anyone had suggested there would be a time when chemotherapy would be over.

In five words, Maria said, "He's given me a sense that there might be a different reality than the chemotherapy life sentence Dr. Huron gave me. It makes me want to cry to know that someone believes I have a future."

SATCHI PLACED A handwritten scrap of paper on the entryway table, where, alongside a wood carved bust of Buddha and a framed photo of Amma when she was in her twenties, it was sure to get our attention. On it was a quote from Alice Schertle's children's book, *Advice for a Frog*. It read, "Concentration is essential: focus on the finish. Dig your toes in, leap off the line, and go for it! No prize for second place. Grab victory by the throat and bring it down."

IN THE EARLY 1940s, when my mother was in her twenties, she discovered a lump in her neck. The night before she had surgery to remove it, she, her Greek aunties, and several older female relatives spent the night in a small Greek church in Astoria, Queens, praying to Christ. The priest, my mother's great uncle, locked the door to the church and left the ladies huddled around a potbelly stove, which served as the only heat in the church. My mom was frightened, having been told that it was likely she would emerge from surgery with frozen facial muscles, or worse, since the tumor was sitting adjacent to an artery and nerves near the spine.

She fell asleep fitfully and awoke in the middle of the night to spy a man walking gracefully from the altar to her side. He looked into her eyes with love and compassion, and placed his hand on her neck, intelligence in his touch, exactly where the tumor was located. Silently, he turned and walked back to the altar, and then disappeared. The next morning, my mom asked her aunties who the man was that had come to her in the middle of the night and touched her neck. The old ladies looked at each other quizzically and said there were no men in the church. The priest had locked them in, and without a key, no one could gain entry.

An auntie pointed to the altar and asked my mother if the man she saw looked like the man in the icon. Startled, my mom said, "Yes, that's the man."

"My child, that's no man, that's Jesus Christ. He must have come to you last night to bless you before your surgery."

When the surgeons removed the tumor in my mother's neck, they biopsied it and learned that it was malignant, though her immediate family didn't tell her (in the old days, family members often kept medical information from their loved ones). She survived not only a dangerous surgery without any complications, but neck cancer, and without any follow-up treatment, she lived cancer-free for over sixty years.

In 2008, my mother's doctors discovered a large tumor in her liver. Given her advanced age and recent medical history, and in the absence of another medical explanation for a mass of that size, they tentatively concluded that she had liver cancer. Treatment options were few, and she refused them, not wanting to live with side effects at her age. Instead, my mother decided to get a blessing from Amma, who was visiting the Bay Area that June.

I brought Mom and Dad to see Amma, and handed her a note explaining that my mom had liver cancer and a slowly progressing dementia and asking her to help.

Four months later, my mother had a second MRI scan to determine how much the tumor had grown. Quite perplexed, the oncologist, who like my mom hailed from Brooklyn, sat my parents and me down and said, "I can't explain what's happened. I've never seen this, but without any treatment, the tumor in your liver has shrunk."

My mom hugged her doctor, said, "You're from Brooklyn, I can kiss you," and then kissed him on the cheek. "It's a miracle," she added, trembling with relief.

On four separate occasions since then, MRIs confirmed that my mother's lesion continued to shrink. One month before Maria was diagnosed with cancer, my mom's oncologist concluded that she no longer needed to see him. She was cancer-free.

SUNDAY, MARCH 21ST

Curled up on the couch, we watched the United States House of Representatives vote to pass the Patient Protection and Affordability Care Act, President Obama's signature first-term legislative priority. The bill is not perfect. In fact, it has serious flaws, but it does acknowledge a fundamental truth about the three hundred million of us who live in this country: our welfare is interconnected.

If over thirty million of us don't have health care insurance, then the rest of us are diminished as a people. And if fourteen thousand of us lose our health insurance every day, then none of us is safe if we get sick.

Being self-employed, Maria and I paid our own health care premiums out of pocket for twenty-five years. My wife was now sick, and I could care less about the politics of it all, from the right or the left. I wanted her to sleep at night secure in the knowledge that she'd never lose her medical coverage. She'd have a better chance of healing if she didn't have to worry about that. Having cancer is bad enough.

I had no idea how closely Satchi had been listening to our conversations about health insurance. He watched the debate with us for an hour and then, when the magic number of 216 votes to pass the legislation was achieved, shouted with exuberance, "We don't need to worry about losing Mommy's insurance anymore."

I felt so sad at how much anxiety our little boy feels. I wondered how many other seven year olds would remember the passage of health care reform as a touchstone of their childhood, the way I, as a seven year old in 1969, remembered Neil Armstrong walking on the moon.

Two weeks before Satchi had given me a ten dollar bill to help pay for doctor bills. He refused to take the money back. After the vote he asked, "Does this mean that I can keep my allowance now?"

THE NEXT NIGHT, after dinner, as I cleaned the dishes, Satchi recited the poem "Dreams," by Langston Hughes, which he'd memorized sometime before, unbeknownst to us. Tears came to my eyes. I took him into the living room, where he recited it again for his mother. Tears came to her eyes, too.

Hold fast to dreams . . .
For when dreams go
Life is a barren field
Frozen with snow.

TUESDAY, MARCH 23RD

Over the weekend, Maria had completed the sixteen-page patient history questionnaire for the Block Medical Center. She'd needed more than ten days to do so. When we first downloaded the questionnaire Maria felt intimidated by its specificity and breadth. It says up front, "The following questionnaire has been designed to better enable the medical and clinical staff of the Block Center to understand the unique needs of each patient."

To the question "What are your expectations for this visit?" Maria first responded, "More specific info about how I can support my healing." Later, she said, "I've been rethinking several of the questions and want to submit an addendum. What I really want to take home from my visit is hope—hope that I can live a long life with cancer, and hope that I can find a team of healers who are attuned to me and can believe in my vision when I lose faith."

SITTING IN "OUR ROOM" at the infusion center, with the first of two units of blood to boost her hemoglobin level already circulating in Maria's body, we talked about our nearly twenty-seven years of being a couple. There was urgency and poignancy to these conversations, knowing that we might not have twenty-seven more years. I mentioned the shift I'd noticed in Maria toward me.

"I feel as though my healing is intertwined with loving you more deeply now." With tears forming in her eyes, she added, "If I could do it all over again, I would love you more."

"You've loved me with every ounce of your being."

"But I know my fears prevented me from giving you everything I have."

"We still have time," I said.

WE DROPPED SATCHI off before school at our neighbor Annie's house. He walked to school with her family when Maria's treatment prevented me from taking him. In the past, Satchi had been anxious about what a transfusion was and how it would affect his mom. "What would it be like to have another person's blood in your veins?" he asked the first time. "Would it hurt? Would it change you somehow?"

The first time, he had a hard time when we left him at Annie's. He was reluctant to leave our side, a little clingy, and worried all day long until we came home. This time, he hugged Maria, ran off into our neighbor's yard to play saying, "I love you, Mommy. Have a good transfusion."

Sometimes you have to flood the rice paddies for the rice to grow strong.

four

◆

STRIKING A DEAL

Maria's tumor marker numbers started heading in the right direction: down, and at a steady clip. We were grateful to Dr. Huron for picking the right sumo medicine. Though we wouldn't know with certainty how fast Maria's tumors were shrinking until we had another set of CT scans to compare to the first, her overall health and steady progress indicated she was making the ascent on Mount Everest. And for that we were relieved. Shrinking tumors meant that her body could start to reorient away from feeding the tumors and toward nourishing itself.

Growing tumors tap into a person's blood and drain the body of iron, hemoglobin, glucose, and other minerals, leaving a cancer patient increasingly at risk for losing energy, weight, and muscle mass. For patients with advanced cancers, stopping the hemorrhage of resources is the first order of business, or else the body never stands a fighting chance. It's a little like trying to pay down your principal when your credit card debt is high: once your debt gets to a certain point, it's hard to keep pace with the accruing interest, let alone pay down the principal. With sumo medicine, we hoped to slow down the interest, and with the Block Center, we hoped to make headway with the principal.

AT THIS TIME, oncologists had one more FDA-approved chemotherapy option at their disposal when FOLFIRI and FOLFOX no longer worked to contain the growth of colon cancer tumors: Erbitux. In a study published in *The New England Journal of Medicine* in 2009, patients who took Erbitux plus FOLFIRI had a response rate (not to be confused with a cure rate) of nearly 60 percent compared to those who did not take Erbitux, meaning almost 60 percent of these patients saw their cancer shrink or disappear for a longer period of time, measured in months, not years. And patients who took Erbitux also showed a 32 percent decreased risk of their colon cancer spreading, compared to patients receiving the other cocktails alone.

Encouraging news, but tragically not every colon cancer patient is responsive to Erbitux. The other 40 percent or so, who don't, don't have a third option. When their colon cancer has progressed to the point where irinotecan and oxaliplatin can no longer keep the interest from ballooning, traditional treatment comes to an end— and clinical trials can begin. In the world of finance, out-of-control credit card debt can lead to bankruptcy, restructuring, and then a fresh start. Sadly, for metastatic cancer patients who have progressed through the treatment options, there are no institutions powerful enough to wipe out your tumor debt and give you a second act.

We didn't yet know whether Maria had the mutation in the KRAS gene that renders Erbitux powerless. The only way to determine whether you're one of the lucky 60 percent is to have a bit of your tumor removed and biopsied to see if the KRAS gene has mutated or is normal, what is called "wild-type." We also didn't know whether the small specimen removed from Maria's colon during her colonoscopy in late January was substantial enough to make this determination, and we were frustrated that Dr. Huron hadn't pushed the pathology lab to run this test sooner. We hoped to hear in time to discuss our options with the Block Center.

SUNDAY, MARCH 28TH

I prayed to Amma all week for a sign that she was watching over us as we prepared to fly to Chicago. I wanted confirmation of her presence before we walked into the fire.

After an easy day of travel, save for the pat-down security gave Maria in San Francisco and an hour wait for our luggage at O'Hare, we settled into our room at the Hotel Orrington in downtown Evanston, five blocks from Lake Michigan and barely a block from Northwestern University. Tired and hungry from our journey, I walked to the nearest Whole Foods. If I hadn't already recognized the signs that week—and there were a few—that though we were already in the fire we weren't alone, I would've had to be blind to miss the one that stood in front of me at the checkout counter of the Whole Foods on the corner of Chicago and Church.

A gray-haired, diminutive Indian woman stood at the end of the counter bagging my groceries. My eyes flashed down from her face to her nametag, which announced in large handwritten letters AMMA. I'd been to India enough to know that many women, especially older ones, are respectfully called Amma, or Mother. The Whole Foods Amma looked at my bracelet, which has a Sanskrit mantra in silver overlaid on brass, copper, and bronze, and said, *"Namah Shivaya"* (Salutations to the Divine within you).

I smiled, returned her greeting, and showed her the mantra on my bracelet, knowing that if she knew Amma, the Hugging Saint, she would recognize the bracelet and the mantra, "*Om Amriteswaryai Namah*" (Salutations to the Mother of Immortal Bliss). She beamed at me and said, "Amma is my guru, too." Then, as if I hadn't noticed, she said, "We"—meaning Amma, the guru, and her—"have the same name." Without waiting for me to respond, she asked where I'm visiting from and why. Her face turned sad when she learned that my wife has cancer and was there for treatment. She said, "May Amma be with you." In that moment, I knew that we were in the right place and that all the Ammas had found me—or had I found them?

Changing topics, I told her that Amma's father had died that week.

"I know," she said, explaining that she was born and raised in Vallikavu, the town adjacent to the fishing village in Kerala where Amma was born in 1953. Her family, who still lived in Kerala, had called her a few nights before to tell her the sad news.

I wanted to ask if she had met or heard about Amma when she herself was young and still living in Vallikavu. Amma, it is said, began to compose and sing devotional music to Lord Krishna when she was a toddler and drew the attention of villagers surrounding her fishing hamlet when, as an older child and teenager, she began to have exalted spiritual experiences. But my own family was hungry and waiting for my return from Whole Foods—and gray-haired Amma, after all, was still bagging groceries. The Amma stories would have to wait. I told her I would see her again, and she gave me her blessing.

Walking back to the Hotel Orrington, I remembered something Amma once said. When you're open to life's lessons, they come to you in a whisper. But sometimes, if you're not, they build to a yell—and then a whack over the head.

I was glad my head was spared.

MONDAY, MARCH 29TH

When we walked through the doors at the Block Center for Integrative Cancer Treatment, I said to Maria, "We're not in Kansas anymore." Under her breath, she said, "No, dear, we're in Illinois."

Kelli, the front-desk receptionist, clearly expecting Maria, greeted her and asked to take her picture, saying, "It helps our doctors remember you."

The waiting room, expansive and filled with sunlight, was decorated with comfortable chairs and couches upholstered in maroon fabric. A wooden bowl with fresh apples and oranges announced that someone was paying attention to healthy snacks. Off to the left, a floor-to-ceiling glass wall separated the kitchen from the waiting area. The kitchen, used for cooking demonstrations throughout the week, is where patients and their families gather to learn about healthy eating from the four Block Center nutritionists.

Along with an individualized integrative program that includes innovative approaches to conventional oncology, the Block anticancer diet is the linchpin of the center's approach to long-term survival with cancer—the idea being that a healthy body can better resist the spread of cancer. Recipes from past cooking demonstrations lay about: "Cilantro Hummus," "Very Green Pea Soup." I thought, Julia Child would never cook in this kitchen; there's no butter.

Behind Kelli was a cozy, partitioned space with an area rug; bookshelves with puzzles, books, videos, and games; and two reclining chairs that faced a large wall-mounted flat-screen television. The television played a soothing video of mountain streams. Down one hall, off the main waiting area to the right, were consulting rooms named for spices, herbs, and greens: Dandelion, Rosemary, Cinnamon, Lavender, Mint, and Basil. Down the other hall, to the left, were rooms with the names of trees: Walnut, Spruce, Maple,

Redwood, Chestnut, and Aspen—nine in all. Patients received sumo medicine in these private, arboreal rooms. A large fish tank with beautiful coral and (strangely) only one fish occupied a wall behind several couches in the infusion room central meeting area. There were also rooms for physical therapy, massage therapy, and yoga. A mezuzah adorned every doorjamb.

Maria and I took our place in Dandelion, overlooking the southwest corner of the Northwestern campus, three stories up. The medical oncologist, Nora Bucher, had hurt her back and was not in the office today. Keith Block had to cover her patients and, as a result, was late to meet with us.

Even before we met, I got the sense that he likes to talk. With a feigned conspiratorial, but good-natured, tone, his staff commented that he liked to spend time with his patients.

DR. BLOCK BREEZED into Dandelion, shook our hands, and apologized for being late. I had the sense that he often apologized often for his lack of punctuality. He was tall, distinguished, and clearly accustomed to commanding attention, and wasted no time in establishing his bona fides as an insider who's also an outsider, a balance that a medical maverick needs to be taken seriously.

He told us that he's been working with patients as an integrative cancer specialist for thirty years and that for the last decade he'd wanted to open a Block Center in Northern California but had struggled to find a medical oncologist who believes deeply in integrated medicine.

It was clear that Dr. Block cares passionately about integrative medicine, not for the money or because it's the new fad, but because he fervently believes it can change people's lives. "At the end of the day, you have to believe you can genuinely change patient outcomes" to do this kind of work, he said, "otherwise you won't be able to provide the rationale and encouragement necessary for your patients, and they will sense a disconnect and know you're not sincere. They can lose the hope and motivation they need to be successful."

Settling into education mode, he explained the distinction between complementary and alternative medicine (CAM), which many doctors now say they practice, and integrative medicine (IM), which forms the basis of his approach to cancer treatment. The former, he said, sees itself as a complement to the "real medicine"—chemotherapy or radiation—and allows you to pick and choose alternative options to round out your care, as though you were picking items haphazardly from a restaurant menu or a hardware store catalogue. CAM might allow for changes in a patient's quality of life, but it doesn't fundamentally re-vision what is responsible for healing and getting well.

With integrative medicine, the logic is different.

"We are thinking about the potential synergy of bringing together a specific group of treatments," he said, "and that is a completely different concept from a philosophical and clinical perspective." Real results are "when you see a blending of these systems so you get a synergistic effect: 2 plus 2 plus 2 may equal 256, something extraordinary," he continued, making the point not just in words but with the force of his presence. "Not 6, not 8. There's this (exponential) effect that actually changes outcome. Though it needs additional research, I believe it may be why some patients do better than others."

A man after my own heart, I thought—a scientist who can see wonder in the world. I knew instinctively that he wasn't speaking literally, that 2 plus 2 plus 2 could equal 256, but poetically, that integrative medicine was more than the sum of its parts. I warmed to him immediately.

To ground his assertion, he returned to science and discussed his study on metastatic breast cancer patients who received integrative treatment at the Block Center. Their outcomes exceeded those of similar patients in the scientific literature who did not receive integrative treatment. "The research needs to be replicated and randomized," he said, "but it does provide patients with the motivation that an integrative program may help them to achieve better outcomes," which I took to mean improving both quality *and* length of life.

For instance, one component that oncologists could, but largely don't, address is "the immediate aftermath of chemotherapy treatment," Block said. Most oncologists prescribe medication to head off side effects, but they don't have a sophisticated strategy for how to protect the body and recover from the ravages of chemotherapy over time.

After each round of chemotherapy, he explained, the body is flooded with toxic metabolites, which cause oxidative, inflammatory, and immune stress. Greater toxicity also can lead to less effective treatment, increased resistance to drugs, and, he stressed, more DNA damage, which can cause cells to replicate and emerge much later as even more aggressive cancer cells. An image of a foreign occupation of a country popped into my mind: the longer you stay, the more resentful, crafty, and desperate the resistance grows.

Catching Block off guard, Maria joked, "We're already sold on your approach. That's why we're here." She could have said, Get on with it. What about me?

Block laughed at himself, admitting that he sometimes goes overboard with his explanations. He then confided in us that he had been "subject to considerable criticism by both mainstream and alternative practitioners" when he began to practice integrative cancer treatment. His "middle-ground" approach to treating cancer, combining the best of both conventional and scientifically sound complementary interventions, wasn't consistent with the false dichotomy in a great deal of medical thinking—of conventional and alternative practitioners alike—that *we* have the real medicine, and the rest is quaint, or even dangerous.

He then laid out the "real" and the "quaint" side by side.

He was comfortable with FOLFIRI, but not with the way it was delivered. The Block Center uses a process called chronomodulated (in essence, time-regulated) chemotherapy to deliver sumo medicine. Traditional colon cancer chemotherapy is delivered at a constant rate throughout the three-day cycle. For Maria, that meant the tiniest amount titrated every minute for forty-six hours. With time-regulated chemotherapy, the sumo medicine is delivered during the best time of day to maximize cancer cell kill and minimize normal cell damage.

"Cancer is a complex disease," he added, "and with this in mind, one should use a multitargeted approach to treatment." FOLFIRI attacks cancer from one angle, but "hitting a single target or just one pathway hasn't been all that effective to date." He stressed the need to address both the primary and secondary pathways a disease uses to spread throughout the body—hence the need for nontoxic supplements, as well as potentially effective off-label uses of certain drugs, to target the cancer from multiple angles.

As he looked at the list of supplements that Broffman prescribed for Maria, he said it was unfortunate that despite the example of practitioners like Broffman, who have tried to bridge integrative medicine into the mainstream, there still aren't more conventional doctors who routinely practice such medicine. With a hint of dejection in his voice, he added, "You have to ask why isn't this routine in every city in North America."

"YOU CAN'T GO spear fishing for cancer cells in polluted, dark waters," Block continued, shifting from what kills cancer to the environment that hosts it. Block talked about the importance of attending to four often-neglected areas of modern life—sleep, exercise, diet, and mind/spirit practices—to keep the body clean and healthy.

We spent nearly an hour talking about how these factors can either favorably or unfavorably affect one's biochemical terrain. The right kind of exercise can "quiet inflammation while rebuilding muscle," he stressed. And the right diet, which is different for different cancers, can also control inflammation and the spread of cancer.

"Every cell in the body," he explained, "is lined with a bilayered membrane filled with fats ingested over the last ninety days. If those fats are pro-inflammatory, pro-oxidative, and immune suppressing, they'll drive cancer in the wrong direction. If they are cancer-inhibiting fats, they'll set you in the right direction. The objective is to favorably change that environment."

Leaning forward and looking Maria straight in the eye, he said, "My program is really about how we transform you so your body is not hospitable to cancer."

"YOU HAVE A serious problem," Dr. Block finally told Maria toward the end of consultation. "In my opinion you should pull out all the stops and do everything that you can." I searched her face to see how these words affected her. To my surprise, she didn't look upset, but, rather, determined, as if she'd been challenged to a fight.

Later I asked Maria how she felt at that moment, and she said, "Oddly, I felt hopeful. What I heard was, this is life-and-death serious, but there are things you can do, and we will be with you every step of the way." It was a message she'd been longing to hear.

Continuing, Block said that living with a chronic disease such as cancer "is not a sprint. It's not even a marathon. It's an ultra-marathon. And no matter how well we get you, you still have to live with a full-court press. We'll help you, and I know tricks that help when people start to get burned out."

Just as quickly as he sowed hope, he offered a sober and realistic assessment.

"In some cases, the first phase of treatment doesn't stop all cancer growth, and patients have to decide if they want to discontinue chemotherapy or continue for the rest of their lives. But I wouldn't get fixated on somebody telling you they know what will happen to you."

"My oncologist told me I'd be on chemotherapy every two to three weeks for the rest of my life," Maria said.

"Well, that's what the data says," he responded straightforwardly, "but it has little to do with you as an individual."

He then explained that "population statistics" are extremely relevant to an oncologist when trying to decide what chemotherapy protocol to give a patient. They indicate what protocol is most effective for 65 to 70 percent of the population. "But," he added emphatically, "to try to predict your outcome based on some kind of database is ridiculous. And it's potentially harmful . . . if I give you a statistic, you're likely to take it in. The danger of giving people a prognosis is that people start to believe the prognosis."

"For that reason," I interrupted, "we haven't asked anyone for a prognosis."

"Good for you. Sometimes you even have to stop people from giving you a prognosis."

BACK IN OUR room at the Hotel Orrington, as the three of us curled up in bed to watch a movie, we noticed the full moon shining through the plantation shutters, illuminating our faces. We opened the blinds to find a distinctive cloud formation framing the moon, like a broad Japanese ink-brush stroke wrapping itself halfway around the rising moon. We marveled as the cloud hung in the sky immobile above the Evanston Public Library, and, like a Greek chorus, we commented on the dramatic sight.

"It looks like the Nike logo," Maria said.

"Perhaps it's telling you to 'Just do it'," I said to Maria, "to come to the Block Center to get your sumo medicine."

"Yes, I need to follow my heart and go for what I want," Maria said, a new fighting timbre in her voice. "Dr. Block emboldened me today to fight harder. I *need* to be here."

Excited, Satchi picked up the theme and shouted, "*Just do it. Just do it!*"

We faced the Nike sign until the moon rose above it, ten minutes later, and knew that we had just struck a deal with the prophetic night sky: even if we didn't know how yet, we would find a way to fly to Chicago for Maria to get her treatment.

TUESDAY, MARCH 30TH

Our first meeting of the day was with Jacki Glew, one of the Block Center's nutritionists. After greeting us, she brought us to the "Cinnamon" room—I made a mental note to ask her if cinnamon is one of the spices Maria could eat—and handed Maria a three-ring binder filled with nutritional guidelines; specific recommendations for supplements, which Dr. Block prescribed yesterday after meeting with us; a list of foods to eat to gain weight and start to correct the good-to-bad-fat ratio; and advice about what name-brand foods the Block Center suggests have the right ingredients for its Life Over Cancer diet.

We talked about Maria's nutritional history and diet, and Jacki offered practical advice about what foods to start with, which sweeteners are best (stevia, agave, and brown rice syrup), which oils to use (olive, sesame, canola, and flax), and why kombu and other seaweeds are so good (they provide essential micronutrients). She then walked us through the thirteen supplements Dr. Block suggested Maria take to strengthen her biochemical environment, many of which Broffman had already prescribed.

I was so intrigued by the conversation that I forgot to ask about cinnamon.

NEXT, LAURETTE FERRARESI, the mind/spirit consultant, a clinical psychologist, arrived to see how Maria was coping emotionally and spiritually with her new diagnosis.

She asked the questions you would expect a psychologist to ask (family of origin, support system, internal resources), but also explained the beneficial effects on the body of full oxygenation of the lungs, and described parasympathetic breathing, a simple deep-breathing practice that interrupts the stress cycle and the cascade of hormones it sets into motion. Maria demonstrated the technique to Laurette's satisfaction. And when Laurette told us that many of Dr. Block's patients are outliers, and that statistics do not account for their success, Maria told her about Dr. Huron, adding, "I feel like she has written me off because of my diagnosis."

"Oncologists and oncology data can inadvertently leave patients feeling hopeless, and that can be damaging," Laurette said. "Statistics don't always apply to individuals."

She encouraged Maria to practice "future adaptive imagery," envisioning herself as she wanted to be in six months, twelve months, five years. By doing so, she added, "you create yourself cellularly in the moment."

Laurette was preaching to the converted. Maria believed that a shift in one's attitude or experience can happen on a cellular level and replicate itself in every cell in the body simultaneously—in other words, the whole system can shift at once. In such a universe, anything is possible, even if statistics don't predict it.

THAT SENSE OF possibility carried over into our last meeting, with Nora Bucher, the Block Center's medical oncologist. From friends, we had heard that Dr. Nora, as she's known at the Block Center, was warm, thoughtful, and intelligent—and within minutes those traits were visible. Twice she asked Maria if she'd been tested for Lynch syndrome, a condition we'd never heard of before.

Aside from lifestyle and dietary reasons, she explained, there are two main reasons people under the age of fifty get colon cancer: one is a family history of polyps, which can become malignant if unattended, and the other is Lynch syndrome, or a nonpolyps inherited cancer, when three specific genes can mutate to cause colon, uterine, ovarian, or gastric cancer. Apparently, individuals with Lynch syndrome have about an 80 percent lifetime risk for colon cancer, and the median age for receiving a colon cancer diagnosis is forty-four.

As parents, she said warmly, it was important for us to get as much information about the etiology of Maria's disease as possible. We liked Dr. Nora right away. A mother herself, she was thinking about our child's welfare. We agreed that it made sense to get the blood test to determine if Maria had this genetic mutation.

Ever aware of the ballooning cost of cancer treatment, I asked her whether it would be feasible for Maria to split chemotherapy between the Block Center and her oncologist back home.

Many patients do, she said, adding that the success of such a split treatment depended on the openness of the oncologist back home. "I would be comfortable consulting with your current oncologist to explain the Block Center approach and would be happy to collaborate with her in an ongoing treatment," Dr. Nora said.

The possibility of a split treatment brought us one step closer to figuring out how to make Maria's desire to travel to Chicago a reality. We left our second day of consultations feeling buoyed and hopeful that we had the beginnings of a solid plan in place.

TUESDAY, APRIL 6TH

When we returned to Berkeley, Maria composed a letter to Dr. Huron about her experience at the Block Center and her desire to split her treatment.

She delivered the letter along with a copy of Dr. Block's book, *Life Over Cancer*, a day in advance of her scheduled sumo medicine treatment. She didn't want Dr. Huron to feel threatened and thought it more respectful to give her a chance to think about the request and formulate a response in advance, rather than feeling compelled to do so in our presence. Exercising her newfound sense of healthy entitlement as a patient, Maria decided to ask exactly for what she wanted: in addition to collaborating with the Block Center, would Dr. Huron be open to providing chronomodulated chemotherapy, so that Maria would not have to travel monthly to Evanston?

During Maria's scheduled appointment, while taking her vital signs, Dr. Huron said, "I read your letter, but I didn't have a chance to look at the book." We then walked into an exam room and started the conversation that had waiting to happen for weeks. Looking down at Maria's medical chart, Dr. Huron asked what chronomodulated chemotherapy was. Maria took the time to answer slowly and carefully.

"This is all new to me, and I'm not an oncologist, so I don't understand a good deal of it. I know there are over forty clinics in

Europe that provide this treatment, and two places in the United States, one of them being the Block Center." Gearing up for the hard part, she said, "From what I understand, colon cancer cells divide twenty-four hours a day, but normal cells divide at different times of the day." She had learned this from Dr. Nora. "The treatment is designed to take advantage of this fact and administer chemotherapy on a sine-wave curve to peak at the most efficient time of the day to kill cancer cells while minimizing the kill of normal cells."

"I have heard of this, but there isn't a lot of data behind it," Dr. Huron said. "It's largely a theoretical thing." My heart began to sink as I anticipated the standard argument used against any innovation not yet considered mainstream. She stated that because it's hard to get enough data on it, the idea provided only a "theoretical advantage," not "a clinical one."

I wanted to jump in and say, It's theoretical for you, but not for the people who experience better outcomes as a result of this treatment, but I waited for Maria to formulate her response.

"Dr. Block is finding that clinically, not just theoretically, it helps patients tolerate chemotherapy better, and, as a result, they don't fall out of treatment along the way when debilitating side effects can make the treatment worse than the progression of the disease."

"None of my patients have ever dropped out of treatment because the side effects were intolerable," Dr. Huron replied. She told us about a patient of hers who benefited from supplements prescribed by a local acupuncture clinic, the Pine Street Clinic. Apparently, her side effects were much worse when she didn't take them during a chemotherapy week.

"Exactly! I've been working with the Pine Street Clinic as well," Maria said, hopefully, sensing the implicit recognition of alternative ways to minimize the side effects of chemotherapy. "I want to do anything I can to improve the quality of my life. I'm a mother, and I want to feel good for as long as I can for my child. Michael Broffman, the director of the Pine Street Clinic, respects Dr. Block and told us that Block's recommendations would supersede his."

Dr. Huron then expressed a concern that antioxidant supplements could interfere with chemotherapy.

"For some reason," Maria said, "unlike Michael Broffman, who divides the chemotherapy cycle into three phases and advises patients not to take antioxidant supplements during the first two phases, Dr. Block advises patients to do so. I know either Dr. Block or Dr. Nora would be willing to explain their thinking."

Yielding—partially—Dr. Huron said that she'd talk instead to Donald Abrams, who, in addition to being a cancer and integrative medicine specialist at the University of California, San Francisco (UCSF) Medical Center was the chief of Hematology and Oncology at San Francisco General Hospital. "I respect his opinion," she said. "I'll ask him about Dr. Block and his program."

Relieved, Maria said, "That's a great idea."

I added, "From what I understand, Dr. Abrams went to Evanston some years ago to shadow Dr. Block for two weeks. They know each other very well." I held back from mentioning that he wrote a blurb for Dr. Block's book, displayed prominently before the title page:

Life Over Cancer provides countless strategies to enable the patient to regain some of the lost sense of control that a diagnosis often carries, empowering them to be a true partner in their fight for life. Dr. Block's counsel and guidance have assisted countless medical professionals hoping to provide their own patients with a comprehensive approach to care.

Curious about chemosensitivity testing, Maria asked, "Do you think it would be useful to test my tumors to see what substances are most effective against them?"

"The problem with such tests," she replied, "is that tumors out of the body don't respond like tumors in the body. A test might determine that a particular agent doesn't work on a tumor in a petri dish, even though the tumor is shrinking in the body. So what will you do with this information? Let's say a chemosensitivity test shows that irinotecan doesn't work, will you stop taking it even if the tumor markers are heading in the right direction and the scans show improvement?"

Her response felt argumentative. She might have been right about how tumors behave in vivo and in vitro, but if she'd been paying attention to Maria, she would have known that Maria would never do such a thing.

"The point might be moot," she continued, "because I might have to do another biopsy to get the tissue, and I'm not inclined to do that right now."

Sensing that Dr. Huron was worried we might act precipitously against her advice, I added, "Maria and I have no intention to act unilaterally; we're not oncologists. That's why we have a team of people, including yourself and the Block Center, to help us make decisions. We want to have a dialogue. And Maria would make up her mind about her treatment."

Her next volley caught me completely off guard. "Traveling to Chicago, even once a month," she said, "is very expensive; only wealthy people can afford this kind of treatment."

I said, "We're not wealthy, but we have family and friends who love Maria and will do anything to help make this happen." My anger rising quickly, I added, "A discussion of whether only rich people can do this is a separate issue, for another time. What is relevant now is whether you'll collaborate with the Block Center." I began to feel worn down, as though only one of us could survive this conversation.

Out of the blue, Dr. Huron then said, "Your options are limited anyway because the KRAS test determined that you have the gene mutation that precludes you from being able to take Erbitux." To add insult to injury, she said, "And oxaliplatin"—the second drug option—"has a lot of toxicity."

My heart stopped. Stunned that she would tell us this now, in this way, I asked, "When did you get the results from the pathologist?"

She peered quickly at Maria's chart and realized she'd been mistaken; in fact, she hadn't received the pathologist report yet. "I'm so sorry I said that. I was confused about whether the lab had returned the results."

"Please be kind with our emotions," I said. "That was a huge thing to drop on us in this manner. We need you to think about the impact of the things you're telling us."

Dr. Huron apologized again and said, "At least I recovered quickly."

"True," I thought. But I still felt elbowed in the solar plexus.

OUR CONSULTATION AT an end, Maria and I walked to the infusion room to prepare for her fifth round of chemotherapy. Despite the rough spots (and they were not inconsequential), Maria and I felt hopeful that Dr. Huron was indeed open to exploring the possibility of working collaboratively with the Block Center. Seated next to Maria, two patients talked about their experience with Dr. Huron. "She's so wonderful and special," one said to other. The other agreed. I wondered what experiences had led to these patients using those adjectives, and why, more often than not, I was left feeling nonplussed and exhausted after our interactions with this doctor.

Toward the end of Maria's treatment, yet another patient in the infusion room turned to Maria and asked how long she's been seeing Dr. Huron. The woman then explained that she'd had another oncologist for ten years, but when her lymphoma returned, it was time to find a new doctor. Her internist recommended Dr. Huron, saying that he'd sent patients with difficult-to-treat cancers to her, and she'd helped them all. "I trusted Dr. Huron the second I met her," she added. "She's so good. She's wonderful." I waited for Maria's response, but she did not reciprocate in the dance of mutual admiration that I've now come to expect in treatment rooms.

I began to wonder why our experience had been different. My high school friend Chrise told me recently that she believed her first husband's oncologist couldn't face his own powerlessness and loss of hope when it became clear Julius wouldn't survive stage IV colon cancer. He declined precipitously when the chemo stopping working, dying within two years of his diagnosis. "The oncologist was distant, discouraging, and insensitive to end-of-life issues," Chrise said. "He kept trying to administer chemo even after it was clear that the chemo was doing more harm than good. He couldn't let go and attend to Tom emotionally and spiritually."

As chance would have it, my mother had the same Bay Area oncologist, and our experience with him had been completely different. But then again, my mom's story was a miracle: her tumor shrank in the absence of any treatment. Who doesn't like to be part of a miracle?

As the oncology nurse prepared Maria's pump, I wondered what kind of emotional pressure oncologists must be under in confronting life-and-death issues on a daily basis. If you know you can help a stage IV colon cancer patient live for one, two, maybe three years, would it be threatening to have them make noise about a program that offers the possibility of more? I, too, would be skeptical: there are a lot of snake oil salesmen willing to take advantage of people's innocence and desire, especially when it comes to terminal cancer patients. I thought how much easier it must be for oncologists to bond with patients who they know will survive their treatment, and how much harder when the statistics are not in their favor. I wondered if oncologists talk about the emotional aspect of their work during regular multidisciplinary meetings with other physicians, or tumor boards, the way psychotherapists do when they discuss a case.

When the pump was nearly connected, Dr. Huron walked into the treatment room and handed me a piece of paper headed "KRAS Gene Mutation Analysis." It was the pathology report on Maria's KRAS status. At Dr. Huron's request, the lab had faxed it over during Maria's treatment. I scanned the report, carefully avoiding Maria's eyes. The first time I learned that Maria had lost the KRAS lottery, that she was not one of the lucky 60 percent who have the "wild type" gene, it was a mistake. The second time, it wasn't.

There was no apology this time.

five

◆

OPENING THE MOUNTAIN

There's a pattern to all things.

By day three of a chemo cycle, Maria began to feel brittle and fatigued. She felt strong, even robust, during the first two days of round five, and walked the hills of our North Berkeley neighborhood throughout the day, starting early in the morning and getting one last walk in before the sun set in the distance over the Golden Gate Bridge and Mount Tamalpais, rising like a bent monk absorbed in prayer—undisturbed, anchored, still.

Dr. Block had motivated her to exercise her heart out, and she was, religiously. If her oncologist had a treadmill in the infusion room, Maria would have been up and running (well, walking briskly) while connected to her IV. She now appreciated the value of a strong and responsive body.

"The more I do, the more energy I have," she told Howard, "and the better I feel."

The persistent drip of 5-FU every ninety seconds could be deceptive, though. For the first two days, it didn't seem like much was happening, but the slow drip eventually added up and crossed a threshold, and then the brittleness would set in, usually by mid-morning of day three. I remember a tenth-grade chemistry experiment in which we slowly added a titrant, drop by drop, from a burette into a flask of acid with unknown concentration. At some point, one additional drop made the acid in the flask cross a critical threshold, and the solution changed color, all at once, just like that. All along, it looked like nothing was happening in the flask, but the titrant was accumulating.

Maria's experience with Dr. Huron was also like this kind of experiment. The slow drip of misattunement, insensitivity, and apology, followed by more misattunement and insensitivity, finally added up and crossed a threshold for her. She decided to look for another oncologist.

Every person has a different titration threshold. Maria had a high threshold for tolerating situations and people that were no longer beneficial to her. She continued to take in that which was not beneficial without outward signs of distress, until, suddenly, her color changed.

I read in a survey recently that seven out of ten survivors (those who've survived a "terminal" diagnosis) change their oncologist at least once. The survey didn't discuss the details of why this was, but I suspect that among the chief reasons is a mismatch between the personality of the doctor and the personality of the patient.

Ultimately, no one is wrong when there's a mismatch; not all patients have the same needs, and not all oncologists have the same strengths and skills. For whatever reason, Maria was leaving her consultations with Dr. Huron feeling less hopeful, empowered, and motivated. Though obviously very smart and fastidious about her work, Dr. Huron was not able to form an emotional connection to Maria. She tried, but got it wrong one too many times.

MARIA FELT RELIEVED to be putting energy into finding a new relationship rather than waiting for the old one to change. Among those we turned to for help in locating oncologists to interview was Donald Abrams. As an integrative specialist, we thought he might know a similarly minded medical oncologist in the Bay Area. We wrote a profile of Maria's perfect oncologist and sent it to him:

> *We are wondering if you know of any oncologists who fit this bill: colorectal specialist; open to co-management of a case with the Block Center; capable of empowering a patient's treatment decisions while still providing standard-of-care feedback; willing to entertain the possibility of offering chronomodulated chemotherapy; and deeply respectful of their clients' emotional and spiritual longings.*

He emailed us immediately with one name, David Gullion, formerly a UCSF medical and integrative oncologist, who was now in private practice in Marin. When I called his office to set up an interview, the receptionist said he was known as the "TLC oncologist" in his six-doctor medical practice.

By the next morning, Maria had rebounded from the brittleness of day three, awaking with a ravenous appetite—always a welcomed sign for a late-stage cancer patient who was once severely anemic. Slowly, she was gaining weight and could sense that she was turning an almost imperceptible corner with the cancer.

"It's more of an intuition than anything else," Maria said. "I'm coming back to life, like the first signs of spring in the middle of winter—crocuses breaking ground, anticipating the warmth of the sun."

On the way to get her second Neupogen shot that day, we drove past Mariposa Bakery, where many of our friends bought gluten-free bread to satisfy Maria's hunger for more calories. A baguette with extra-virgin olive oil—at 120 calories per tablespoon—is a sure way to gain weight. So when I realized that Maria hadn't had that bread since we returned from Chicago, I wondered why. She said it was made with honey, "and honey is not good for me. The yeast in the bread doesn't eat up all the honey, and the leftover honey feeds the cancer cells."

Inspired and surprised by the extent of her resolve, I said, "You are *really* with the Block program."

MONDAY, APRIL 12TH

Maria emerged from round five stronger, with fewer side effects, and feeling uplifted and determined. She took over many of the jobs I had performed as she recovered from anemia. Sunday morning, I came downstairs to find her distributing the scores of supplements she needed to take every day into her seven-day, multicolored pillbox. Delighted, I thought, "One less job for me to do on Saturday night."

As Maria rebounded and I begin to drop my protective vigilance, I could feel the weight I had been carrying as a caregiver. A dream over the weekend signaled how burdened and worried I'd been.

I had to get somewhere urgently; my family depended on it. The only vehicle available was a large fish truck. Driving frantically along perilous mountain roads, I realized I didn't know how to get to my destination. I parked haphazardly and illegally, went to ask for directions, and returned to find the truck had been towed. Frantic once again, I realized the fish I was carrying would spoil if I didn't find the truck and put the fish on ice.

I awoke just then, feeling relieved that the fish had not yet started to smell. I imagine that some version of this anxiety dream must be fairly common for caregivers: You have to get somewhere quickly. Your family depends on you, but you don't know where you're going. The road seems perilous, and you have setbacks along the way. You feel terribly burdened that the whole enterprise rests on your shoulders. And if you don't succeed, the fish will start to smell.

TUESDAY, APRIL 13TH

You know cancer is a topic of conversation in your home when your seven-year-old child hops into bed with you and, even before you've had a chance to open your eyes, says, "Trophoblasts and the origins of cancer." That's how we started our day. Then we all fell asleep again.

When I eventually stirred, I asked Satchi if he knew what a trophoblast was. He did not, but he liked the sound of the words put together like that. The book, *The Trophoblast and the Origins of Cancer: One Solution to the Medical Enigma of Our Time* (what we called "the blue book" for its cover in shades of blue), had been lying around the house for two months. No doubt Satchi heard me ask anyone who might know anything about the trophoblast what he or she knows. I was on a mission to understand the mind of the trophoblast.

The last time I'd heard the word *trophoblast* I was in a high school physiology class and thought the term referred to a kind of prehistoric fish. When Maria was diagnosed with cancer, one of our doctor friends, Edison de Mello, who himself works with cancer patients as the director of the Akasha Center for Integrative Medicine in Santa Monica, California, suggested that Maria and I read *The Trophoblast and the Origins of Cancer,* (by Nicholas J. Gonzalez and Linda L. Isaacs). The authors, he said, made an interesting case that cancer cells share many of the characteristics of the embryonic trophoblast, the cells that form in mammals during the first stage of pregnancy and later develop into the placenta. "The book might stimulate you to think outside the box with respect to the mind of cancer cells," he added.

I had no idea what he was talking about, but Maria knew immediately. She'd studied early embryonic development and knew that trophoblasts are idiosyncratic cells with a distinctive character.

Not a biologist by training, I felt apprehensive about reading a semitechnical book, but once I let go of the need to evaluate the merits of the argument, I started to enjoy the powerful metaphors that arose in relationship to the trophoblast. To wit: as the first cells to differentiate from the fertilized egg, the trophoblasts implant in the endometrial wall of the uterus and help to establish the necessary blood supply, which the developing embryo needs to grow. Without this connection to the mother, the embryo cannot survive; it's helpless.

To implant in the uterine wall, however, the embryo must trick the mother's immune system into believing it doesn't pose a threat. After all, it has a different genetic fingerprint than the mother's, since half its genes come from the father. That's where the trophoblast comes in. Unlike any other cells in the human embryo, and much like malignant cancer cells, the trophoblast can conceal its true identity by erecting a shield and making itself invisible to the watchful eyes of the mother's immune system.

Cancer cells use the same molecular techniques to invade, colonize, and spread throughout the body that trophoblasts use to implant in the endometrium. Mimicking the surrounding epithelial tissue, cancer cells appear to be friendly cells just knocking on the front door for a neighborly visit. Seeing no threat, the surrounding tissue loosens the molecular matrix that binds its cells together and allows the invading cancer cells to penetrate deeper into the underlying connective tissue (the stroma), the superhighway for metastasis. About 90 percent of all malignancies, including lung, breast, pancreatic, prostate, and, yes, colon cancer, develop in these receptive epithelial tissues.

The great irony, the authors suggest, is that cancer cells take advantage of the epithelial cells' programmed desire to be of service to new life:

> *Why would our normal tissues work so hard to help a tumor survive, grow, and invade? This molecular scenario makes no sense—it makes no sense, that is, unless the epithelial cells and stromal tissues have been fooled into thinking that tumor invasion is a good thing . . . a normal healthy process. Why else would they cooperate?*

And here's the kicker: the authors suggest that in all epithelial tissues, "a genetic memory remains," which "provokes them into behaving like the receptive endometrium receiving an embryo." In other words, the body allows cancer to spread because it believes it's helping an embryo.

Unlike cancer cells, the trophoblasts know when to stop invading the mother's body. Once implantation is complete, a series of molecular signals from within the developing embryo say, Mission accomplished. You can stop now. The embryo is securely attached. And on cue, eight weeks into gestation, the once primitive, stealthy, and aggressively invasive trophoblasts change character and transform into the mature, noninvasive placenta, the symbol of a mother's holding love and compassion.

I like to think of a school of fish changing direction all at once, as if attuned to the same mysterious call. But cancer cells do not respond to any such call. They are sharks and take no direction from anyone. Tragically, the mechanism that turns off trophoblasts is missing in cancer cells.

I have no idea if the science behind this theory is solid—if cancer cells are indeed trophoblasts, as the authors suggest—but the metaphors are elegant, especially if one is trying to understand the "mind" of cancer cells. Cancer cells proliferate wildly, invade without difficulty, and migrate easily through tissue, but what motivates them may not be maliciousness and life-negating psychosis. Like trophoblasts, they may have started with a desire to embed; to find Mother, take root, and attach; and to locate resources to sustain life, just like the rest of us. Along the way, they have forgotten, or lost, their connection to the whole. They now believe their sole purpose is to invade and find blood on which to feed.

As my sister, Ariste, who teaches English literature and cinema in northern England, likes to say, "They've lost the plot."

FRIDAY, APRIL 16TH

Maria had hoped to split her treatment between the Block Center and a new Bay Area oncologist, but she was no longer certain how often she needed to travel to Chicago: every month (not likely), every two months (perhaps), or every three months (more likely). She'd discovered that it's no easy task, with a child and all the moving parts associated with travel, to uproot your life for five days when you cannot be certain how you'll be feeling.

In the meantime, we began to interview new oncologists. The first was Dr. May Chen, who specialized in gastrointestinal cancers and women's health, and was described by other colon cancer patients as "super-kind" and "very proactive." Though she practices an hour south of our home, in Campbell, we drove to the South Bay to see if she might become a part of Maria's new team.

With sensitivity, Dr. Chen started the consultation by asking Maria why she'd come so far to meet her. The tone in her voice—and the awareness that something was amiss—put Maria at ease immediately, and she began to tell the story I had heard many times before but which this time came alive in a new way, as though she sensed she was in the presence of someone who knew how to listen deeply.

When Maria finished, Dr. Chen said, "Let's start from the beginning again to see if I can add anything to what you're doing." She knew her place was to add to Maria's treatment, not to take charge. She'd been listening.

When Maria talked about side effects, Dr. Chen noticed that Maria still had her hair.

"It's good for your son to see to that his mommy is normal," she said, knowing that for a mother who has cancer her children are never far from her mind. And in the first of many hopeful comments, she said, "It's a good sign that you haven't had a lot of side effects with the FOLFIRI. That means the chemotherapy is working," she said matter-of-factly, but with great impact. I could see Maria soften.

Maria told her that she sees an acupuncturist. "Yes, I have a number of patients who do acupuncture," she said. "They recover more quickly from chemotherapy." When examining Maria's abdomen, she saw an herbal patch that Maria wore on her stomach, Lam and Howard Kong's special herbal mixture designed to improve yang energy (to fight cancer) without draining yin (to sustain the body through treatment).

Maria said, "I can take it off for you."

"No, I recognize it. I know what it is."

Maria told her what she knew of the patch just to make sure they were on the same page. They were, and the difference was palpable; we didn't have to defend anything or endure arguments about why such alternative practices weren't standard of care for cancer patients.

AFTER THE EXAM Dr. Chen asked if we wanted to retreat to her office, which was a more comfortable setting in which to talk. Attractive in a dignified way, with jet-black hair set off by rimless glasses, and an imperturbable presence, she sat down at her desk. Pictures of her family occupied the bookshelves to her left, and diplomas from some of the best universities in the country hung on the wall behind her: Harvard, Yale Medical School, a Stanford residency. She looked at Maria probingly and said kindly, "What are your goals with this treatment, and how do you want to incorporate this into your life?"

Maria closed her eyes and reflected for a moment. "To contain this cancer and to live as long as I can so that I can benefit from future advances in cancer treatment. And I want to watch my child grow old."

"Those are good goals," Dr. Chen said slowly, each word having its own space.

"My complaints aside, I'm very grateful to my current oncologist for bringing me back to life from when I was almost catatonically anemic in the winter."

Again Dr. Chen observed that Maria'd had a pretty good start on FOLFIRI. "In fact, you haven't had bad side effects and you're on schedule," she said, explaining that some patients have to slow down their chemotherapy schedule because their bodies can't keep pace with the toxicity. "These are good signs."

Then she continued, "Looking at your scans, I have concerns about the lesions in your liver." That was the most troubling piece of Maria's profile, she said, and the one that needed to be addressed in treatment.

"Several of my patients have done well after a diagnosis of stage IV colon cancer and a metastasis to the liver," she said. "Each of them had chemotherapy to shrink their tumors, followed by a resection, or surgical removal, of a part of the liver that has the malignancy. One is now ten years out," she continued. "He had a liver resection; when the disease returned, he had another resection; and last time, when the disease returned again, he had chemotherapy."

"That's impressive," I said.

"Is it possible with chemotherapy alone for the tumors to shrink to the point where surgery would not be necessary?" Maria asked.

"It's very, very possible," she answered positively. "Some of it has to do with the disease itself, if it will behave in a fashion that will allow us to manage it" without surgery. "But the biology of the tumor dictates the course of treatment." Again, she noted that Maria was responding well to the chemotherapy and added, "If you can take the chemo, we can manage the cancer. And if you were to have had a problem with the tumors in your colon, that would have shown up by now."

Looking relieved, Maria said, "That's so good to hear."

"We can be aggressive about the liver lesions," Dr. Chen said. "I'm very aggressive with treating colon cancer. If you can control the liver lesions and keep them to under 3 centimeters, then you can control the disease."

She then described a new treatment called Cyberknife, developed at Stanford University, where she completed her medical oncology fellowship. Officially known as the Cyberknife Robotic Radiosurgery System, it is a nonsurgical technology that can reduce or eliminate tumors once considered to be inoperable. It delivers high doses of radiation directly to the liver lesions, effectively burning them and killing disease without the side effects of long-term chemotherapy. Cyberknife, I later read, can burn the last remaining layers of a lesion, even if they're only a few molecules thick.

"I know all the doctors at Stanford who've been pioneering this new technology," she said, "and would be able, if your tumors respond to the chemotherapy, to guide you into this treatment." The game plan, she repeated, would be to shrink the tumors enough that Maria could benefit from Cyberknife and, if the liver lesions did not shrunk enough, to get a biopsy to see what else is happening in the liver. "Cyberknife can prolong your life and keep chemo for when you really need it down the road."

TURNING TO INTEGRATIVE medicine, Dr. Chen said, "I have found with my patients who do acupuncture and alternative treatments, they do better and have fewer side effects—and frankly, do better overall. One's attitude controls the rest of what is happening in the body. I have seen the mind-body connection make a difference in my practice." She talked about chronomodulated chemotherapy, quoting studies indicating its effectiveness with certain patients, especially those with pancreatic cancer, and added she would use it if a patient were not responding in the way she wanted. "I'm willing to be whatever part of the team you need me to be and would be glad to collaborate with the Block Center on your behalf." She added, in a way that was reassuring without sounding Pollyanna-ish, "It will all work itself out."

As we ended, Maria again asked, "Is it possible for the tumors in my abdomen to disappear with just the chemotherapy alone?"

"Yes," she said, "but we would not be able to see any evidence of molecular disease that remained. That's why we need to work to contain the disease even when there's no evidence of disease anymore."

"I'm starting to understand that there's a new way to think about cancer, more like a chronic disease, like, say, AIDS—something you can live with," Maria said.

"Yes. There has been a whole shift in paradigm with respect to cancer," she said, reeling off a list of chronic diseases, such as diabetes and heart disease. "It's a totally different game. As long as you're around, there'll be new treatments down the road. That's the game. You have to be positive."

ON THE WAY to Campbell, Maria had taken my hand and asked evocatively, "Honey, do you remember what day this is?"

"Give me a hint."

"Twenty-seven years ago today."

Quickly putting the pieces together, I asked, "Well, that places it at Princeton, in the spring. Right? The day you turned in your thesis?"

"Yes. And the day we first kissed. Do you remember? You were waiting for me outside the Religion Department after I turned in my thesis . . ."

"And I had a bottle of champagne and Orange Milano cookies," I interrupted, completing her sentence. "And we celebrated the end of your resistance to letting me in."

"I had to keep you at arm's length while I wrote my thesis, or else I would never have finished it on time. I wanted you so much. I couldn't handle both you and my thesis."

I smiled. "I know. Three months of torture. When we fell in the snow, after I got back from London, I knew then that I wanted you. I'd been waiting all spring to seduce you. But as we started to flirt with kissing, I got scared. I wanted you so much, but I didn't want to lose our friendship."

Maria nodded in agreement. "Me too. Our friendship was too special to risk. I didn't know if what we had was a lifelong friendship or a romance. I wanted both, but I knew once we crossed the threshold there was no going back."

"I guess we got both," I said.

The atmosphere in the car shifted as Maria told me about a front-page article she'd read that morning in our local newspaper. The story was about Alicia Parlette, a twenty-eight-year-old San Francisco writer who was diagnosed with a rare and incurable form of cancer when she was twenty-three. She chronicled her story in a book, *Alicia's Story*, which first appeared as a seventeen-part series in the *San Francisco Chronicle*.

The current article updated readers on Alicia's illness, saying that her cancer had progressed to where treatment was no longer possible, and she was now living her last days in the hospital surrounded by family and friends. Maria began to cry as she told me that Alicia had met a man the previous fall, and they'd exchanged wedding vows two days before, in the hospital.

"She's going to die, and she's still living her life," Maria said, crying. She took my hand again, and we drove south, listening to Norah Jones on our car stereo.

MONDAY, APRIL 19TH

Sitting in Dr. Huron's infusion room, Maria and I looked out over a panorama of the San Francisco Bay, with the Golden Gate Bridge to our left in the distance and Tiburon and Angel Island straight ahead across the water. A tangle of San Francisco streets, reminiscent of the IV lines dangling on Maria's blouse, crisscrossed below us.

We'd just learned that Maria's hemoglobin count had gone up slightly in the last two weeks, the first time it increased without a transfusion since she began this journey three months before—it may very well have been for the first time in years.

Maria and I celebrated the good news: it meant she was no longer bleeding internally. It was likely that her tumors had shrunk enough that their extra weight was no longer tearing the tissue in which they were embedded. We had been waiting for this milestone.

THE DAY BEFORE, we had celebrated our wedding anniversary and reminisced, as we did every year, on how we'd changed—and how stayed the same—since the day we married twenty-two years before. It was also an opportunity to revisit one of the most painful events of Maria's adult life: that her father and mother did not attend our wedding. Though knowing that they didn't bless our union, we had accepted her mother's invitation to come to their home after the ceremony to celebrate with a bottle of champagne—despite the obvious tension and hurt. When we arrived, Maria's father was not there. He'd slipped out of the house to get a haircut and didn't return until after we'd left his home for the first time as a married couple.

Retelling the story, Maria added a new twist to a familiar narrative. Shortly after our wedding, Maria asked her family to come to Los Angeles (to my parents' house) to celebrate our marriage at a party we threw ourselves. Already hurt, we didn't want to be beholden to them, or anyone, for our celebration. Her mother agreed to come, but her father said, "Why would I want to spend money I don't have, to go to a place I don't like, to see people I will never see again?"

As Maria spoke, I noticed that the last of the cherry blossoms outside our bedroom window had fallen, leaving a soft carpet of pink in our backyard. Remembering the rejection, Maria cried. "I wasn't able to give my dad an answer to his question then, and I haven't been able to for all this time." Then she added, "But I now know what I wish I could have said to him. I wish I had said, All of that may be true. And then the only possible reason to come would be to celebrate your daughter's happiness."

Billy Hanahan had barely a year left to live at that point; he already had cancer of the throat and tongue.

"I can better understand why my dad would feel that way," Maria explained. "He had cancer and didn't have much time to waste. Maybe he didn't have the energy to travel cross-country, given his condition, and maybe he didn't know how to tell me that."

A year later, at her father's side, on his deathbed, Maria felt that there was a moment of grace when, for the first time, he asked how I was doing. Maria responded simply, telling him I was okay, though she believed this was his way of saying, Van is your husband, and I am leaving you to him, with my blessings. He died the next day, alone in the room with Maria, his oldest child.

DR. HURON CALLED us into the Venice room for Maria's pre-chemo consultation. We learned that Maria had gained four pounds since her Block Center diet adjustment and that her hemoglobin level had remained steady. Maria and I were delighted by the news, and even Dr. Huron seemed lighter and warmer.

"When I saw you in the chemo room," Dr. Huron said, "I said, 'She looks really good today.' I could tell you gained weight just by looking at you." She then reminded Maria that she had two more rounds of chemotherapy before her next CT scan.

"What will we be talking about after the scans?" Maria asked. I was surprised by the question, knowing Maria would soon choose another oncologist. But I could sense that, after meeting with Dr. Chen, Maria, who did not have a devious bone in her body, was genuinely curious about the next part of her journey—how to contain her liver lesions—and about Dr. Huron's long-term plan, which had always seemed a little one-dimensional to us: chemotherapy followed by more chemotherapy, until nothing more could be done.

"You'll need to continue with the chemotherapy until the 'maximum benefit' has been derived," Dr. Huron said.

"What does 'maximum benefit' mean?" Maria asked.

"Until the chemotherapy is not working anymore, or you're not tolerating it."

I started to feel depressed, as if Dr. Huron had put me back into the no exit of the chemotherapy-until-you-die box. Now *I* wanted to know Dr. Huron's game plan, after the maximum benefit had been derived, but I also knew that her answer was not that important to me anymore.

Frowning, Maria persisted. "But what happens if the chemotherapy substantially shrinks the tumors in my liver, and they disappear? Would I be cancer-free?"

"The old dogma is that once chemotherapy shrinks the primary tumor it gets the metastases everywhere else. But now we know that subtle genetic changes occur when cancer cells leave the primary location and go somewhere else."

Taking that to mean that, even if the primary tumor in the colon disappeared, Maria might be left with disease in the liver whose genetic fingerprint was less responsive to chemotherapy, I asked, "What nonchemo options will be available to Maria once the liver tumors have shrunk?"

"There's a noninvasive treatment for inoperable liver malignancies called Radio Frequency Ablation, or RFA," she explained, where radio frequency waves are directed into small tumors to increase their temperature and destroy them.

"And what about using Cyberknife technology to destroy lesions in the liver?"

"This technology is used primarily in other organs, but not the liver, which is sensitive to radiation."

"I understand doctors at Stanford are using this technology on liver lesions," Maria said.

"I'm not aware of there being large-scale data on its success with the liver."

Maria and I exchanged a glance. I know Maria doesn't feel as though she has the time to wait for large-scale studies.

"Maria and I are worried about her liver metastases," I said. Remembering what Dr. Chen advised, I asked, "Would you advise Maria to biopsy the liver tumors if the CT scan indicated that they hadn't shrunk?"

"The liver tumors could be filled with necrotic (dead) tissue," she said, adding that she wouldn't rush to biopsy them. She explained that some liver tumors retain their basic architecture and size despite successful treatment, and only a PET scan, which measures metabolic activity, can determine the tumor's density and how quickly its cells are dividing. "It's definitely not urgent and pressing to attend to the liver mets," Dr. Huron concluded. "We can wait and see what happens."

She advised Maria to do CT and PET scans after another eight rounds of chemotherapy and then to see what changes had occurred in the liver. "We don't have to be aggressive with the liver. We can take out most of it, if we have to, and it will regenerate enough to pick up the functions it now provides."

By this point I felt confused: in the span of four days, two separate oncologists had presented different conclusions about the urgency of addressing Maria's liver mets.

Just to confirm what we both already knew, Maria asked, "By the way, have you had a chance to speak to Donald Abrams about the Block Center?"

"I've not had the time."

DRIVING HOME, MARIA didn't know if she would have one more round of sumo medicine with Dr. Huron, but she knew that her trust had been irreparably damaged.

"She may be right about everything she has told us, but I simply can't hear her message when she's so insensitive to my sense of urgency," Maria said, her indignation growing. "And not once did she lay out my options and ask me what *I* thought or wanted for my own treatment. I'm not waiting around for my mets to get out of control and for her to get comfortable with large-scale studies of treatments that could prolong my life. That's not the party I'm going to." Almost apoplectic, Maria added, "I want to be aggressive with this cancer. I want to be around a long time. I want to be an outlier, but that won't happen if I sit back and wait for chemotherapy to run its course without doing anything else."

"I know. Dr. Huron's laissez-faire attitude feels like a death sentence."

"I need to work with a warrior, someone who mirrors the fierceness I feel in my gut. I want to attack this cancer, take the battle to the enemy, catch it off guard, confuse it, outflank it. I don't want to sit back and wait. Waiting—that's no way to live your life."

LISTENING TO MARIA, the opening lines of the poem "Waiting for the Barbarians," by the Greek poet Constantine Cavafy came to mind. In it, the narrator observes that everyone seems stunned into indolence as they wait to be overtaken by the barbarians:

> *What are we waiting for, assembled in the forum?*
> *The barbarians are due here today.*
> *Why isn't anything going on in the senate?*
> *Why are the senators sitting there without legislating?*

Because the barbarians are coming today.

What's the point of senators making laws now?

Once the barbarians are here, they'll do the legislating.

Maria wasn't waiting for the barbarians. She would do the legislating when it came to her life and happiness.

MONDAY, APRIL 26TH

This morning we drove to Marin County over the Richmond–San Rafael Bridge to continue our search for a new oncologist. When we arrived at Dr. Gullion's office, we looked up to find that we were on the plain below Mount Tamalpais, the highest peak in the Marin hills at 2,572 feet, and for many the most sacred spot in the Bay Area.

Arriving early, we walked along a low berm next to Corte Madera Creek, which winds its way from the San Francisco Bay through the valley's communities, with Mount Tam standing between it and the Pacific Ocean. Salt marshes extend in both directions.

"This is so beautiful," Maria said. "I would love to do my sumo medicine here at the foot of Mount Tam. I don't think they'd let me walk on the mountain, but maybe I can even walk along the creek while getting chemo."

Circumambulating the mountain is a time-honored tradition here. In 1965, three Buddhist poets (two Beats among them)—Allen Ginsberg, Gary Snyder, and Philip Whalen—gathered at the base of Mount Tam and, inspired by the Tibetan and Indian practice of walking clockwise around a venerated object, "opened the mountain" by completing their first circumambulation, starting a tradition that continues to this day.

INSIDE THE MARIN Cancer Institute, which housed Dr. Gullion's medical practice, Marin Specialty Care, quilts from a local artist adorned the walls in what we learned was a rotating exhibit of local artists. A large mobile hung from an atrium ceiling in the center of the building. In the exam room, a wall-mounted plastic brochure holder displayed six handouts, each one describing a different complementary service provided by the Integrative Oncology program, which Gullion directed: Massage Therapy, Acupuncture, Jin Shin Jyutsu, Nutritional Counseling, Gentle Bodywork for Wellness, and Supporting the Healing Process through Art.

Dr. Gullion walked into the exam room punctually, and shook both our hands. A tall, handsome man in his mid-sixties, he had a bearing that suggested an active life outside the consulting room. He wore a heart-shaped pin over his shirt pocket: two hands—one silver, one bronze—holding a gold heart. His light blue eyes looked darker against an impressive tan and blue shirt. He had just returned from a two-week vacation in Hawaii, and Maria was his first patient.

Turning his attention to Maria, he said, "So, you've been through quite a bit to get here."

"Yes, and I'm here."

"What brings you to see me?"

"To be frank, I'm out of sync with my current oncologist. And I need to work with someone who can stay hopeful in my treatment and convey that to me."

The Block Center program and their staff, she added, had inspired her to believe that she could make a difference in her own life by devoting herself to an integrative program. "I feel ten times better now than I felt before I started implementing their suggestions." Bottom line, she said, sounding clear and forceful, entitled to what she wanted, "I want to work with an oncologist who can collaborate with the Block Center to develop a more positive plan of action. Doing chemotherapy alone, every two weeks for the rest of my life, is not a plan."

Dr. Gullion seemed unfazed, perhaps even intrigued, by her clarity. Before him sat a woman who had been emboldened in three short months to take her care into her own hands. There can be something attractive about that in a patient who, like Maria, was assertive yet vulnerable, but not belligerent.

He asked her many of the same assessment questions we'd heard from others, but he seemed surprised that she was getting four Neupogen shots. He explained that he would only prescribe a white blood cell booster if a FOLFIRI patient was coming up to their next cycle, their blood counts were low, and they needed a boost to keep them on their chemotherapy schedule.

Maria, relieved not to have to get four injections again, agreed to continue to negotiate with him about what is appropriate for her, based on her ongoing blood tests.

They're already collaborating, I thought.

Reviewing Maria's electronic medical records, he declared, "Everything points to a response with the treatment," and he listed all the indicators: Maria's feeling better, tumor marker numbers dropping, tolerating the FOLFIRI without major side effects.

"The best part of the whole thing," he added, "is that people with a dramatic response fare much better." Maria was visibly relieved to hear that, much as she was when Dr. Chen told her the same thing.

THE EXAM OVER, Dr. Gullion said, "I'd be glad to help you in any way I can." He was not as forward and opinionated as Dr. Chen, and started slowly, if not carefully. "In your situation, I think nutrition is on top of the list, followed by exercise."

He acknowledged that he agreed with Keith Block's recommendations, noting that Maria was already doing much of what his Integrative Oncology program would recommend. Keith, he added, was looking into whether patients do better if they exercise while receiving chemo, and said his own patients sometimes walk along the creek *before* treatments.

I interrupted. "Can they walk along the creek *during* treatments?" I imagined he thought I was joking, but he didn't know Maria yet.

The liver on her mind, Maria asked about the feasibility of Cyberknife. "Liver-directed treatment can be fairly invasive," he stated, especially with RFA and to a lesser extent Cyberknife, and cautioned that whether Cyberknife can be used depends on the precise location of the lesions in the lobes of the liver. If they were adjacent to vein structures, you would run the risk of destroying tissue close to blood vessels. He advised Maria to push on with the chemotherapy "to get the maximum benefit." By then I wasn't so angry when I heard these words.

"Does it make sense to throw a changeup," Maria asked, "to switch to FOLFOX, and catch the cancer cells off guard?"

"Toxicity can begin to outweigh the benefits of a drug, even when it's working," he answered, "but in general you don't want to switch drugs until you have to. Cancer cells become resistant, and if you expose them to multiple drugs at once they adjust and develop multiple resistances." He said researchers at Stanford University Hospital were currently studying this phenomenon.

"The next scan will be critical," he said, summing up. "It'll determine what course of action to take." If all the lesions were shrinking (in the colon, pelvis, and liver), then Maria could be aggressive and, essentially, pursue the treatment plan that Dr. Chen recommended. If the liver lesions looked better, but there was still evidence of pelvic and abdominal disease, then she wouldn't be able to go after the liver lesions until the pelvic disease was contained.

I made a mental note that he didn't mention a third possible scenario: the tumors shrink everywhere except the liver. I realized for the first time that all of Maria's lesions had to be contained, if not quiet, for other nonchemotherapy options to be viable, and I felt that familiar anxiety that lurked in the background even when I was hopeful. My wife was climbing a formidable mountain, and though others have climbed it, each attempt is unlike any other.

Dr. Gullion walked us to see the treatment room, a long, narrow room with a strikingly beautiful view of Corte Madera Creek and Mount Tam, which, because of an abnormally wet winter, was lush and green. We stopped to admire the mountain's presence. Dr. Gullion paused, then said, "The Dalai Lama says Mount Tam is a healing mountain. He has made pilgrimages to Mount Tam when he's here."

Maria lingered in the infusion room, sensing the mountain, taking in the activity in the room: the oncology nurses, the other patients, the classical music in the background. I could tell what she was thinking: Just do it.

DRIVING HOME, WITH Mount Tamalpais at our backs, Maria told me that she wanted to switch her treatment to Dr. Gullion. "I would've told him in person, but I needed a few moments alone with you first to allow myself to desire what I desire."

Remembering the lines Satchi had placed on the hallway table recently, I said, "Dig your toes in, leap off the line, and go for it!"

Maria picked up her cell phone, called Dr. Gullion, and told him she wanted to transfer her treatment to him. She crossed the threshold and opened the mountain.

six

◆

THE DIAMOND OF HEALING

I was eavesdropping on Maria and Satchi. Walking into earshot, I heard Satchi and Maria talking in the kitchen. "Mommy, why did you cry when you found out you had cancer?"

Maria chose her words carefully, as though her brain hadn't caught up with her heart yet. "In the old days," Maria started, not talking at her normal pace, "when people were told they had cancer, they knew it meant that they were going to live a short life. . . . It's different today. . . . Doctors know so much more now about how to help people live long lives with cancer. I'm doing everything I can do to make sure of that."

From where I was standing in the dining room, I could see into the kitchen. Satchi looked half-satisfied, half-confused. Maria noticed his frown, met his eyes, and said, simply, "I was scared, honey."

That seemed to make more sense to him. He put his lips to her ear and whispered, "I've been scared you're gonna die."

In an email to all our loved ones, Maria wrote:

I have to share with you some news from today's San Francisco Chronicle *that is cause for great celebration. To quote: "Health insurer WellPoint Inc. said Tuesday beginning May 1, it will comply with a provision of health care reform that limits cases in which insurers can cancel coverage when a customer gets sick. The Indianapolis insurer said that . . . it will follow a reform guideline that restricts cases of rescission only to instances where a patient committed fraud or intentional misrepresentation."*

This means that as of today, my health insurer (a subsidiary of WellPoint) can't cancel my insurance just because I have cancer. Woo hoo! What a relief! Of course, they can raise the rates as much as they want between now and 2014—and they most certainly will—but they can't just throw me out. I thought this provision wouldn't take effect until September, but it seems WellPoint is voluntarily complying now. I can't tell you what a relief that is. Whatever your feelings about health care reform, please give thanks today for me and the millions of American who suffer from chronic disease. We will not be left behind.

David Gullion, a heart-shaped green-enamel brooch pinned to his shirt, walked into the exam room for Maria's first prechemo consultation as his patient. Maria must have looked upset, since he sat down, made eye contact immediately, and asked if she was okay.

"Well, I'm feeling stressed today."

"Is your stress related to being here for your first treatment?

"No, emotional stress in my life in general."

She didn't mention that she and I had just fought in the car and both felt terrible as a result. Sitting next to her, I could feel my own upset close to the surface. I felt unappreciated trying to get Maria, Satchi, and me prepared for a chemo day—a juggling act complicated by Maria's fragility and bossiness on these mornings—and demonstrated my displeasure by criticizing her for not being more sensitive to me. Maria reacted by withdrawing emotionally, and I felt a wilting combination of aloneness and guilt—guilt for not being able to handle my own need for recognition without snapping, and for contributing to Maria's chemo-day burdens.

Dr. Gullion said kindly, "It's a roller-coaster ride sometimes with cancer, besides life." He wondered if Maria had a therapist, explaining that if she felt emotionally secure it would contribute to her sense of well-being—and that would help her treatment. Maria's eyes flicked from his face to mine, searching for our familiar comfort, and back to his. I remembered something the Vietnamese Buddhist teacher Thich Nhat Hanh wrote: when you're angry at your beloved, imagine yourself and your beloved one hundred years from now, and your anger will evaporate. I reached out and squeezed Maria's thigh.

Reviewing the need for Neupogen shots, Dr. Gullion advised Maria to continue the shots for the time being, especially since we would be traveling to the Block Center in two weeks and needed her immune system to be strong for the journey. But depending on our insurance benefits, he said, it might be preferable for Maria or me to administer the shots at home, where Maria might be more comfortable.

"That would make me happy," Maria said.

Overwhelmed by the cancer research I was doing, I asked Dr. Gullion if he'd be willing to help me think about potential new treatments. He took a stack of articles I copied for him, perused the first one on PP224, a drug being tested to regulate apoptosis in cancer cells, and expressed curiosity about the new research, adding that clinical results with the first generation of this drug ended dismally.

"It's indeed overwhelming to keep up with the amount of ongoing cancer research," he said. I was only researching new treatments for one cancer, colon cancer; I couldn't imagine how difficult it would be for an oncologist to stay abreast of research for ten or twenty different kinds of cancer. At some point, the amount of knowledge generated must outstrip one's capacity to integrate and utilize it meaningfully. In a way, cancer cells employ the same strategy: they overwhelm the body with the sheer force of their exponential persistence.

ONCE IN THE infusion room, Maria and I were surprised that the consultation was so short and we had so little to say. The relief of being in a new setting, with a new and collaborative doctor, must have quieted our minds. Plus, Dr. Gullion's bearing was reassuring and comforting; his presence didn't generate new anxieties.

A day earlier, Maria had hand-delivered a letter to Dr. Huron saying that she was transferring her treatment to a different team of oncologists, including the doctors at the Block Center, a South Bay oncologist who specializes in gastrointestinal cancers, and a local oncologist who offers integrative care.

"I feel so much lighter now," Maria told me, "I'm ready to scale the mountain."

In her letter, Maria wrote that she'd be forever grateful to Dr. Huron for getting her on her feet again and, using a chess metaphor, added that she knew that she was still in the opening game but that it was time to mobilize for the middle game. "I am confident," she wrote, "that this team can continue your good care as I enter the next stage."

Maria knew Dr. Huron cared for her, but also realized that their particular doctor-patient relationship was simply a mismatch from the beginning. This happens with all doctors. It certainly happens routinely in psychotherapy that both therapist and patient sense a mismatch.

Sometimes, in the hands of a skilled clinician, the mismatch can be used to facilitate growth, but sometimes it cannot. It's a sign of maturity to acknowledge such a dilemma.

BY DAY'S END, Dr. Gullion returned to the infusion room to check on Maria. He noticed the food in front of her—halibut steak, sautéed spinach, quinoa. "You have your own little buffet going. Very healthy—fish and vegetables." He then joked, "Keith Block can get anyone to eat a healthy diet."

We all laughed. "That's true," Maria responded. And then, "I'm on a short leash with Dr. Block."

"Do you know Keith Block?" I asked.

Smiling, he said, "I've known Keith for over ten years. We've collaborated many times." As members of a small but growing cohort in the oncology world, he and Block had participated in conferences at the Commonweal Cancer Project in Bolinas, California.

"Keith has moved in the direction of supplements and blood testing and matching supplements to your body's needs," he said. "I, on the other hand, have pursued mind-body modalities, like expressive art therapy." As he spoke, I found myself thinking that while Dr. Block had focused on changing outcomes with his 2 + 2 + 2 = 256 philosophy and plan, Dr. Gullion seemed to be focused on providing complementary modalities that reduce stress, minimize side effects, and improve well-being, with the hope that outcomes can be affected.

He didn't seem to share Dr. Block's conviction that the synergy of integrative medicine can improve life expectancies. Whatever their differences, I was relieved that Maria would benefit from *their* synergy.

"Keith likes to come to San Francisco to surf with his buddy, Mark Renneker," Dr. Gullion added.

Maria laughed; she'd known about Renneker, known locally as the "surfing doctor," for over a decade, since she herself started to surf in her mid-thirties. Over the years, Renneker had built a medical consultation practice whose focus was to provide patients and family members with practical information and strategies for achieving the best possible, most comprehensive cancer care. He also helps patients locate the right doctor if they're at an impasse with their current one (apparently, this is a common problem in cancer treatment).

"Oh, I know of Mark Renneker," Maria said cryptically.

"You don't need Mark," Gullion quipped. "You're doing all the research you need to be in charge of your treatment."

SUNDAY, MAY 9TH

Maria was jonesing for my chocolate. I was just about to finish my piece of dark raspberry chocolate when I looked across the table at Maria. On most days, she was only mildly annoyed when Satchi and I enjoyed dessert openly in her presence; she hadn't been able to eat sugar for many years prior to her cancer diagnosis. On sumo medicine days, however, her annoyance approached envy, if not murderous proportions.

"I can tell those little cancer boogers are dying, because I want sweets. And I want to kill to get sweets in my body," Maria said, exaggerating.

"Give me sweets!" she commanded.

The craving would last for thirty-six to forty-eight hours, then being to taper off, until it disappeared on day four of sumo medicine, as the 5-FU pogrom began to wind down. Maria sensed that the craving is the last breath of the dying cancer cells. They need glucose to survive, and in the moments before they die, they send out one last distress signal: Feed me. *Now!*

Curiously, in every chemotherapy treatment room I have been in, except the one at the Block Center, candy (Tootsie Rolls, hard candies, even chocolate) is usually available for the taking. The problem is, chemotherapy takes life with one hand and sugar gives with the other. Most people can't imagine a life without sugar; Maria couldn't imagine a life with it.

THE GERMAN SCIENTIST Otto Warburg won the Nobel Prize in 1931 for his work on the metabolism of tumors and the respiration of cells, particularly cancer cells. He hypothesized that cancer growth is caused by "the replacement of the respiration of oxygen in normal body cells by a fermentation of sugar." Normal cells generate energy from oxygen within the mitochondria; cancer cells generate energy from the breakdown of glucose.

In other words, cancer cells are sugar junkies (they have sixteen times the number of insulin and insulin-like receptor sites as healthy cells); the more sugar, or carbohydrates, in the diet, the faster cancer grows. It literally steals glucose from the body's normal cells. Take away sugar and you starve cancer cells.

Known as the Warburg Effect, this phenomenon is one of the pillars of the anticancer diet now espoused by nutritionists and authors, including David Servan-Schreiber in his widely popular book, *Anticancer: A New Way of Life*, and in cookbooks, such as *The Cancer-Fighting Kitchen*, by Rebecca Katz.

In his book, Keith Block bemoans how many oncologists encourage cancer patients who have lost weight precipitously (when malignancies hijack the body's nutrients) to fatten up after chemotherapy by eating ice cream and high-carbohydrate, high-fat snacks and meals. Paradoxically, the benefits of chemotherapy are attenuated by a diet that misguidedly strengthens the tumors even as it's supposed to nourish and strengthen the ailing body.

FRIDAY, MAY 14TH

"Cancer thrives in dark, closed spaces," I overheard Maria say on the phone one night. "Letting in the light, letting out the secrets, and cleaning out everything: that is my agenda right now."

I'm not sure to whom she was talking, or if she was talking symbolically or concretely, or both. But what she said captured in an elegant way something I also believe to be true, and which became clearer the further we moved from the crushing news of her diagnosis: cancer is an opportunity for the mind and heart to heal as much as it is for the body.

MONDAY, MAY 17TH

Maria eagerly awaited her return to the Block Center for round eight of sumo medicine so she could experience chronomodulated chemotherapy for herself. The Greeks have an expression, *teliósane tá psémata*. It literally translates as, "The lies are over," but more commonly it means, "Now we'll finally find out for ourselves."

The night before, as we prepared for our journey, Maria said, "Seventy-five percent of what the Block Center has told me to do is what I've known I need to do all along, but I haven't been willing to fully show up for it. The cancer is like the universe saying, Hello, wake up! You really need to be focused now. You have no more leeway." Pausing, she added, "With all that I'm doing, I feel more aligned physically, emotionally, and spiritually—from my cells to my soul."

I liked the sound of that, "from my cells to my soul," and said, "You're a poet."

She blushed and said, "The three of us are creating the new poem of our lives."

"Yes, we are. And sometimes we're angry poets, and sometimes we're poets of the heart."

"You know, I'm getting more comfortable not knowing what to expect anymore," Maria said. "How far north do you think this bus is heading?" It was an inside joke, and we both laughed. In my early twenties, while traveling in Greece, I would board buses not knowing where they would let off, and then spend the rest of the day exploring unexpected delights.

"SUCCESS IS NEVER final, and failure is never fatal. It's courage that counts." Below this quote, on a whiteboard in the Block Center infusion room, is another: "Every now and then life throws you a curve ball. If you can't hit the curve, you can't stay in the majors. SWING AWAY!!!"

I wonder how often they change the quotes. On the wall adjacent to the coral tank with one fish is a poem from an unknown author:

What Cancer Cannot Do
Cancer is so limited . . .
It cannot cripple Love.
It cannot shatter Hope.
It cannot corrode Faith.
It cannot destroy Peace.
It cannot kill Friendship.
It cannot suppress Memories.
It cannot silence Courage.
It cannot invade the Soul.
It cannot steal eternal Life.
It cannot conquer the Spirit.

The Block Center infusion room was crowded. By the time we arrived, the tree rooms were already occupied and we had to settle for one of the herb rooms. The oncology nurse hooked Maria up to her prechemo IV drugs, which included dexamethasone, a corticosteroid to prevent nausea, and a mixture of micronutrients (vitamins C, A, D3, B1, B2, B6, B12, niacinamide, E, K, folic acid, and biotin), which support the body and help to minimize side effects. While waiting for the sumo medicine, Maria met with Sarah Kranz, the physical therapist, to talk about the restricted range of motion in her left arm and exercise in general. Maria explained that since the portacath surgery her shoulder clenched whenever her port was accessed. "The clenching can continue for days," Maria said. "And the muscles under my port are cranky."

Sarah carefully moved Maria's arm and observed, "The port is set very low in your chest, right in the meat of the muscle." She added, "Usually, it's higher, near the collarbone."

Maria perked up, "That's what it feels like to me. When I met with my surgeon to discuss the portacath, he said he would place it lower so I could wear low-cut dresses. Had I known it would be this painful, especially in someone as thin as me, I would have told him, No, thank you. To hell with the low-cut dresses."

Sarah showed Maria exercises to build strength in her shoulder but speculated that the tissue and muscle were holding a memory of repeated trauma—from surgery and biweekly accessing of the port. Physical manipulation alone might not be enough to help the shoulder, Sarah said, but it was likely that together physical and emotional attention would, and encouraged her to look into Somatic Experiencing, a body-awareness approach to releasing trauma, which Maria was familiar with in her own work.

Turning to exercise, Sarah explained that Maria's blood tests would determine how much cardiovascular exercise and resistance training she could handle. If her hemoglobin and hematocrit levels were low, too much exercise would challenge the body and deplete her reserves.

"Overall, fatigue that comes from cancer—and the treatment of cancer—is different than fatigue that comes from a hard workout. Fatigue from a hard workout feels better, with quality sleep." But with cancer and treatment-related fatigue, rest alone doesn't help. What helps, she said, is a consistent level of activity.

Next, she reviewed Maria's FOLFIRI side effects, identifying three problem areas: fingertips, feet, and mouth. I thought it odd that a physical therapist would review chemotherapy side effects, but I later learned this is how the Block Center team works: each specialist asks similar questions of patients, then pools what they have learned to develop a multilayered team response to problems.

Examining Maria's fingertips and the soles of her feet, she saw that her fingertips were starting to crack. "Your fingertips have the presentation of hand-foot syndrome," she said. Small amounts of 5-FU leak out of the capillaries and can cause redness, tenderness, and peeling. "The problem is interconnected with your overall health," Sarah explained. "These treatments affect your whole body. The stronger your whole body is, the less hospitable it will be to cancer. If your hands and feet hurt, you're less likely to want to be active, and if you're not active, you'll not be able to sustain the level of exercise you need to stay strong." The domino effect of inactivity is a weakened body.

By the time Jennifer Ellis, the physician's assistant, greeted us, she'd already consulted with Sarah and offered Maria simple treatments to control 5-FU toxicity, including the option to eliminate an extra shot, or bolus, of 5-FU during the daylong infusion. "Even the Mayo Clinics have discontinued the 5-FU bolus with FOLFIRI, believing it adds too much toxicity to the body without added benefits."

She then explained that because we were in Evanston for only three days, and not four, Maria wasn't a candidate for chronomodulated FOLFIRI, which requires an extra night and day. Though disappointed—her experiment with chronomodulation would have to wait—Maria was still relieved to be spared the extra 5-FU toxicity.

As Jen stood to leave, I asked her to interpret the results of genetic tests for Lynch syndrome, which we'd received a few days before. "No mutation was detected in any of the tests," Jen said, "so you're not a genetic carrier of Lynch syndrome. Satchi will not be at high risk for colon cancer because of a genetic mutation."

Maria and I felt a burden lift. Given how young Maria was to have developed colon cancer, a disease which typically strikes later in life, we'd been worrying about the trajectory of Satchi's health. Jen then added, "It takes five to ten years for polyps in the colon to turn into cancer, and then another five years for them to metastasize. So for you, it's probably taken at least fifteen years to arrive at this point."

Maria and I quickly did the math in our heads. "That means I probably started to develop these polyps when I was in my early thirties."

"Satchi should probably start getting screened for polyps when he's thirty years old at the latest," Jen said, "but to play it safe, when he's twenty-five."

Whatever led to Maria's polyps may not be a factor in Satchi's life, but we'll have to educate him about his family history and how to make proactive choices about his diet and health. The habits he develops now will become the lifestyle he adopts in his twenties.

THE INFUSION ROOM crowd thinned by midafternoon and we moved to Oak, a room with an inward feeling. At day's end, the wife of another patient with stage IV colon cancer walked in and introduced herself. She held a book called *A Homeopathic Approach to Cancer* and told us that her husband was from Germany, where homeopathy is commonly practiced, even for chronic diseases such as cancer. His German doctors were encouraging him to stop che-motherapy once his tumors were contained and to continue with homeopathy. We commiserated on how hard it would be to make such a decision to get off the traditional oncology train.

Sharing more of her research, she told us that extract of olean-der is a promising off-label, nontoxic, natural compound for colon cancer. A scientist from MD Anderson Cancer Center, in Houston, she reported, had published studies in peer-reviewed journals that indicate oleander not only stimulates the immune system but also attacks cancer cells without posing a threat to normal cells. "My husband is leaning toward using homeopathy, oleander, and other off-label compounds to contain molecular cancer cell growth once he's cancer-free."

Maria was intrigued and inspired to hear of another stage IV colon cancer patient who was making plans for a post-chemotherapy life and asked me to order the homeopathy book when we got back to the hotel.

AFTER DINNER, MARIA and I strolled across the Northwestern campus and began to integrate the day's information.

"I had cancer when I was pregnant with Satchi," Maria said, obviously shaken by the unimaginable realization. "It's going to take me a long time to digest that I've had tumors growing in me since I was in my early thirties. I need to create a whole new narrative that takes into account that most of my adult life has been moving in this direction."

We walked in silence as the new narrative began to take shape. A cold wind blew in off Lake Michigan, and we turned to hurry back to the Orrington. Breaking the silence, Maria asked, "How do you feel about the Block Center?"

"I feel very well held there."

"Me, too," Maria said, "but it's more than that for me. I feel like there's a field of love beneath what they provide, as if they planted a seed of love many years ago and the field has blossomed. I feel loved there."

WE SKYPED WITH Satchi before he went to bed. We'd spoken with him nine times since we said good-bye at the airport (once, while meeting with Jen, I had to end our conversation abruptly). It was the first time we'd both been away from him for more than a weekend, and we wanted to stay connected through this experience.

"You won't believe it," I said. "The movie playing on our flight was the same one we rented in the Hotel Orrington the night 'our' moon rose over the Evanston Public Library."

He laughed and said excitedly, "Really? The night we saw the Nike sign?" We were in sync again. "I miss you guys. Let's hug." We hugged our computer monitors so that it looked like we were hugging each other, two thousand miles apart.

BULOOP! WE WOKE up Tuesday morning to a *buloop!* sound from my laptop. Satchi was Skyping us. Once connected, much to our surprise, Satchi held up a page from his journal to the camera so we could read it for ourselves. Then he read it out loud as well:

Monday, May 17: When I got up I went downstairs and Skyped my parents. Their first room in the hotel was too small so they moved. But just down the hall. My mom walked all the way to the university and around it . . . I called my dad and he literally said, 'I'm meeting with the doctor, I can't talk.' I cried. Now whenever they call I hang up.

"You must have been very disappointed, and angry, when I told you we couldn't talk," I said.

"I can understand how you would want to hang up to let him know that," Maria said, the two of us talking in tandem. "I'm so glad that you found your words, that you're telling us now."

He listened carefully, "Uh huh. Uh huh. Yeah. Uh huh . . ." And then said, "But that was yesterday and today's a new day."

THURSDAY, MAY 20TH

On our last day at the Block Center, Maria's nurse told her that Dr. Nora would like to run a test to determine if the 5-FU levels in her blood were within the therapeutic range or too high—and potentially toxic.

Delighted to give blood for this reason, Maria wondered why other oncologists had not monitored these levels. The test, the nurse said, is not considered standard of care yet, even though it's covered by insurance.

"Old ways are hard to change," Maria commented. She then told the nurse that, even without the 5-FU bolus, she feels the heat from the 5-FU intensifying in her hands and mouth. "I feel like I have hot sauce in my mouth, and that I have sunburn from the inside out in my fingertips."

Deluged with new patients, Dr. Nora was unable to meet with Maria before we returned to California. Maria walked back to the Orrington feeling dispirited, the first time she's felt this way at the Block Center. That night, as we packed our bags, Maria received a call. It was Dr. Nora. She called to apologize and to make sure she and Maria had a chance to discuss anything important. Concerned about what scans to have back in California—CT, or CT and PET—Maria asked Dr. Nora what she wanted to see.

"Improvement," Dr. Nora said, not missing a beat.

WEDNESDAY, MAY 26TH

"I hate needles," Maria cried, almost inconsolably, as she lay down on the couch to get the third of four Neupogen shots, spread out over four days. "I don't want another shot. If I'm going to die anyway, why do I have to get another shot? It's cruel. I hate this. I want it all to stop."

I felt horrible looking into Maria's anguished face. It's how I would imagine feeling if I had to subject a very small child to a procedure that, though in her best interest, caused incomprehensible pain or fear, and no amount of explaining could make it better. And yet, with the hypodermic in my hand, I wanted to tell Maria to snap out of it. After all, we'd agreed I was going to give her shots at home instead of driving half an hour each way to Dr. Gullion's office. But looking into her face, I knew that tough love would not work, nor would it be kind.

Despite our attempt at forbearance, we slipped into a fight. Maria became agitated as the time approached to inject the needle into her belly. She didn't like the way I pinched her belly between my thumb and forefinger, and thought I was being abrupt and insensitive. I felt criticized and blamed, as though it were my idea to give her a shot in the first place.

"Whatever's going on, don't take it out on me," I barked. "I'm just here to help. Stop pushing me away."

To which Maria, with a hot and peremptory look, said, "Well, just forget the goddamn shot. Screw it. Don't give it to me tonight."

I pounced back, "Well, I don't want to give you the fucking shot anyway."

As a marriage therapist, I specialize in helping couples to recover and repair quickly after fights (the faster couples repair, the more secure their marriage, and the better their overall health). We raised our eyes to meet each other. An almost imperceptible smile crossed her lips. I softened. We found our nonreactive selves (or, to be more precise, our orbitofrontal cortexes) and apologized. I said, "Whatever led to that, let's put it aside. We need to make this shot happen tonight."

Maria got comfortable on the couch and started to cry. She'd received fifteen shots over the first six rounds of sumo medicine (three

Neulasta shots and then twelve Neupogen shots), all, save the last two, at the doctor's office, and there simply wasn't the time or the emotional space to say to the oncology nurses, "Hey wait, I'm feeling very scared. I have to process my feelings." But on this night, there was, and she said, "The last few nights, the shots stung. I think I'm anticipating more pain, and my whole being is preparing for a fight."

Maria had actually made great progress in getting shots. Recently, our friend Dawn, who's a doctor of endocrinology, had recommended a homeopathic remedy—Silicea—to ease the fear of shots. Since starting to take it, Maria had noticed a difference: the fear had been coming to the surface more gently, less like a tsunami. But several nights of stinging pushed Maria back into the red zone. After averting a full-on fight—with me feeling unappreciated and aggressively pushing for recognition, and Maria feeling scared and aggressively trying to control her environment—we slowed down to make room for the underlying feelings.

"I've had to be vigilant my whole life," Maria said. "I've erected rigid boundaries to not let people in and to defend myself. I haven't been able to relax and just listen to what's inside myself because I've been so scared of what might come at me from the outside." She paused, listening internally, and then said, "I think this must be true on a cellular level."

"How does that relate to getting an injection?" I asked.

"Well, I'm always on alert," she said. "I'm sensitive to being intruded upon, to invasion, so much so that when I'm scared I get hard and thick-skinned, like leather. It hurts even more to get an injection when this is the underlying drama that's moving through your emotional body *and* your physical body—and probably your cell membranes, too. A shot is not just a shot; it's almost a cataclysmic event."

Then she said she was feeling sad—sad for how much she has sacrificed in life by being preoccupied with her safety.

"I'm ready for the shot," she said, without fear.

I rubbed the alcohol swab on her belly, clockwise, an inch and a half from her belly button. The astringent alcohol smell pierced the air, then evaporated. I pinched her skin between my fingers, counted to three, and pushed the needle into her belly. Maria did not wince. Sometimes the first push is the hardest; the plunger can stick and then jump, spurting too much liquid at once. I was relieved that it didn't jump this time. I pushed the plunger steadily until there was no Neupogen left in the barrel. There was no stinging.

TUESDAY, JUNE 1ST

Maria had her second CT scan last week. Over the weekend, we had the fantasy that the radiologist would call and say, Uh, I'm so sorry. The technician screwed up your scans. There are no tumors in your body. We don't know what happened. Come in so we can do another scan. The other half of the fantasy is that the technician didn't screw up at all; the treatment destroyed all the tumors and Maria is now cancer-free: a miracle in four short months of treatment.

Sadly, neither happened. But the scan confirmed what Maria already knew to be true in her own body: the tumors, though still there, were shrinking.

"This is great news," Dr. Gullion said, explaining that most of the tumors had shrunk: some by over 40 percent, the largest lesion in the left lobe of the liver by almost 70 percent. Confusingly, there was also evidence of several very small new liver lesions, which might not have been clearly seen on the first scan.

The previous week, Maria also received the results of extensive blood work from the Block Center and learned that the inflammatory markers in her body, which were 900 percent over normal in late March, before she started the Block program, were now within normal range. In two months, Maria had been able to make her body a less hospitable place for cancer, and had gained eight pounds to boot!

Maria briefed Dr. Gullion on her visit to the Block Center and on the new treatments that she wanted to include in her program—homeopathy and Anvirzel, a patented oleander extract.

"I'm comfortable with both, though there's a reason," he quipped, "why deer know to avoid eating the oleander leaves—ingesting a leaf can kill you."

"That's the idea with the cancer," Maria said. "Preliminary research indicates that the extract is nontoxic to the body but highly toxic to cancer cells."

Though familiar with early, phase I clinical trials of Anvirzel, designed to determine the right dose for humans, Dr. Gullion hadn't heard about subsequent developments. "Keith might have an insider's knowledge of Anvirzel. He'll have to direct that part of the treatment."

As Maria stood to leave, Dr. Gullion may have sensed her disappointment that the scan report was not unambiguously good. He gave her a warm hug before she walked down the long corridor to the treatment room.

THE THREE OF us had dinner in bed that night. Maria needed to rest after chemo, and Satchi and I wanted to be with her. After dinner, I went downstairs to clean the dishes and, standing at the sink, heard beautiful music in the distance. At first, I thought one of our neighbors might be playing devotional music. As I listened, I realized the music was coming from our living room, and it was one of our favorite devotional yoga CDs, *Light of the Sun,* by Mukti.

I walked into the living room to see if Satchi had turned the stereo on and saw only our cat asleep on the rug. I asked Maria and Satchi if they had turned on the stereo, which requires pressing three separate buttons, a feat beyond even our very smart Abyssinian. Much to my surprise, neither of them had turned on the music. Delighted by the mystery, we lay in bed and listened to Mukti celebrating the Divine Mother.

TUESDAY, JUNE 8TH

Amma was appearing in the temple in San Ramon, blessing whomever came to her without regard to race, creed, or nationality. She had arrived in the Bay Area a week ago, by way of Buffalo, New York, where she received an honorary degree, a Doctorate of Humane Letters. The State University of New York recognized her commitment to education and "the humanitarian institutions and services she has inspired and supported for over three decades."

Maria, Satchi, and I arrived early to find seats in the front of the temple, a large A-frame wood building that looks like a country barn, except for the pictures of an Indian woman on the walls and the stage at the front, which is framed with a backdrop of colorful Indian silks rising twenty feet to the ceiling. We sat in a second row of chairs on the side, but the hall monitors, who knew of Maria's fragility, asked her if she wanted to sit in the front row. One added, "We'll move chairs for you, if you want."

Feeling biblical, I whispered to Maria, "We'll move chairs and mountains."

On cue, Satchi said, "We'll move cancer for you."

"An auspicious beginning," I thought. "The metaphors are all in place."

Within moments of sitting down, waves of grief rolled slowly from my heart and broke into tears. My eyes met Maria's and she shook her head as if to acknowledge the heaviness in my heart. Satchi smiled at me, sat on my lap, and, teasingly, said, "You're a crybaby, Dad." I could feel his seven-year-old love.

Our friend Prana, whom we'd asked before Satchi was born to be his godmother, spotted us from across the temple and made a bee-line for Satchi. She'd moved to Amma's Kerala ashram in the mid-'90s after her husband, Phil, died tragically on their honeymoon—a cliff that he was standing on in southern India gave way, and he fell to his death. Since then, she's traveled the world with Amma, when not serving her in India.

Later, Maria and I held hands as we waited our turn to get a family *darshan*, a Sanskrit term for seeing or being blessed by a holy person. Accompanied by Prana, the three of us made our way to the front of the line, ten feet from Amma. A small child in front of Maria fussed. Satchi smiled, remembering when we held him against our chests for a blessing.

Maria leaned over to the child and said, "She'll give you a hug, and then she'll give you a chocolate." The boy looked confused, then intrigued, and quieted down. Maybe this wouldn't be so bad after all!

When our turn arrived, Satchi handed Amma's attendant a piece of paper with two questions written on it: "Was that you turning the stereo on?" and "When will my Mom get better?" The attendant translated both questions for Amma. Amma pulled me to her body, and said, "My darling, darling, darling son." I held her tight. She whispered "my darling son" several more times before she released me, looking probingly into my eyes. I felt held in her gaze—at home, seen, recognized.

Then she pulled Maria and me to her bosom, and Satchi to our backs, and held us all for a long time, whispering into Maria's ear. When she released us, she affectionately squeezed Maria's and my cheeks, looked from Maria to me and back to Maria again, and then showered our family with rose petals. She handed us each a chocolate kiss and flower petal as we rose to leave.

As we stood to leave, the attendant told Satchi, "Amma said, 'That was me who turned your stereo on, so you could listen to *bhajans*'"—devotional songs.

Satchi turned to me quizzically, "She didn't answer the second question."

I shook my head. Some things will remain a mystery until they're ready to be revealed.

MARIA GAVE ME a recital tonight. She's been teaching herself to play the piano. She used to play the guitar, but this is the first time in years I've seen her delight in sharing music with me. She's lighter and happier when Amma is here, as if she's no longer fighting the ghosts of her past and instead is focused on the life in front of her. I listened with eyes closed as she played the melody of the "Ode to Joy," from the last movement of Beethoven's Ninth Symphony.

She stopped midway into her recital to tell me about a healing session she'd had at the ashram today with a Tibetan Buddhist priest named Pujitha. Prana had introduced them. "She travels around the world with Amma and offers a form of energy work called Radiance Energy," Maria said. "It's her mission to help people reconnect to this energy, which she described as a universal radiant white light in the form of a double helix."

"Wow! That's trippy. What was it like to have her direct energy into your body?"

"It was deeply relaxing, as if a field of warm love were moving through me. She said she'll transmit this energy to me all year long, at the same time every day, from wherever she is on the planet."

Maria restarted the "Ode to Joy." I imagined that she and I had no future, only the present moment, and the present had no end, and we were encircled in a double helix of radiant white healing light.

MONDAY, JUNE 14TH

"I will see a Tibetan doctor in a few days," Maria told Dr. Nora during a phone consultation.

For weeks, our friend Michelle had been telling us about a Tibetan doctor named Dr. Dickey Palden Nyerongsha, a seventh-generation doctor from a renowned Tibetan medical family, who rotated her practice among Tucson, Arizona, and several cities in California, including Berkeley, and who specializes in working with individuals who have advanced colon cancer diagnoses. Maria didn't think it necessary to add to her medical team but had relented, sensing the strength of Michelle's conviction.

"Apparently, many oncologists refer their cancer patients to her when they can't do any more for them, when they've come to the end of the road," Maria told Dr. Nora. "Do you know anything about Tibetan medicine?"

"I don't, but that's pretty amazing that oncologists refer to her," Dr. Nora said. "There's so much we don't know in medicine. I wouldn't want her to tell you to stop chemotherapy, but she probably has a lot to offer, and we can keep talking about what she recommends."

"No need to worry about stopping chemotherapy, I'm not going to do that," Maria said. "But I appreciate you holding the big picture, staying open to whatever might work to help me."

"Yes, that is the goal."

"I believe there's a great mystery around what ends up making a difference in an individual's treatment," Maria said.

"What we know in traditional oncology is from what we've studied," Dr. Nora said, "but if you get all the Tibetan colon cancer patients in a room and do a study, you might find something meaningful, by virtue of directing your attention there. It just hasn't been studied."

I wondered if Dr. Nora has read much in quantum physics, which says that the observer is the observed, or, to be more prosaic, you find what you're looking for in science and medicine, as in life.

AFTER TELLING DR. Nora about the Tibetan doctor, Maria then mentioned the homeopath she'd seen the day before, Christine Ciavarella, a warm and nurturing practitioner of Greek-Italian descent who had served, alongside the Kongs, as our first line of defense when one of us was ill.

During the consultation, Christine explained that she would be trying to determine what two remedies would help Maria's body fight cancer. One remedy would be a constitutional, the other a nosode. Both take into account all the symptoms—emotional and physical—that a patient expresses at the time of illness, but they address different problems.

Samuel Hahnemann, the German physician who developed homeopathy in the 1790s, believed that one's parents' lifestyle, their emotional states and diet, as well as the environmental conditions at the time of conception, would affect the kind and severity of "miasmas"— deep-seated chronic patterns—that interfere with one's vital life force. Constitutional remedies are designed to address miasmas. A nosode, on the other hand, is intended to address a more acute imbalance that is the result of a present-day situation, like, for instance the impact of cancer or chemotherapy on the body. It is not unlike a vaccine and is prepared from a pathological specimen, like, say, the saliva, pus, blood, or tissue of an animal or person, and signals to the body to fight against the specific symptoms present in the moment.

I once had a client who was depressed and angry; her homeopath prescribed a remedy made from the saliva of a rabid dog. Her depression lifted after taking the remedy.

After asking Maria a detailed list of seemingly unrelated questions (among them: "In general, when you come up against authority, do you get naturally fearful or combative?" "Are you more at home in the mountains or at the sea?" "Do you go crazy when it's humid?" "Are you drawn to animals? Cats or dogs?"), Christine chose *Tuberculinum bovinum*, a nosode made from cow tuberculosis. She explained that *Tuberculinum* was indicated for people who have wasting diseases (and who are drawn to trees; prefer cool and dry climates to hot and humid ones; prefer cats to dogs; and have an affinity for the mountains).

Almost immediately, Maria said, "*Tuberculinum* resonates for me. . . . In the antebellum South, tuberculosis was fairly common. I wouldn't be surprised if some of my ancestors died from TB."

The constitutional remedy proved to be more challenging, though Christine narrowed it to several remedies derived from tropical fish that live in coral reefs and inshore grassy areas, among them, the Atlantic blue tang surgeonfish (*Acanthurus coeruleus*).

"I need to do more research to pick the right constitutional, but these blue tang tropical fish remedies are often prescribed when there are issues relating to wasting away" at the heart of the miasma. Blue tangs, I later learned, live in holes and crevices where they can shelter from predators while they sleep at night. Because they're small and need constant protection, baby blue tangs are rarely seen on the reef. If their environment is compromised (or destroyed), they have no place to hide, and they waste away.

"Can I ask one more question?" Christine said. "I'm sure you have days when you feel very low, but in general how is your mental game right now? Overall?"

Maria thought for a moment. "Pretty good, maybe 80 to 85 percent. When I'm feeling good, though, I can get scared. Sometimes the better I feel, the more scared I get." She turned to look at me, tears started to shine out of the corners of her eyes. "Lance Armstrong said cancer is the best thing that ever happened to him. I can't say that, but I'm grateful for how much it has allowed me to open up and receive my life. It has knocked me off the wheel I've been on."

THURSDAY, JUNE 17TH

The night before day one of round ten, Satchi presented a drawing to Maria after dinner. He'd been working on it for several days and was eager to give it to her.

He had just finished reading Ursula Le Guin's *A Wizard of Earthsea* and *The Tombs of Atuan*, the first two books of the

Earthsea cycle, and was intrigued by the young wizard, Ged, who uses his powers to restore balance to the Earthsea archipelago after he has summoned a nameless shadow spirit from the dead and disrupted the boundary between the living and the dead.

Handing his drawing to Maria, Satchi explained that the tree of life framing the drawing on the left and top protects Ged, who's pointing his mighty staff at cancer. Ged shouts the cancer's true name to establish control over it. An eagle with long talons, holding healing herbs, flies in under the tree of life to engage the cancer.

"Ged, who's love, is pointing his chemotherapy staff at the cancer. The light coming out the staff is power. And the eagle, which is homeopathy, is dropping Tibetan medicine on the cancer," he said.

DRESSED IN A beautiful turquoise-blue Tibetan silk robe, Dr. Dickey invited us into a small, unadorned office in downtown Berkeley, barely two miles from our home. She was younger than I had expected, our contemporary in years, and reminded me of a still mountain lake. A small *thangka* of the Medicine Buddha—the dark blue master of remedies, who sits in the center of a celestial paradise surrounded by healing gods, sages, exalted beings, and medicinal plants and trees—adorned one wall. Colorful silk pouches containing traditional Tibetan herbs filled a table behind her desk.

Within moments, she'd taken Maria's right forearm and placed her three middle fingers perpendicular to Maria's wrist, slowly raising one finger, then another, then placing all three down, a little like playing a trumpet. She interspersed questions with observations as she listened to Maria's pulses.

"Still kind of anemic . . . Chemo rather strong for you . . . Still kind of depleted, extremely yin-deficient . . . Seems like you're not over from trauma—from diagnosis, treatment, procedures.

Everything still really shaky: it's like watching an intense movie, and you're still in the middle; the beginning is dramatic, but you're still in it."

I could tell that Dr. Dickey had found a metaphor that spoke to Maria about the weariness that comes after five months of continual chemotherapy.

After six minutes, she reached out to read the pulses on Maria's left forearm. She asked to look at Maria's eyes and said, "Your eyes are pale . . . Chemo hard on the liver." Examining a jar of Maria's urine, she observed that Maria likely has *Candida*, often an invisible side effect of chemotherapy, and that her kidneys were not filtering well.

When she learned that Decadron, a corticosteroid to prevent nausea and vomiting, is part of Maria's prechemo IV drugs, she said, "The steroid not good for your kidneys," and suggested they work to eliminate it over time. "Chemo is killing cancer cells, but your cells too. You're not getting good results with well-being," she told Maria. "If you will eliminate all the things that go with chemo, that would be good." They devised a plan to substitute Tibetan herbs for some of the pharmaceuticals.

Standing to collect pills from the silk pouches, she explained that some of the herbs would prevent nausea and diarrhea during the first five days of the chemo cycle, and some would fight the cancer and stimulate the immune system during the rebuilding phase. One of the off-chemo herbs is supposed to aid in clearing one's karma, getting at the root of why an individual in a particular lifetime may be predisposed toward cancer, while another with very similar habits is not, family history aside.

She encouraged Maria to speak to her spiritual teacher about other ways to address the karmic level of healing and gave Maria another Tibetan herbal mixture called *sorig tsephel dhutse*, or "elixir of life," to prolong the life span. Maria would need to take the elixir of life first thing in the morning, while chanting a Tibetan mantra.

In a surreal confluence of the ancient and the modern, Dr. Dickey invited Maria to download a YouTube video of a Tibetan monk chanting the mantra in order to get the pronunciation correct. I knew the Dalai Lama would approve.

DR. DICKEY DID not promise anything, but Maria and I felt more hopeful after meeting with her. Perhaps it was her presence; perhaps it was that she listened with *bodhicitta*, the Tibetan word for compassion—literally "awakened heart." Whatever the case, Maria felt immediately bonded to this woman and knew that Tibetan medicine would play a central role in her integrative treatment.

As we drove home, Maria and I realized that each of her doctors, whether allopathic or Eastern, was trying to find the true name of what needed healing. The traditional oncologists said Maria had an adenocarcinoma that needed to be poisoned or zapped. The integrative oncologists said her whole body had been hospitable to cancer and needed to be rebalanced. The acupuncturist and Tibetan doctor said she had a yin-deficiency and needed karmic clearing. The homeopath said she had a hole in her system that needed plugging. The radiant energy healer said she needed to reconnect to the radiant double helix of white light that permeates the universe. Six practitioners: six facets of the diamond of healing.

seven

◆

SHORING UP THE LEVEES

Christine Ciavarella called to say she'd decided on a constitutional remedy. At first, she'd thought Atlantic blue tang would be the right remedy, but after consulting with other clinicians, researching case studies, and reflecting on Maria, she decided on another remedy from the sea family: *lac delphinum*, or dolphin's milk.

By way of explaining why she chose it, she said, "We're treating the person, not the disease. The nature of the disease doesn't matter as much as how the person who's being treated lives in their skin." *Lac delphinum* is one among a small group of remedies (referred to as the milk remedies, or "the lacs") derived from mammalian milk and prescribed for individuals sharing a variety of early childhood similarities, such as a history of poor bonding, feeling unloved, and anxiety about belonging. These individuals often crave mothering, warmth, and family, but can feel empty, worthless, and forsaken. They tend to feel timid, are sensitive to reprimand, and seek security by clinging.

Among the milk remedies, the *lac delphinum* has its own distinct signature. "Dolphins are playful, loving, and happy," Christine explained. "They play a serious role in the world, working as ambassadors and healers of the sea. But there's also a shadow side to people who need this remedy. They often have a family history of trauma, as well as family secrets."

I walked upstairs to tell Maria about Christine's choice for a constitutional. Maria was on the bed talking to her sister, Anne, who was visiting from Charleston with her children. A diptych of two pictures of Maria, nine months pregnant and draped in an aubergine shawl, the late afternoon sun illuminating her belly, sat atop the dresser, next to the bed.

"Dolphin's milk makes more sense to me than blue tang," Maria said. "Maybe blue tang will be useful later, but for now, I think she hit the nail on the head."

The next day, Maria called Christine to thank her for the new remedy and to tell her about *China officinalis* and *hypericum*, two remedies she'd been taking recently to help with dizziness. "They're good choices for you," Christine said, explaining that *hypericum* (also called St. John's wort) was used extensively during the Civil War to treat soldiers on the battlefield.

Raised in the Lowcountry, the coastal area of South Carolina, Maria joked with Christine, "Sometime down the road we might consider remedies made from kudzu, pluff mud, and Kentucky Gentlemen," her dad's bourbon of choice.

MARIA WOKE UP feeling dizzy and sludgy today, took *China officinalis* and *hypericum* again, and called Howard to see if she could come in earlier. He greeted us in his slightly soiled white lab coat and, even before we sat down, started to explain that dizziness is an aspect of nausea and asked her if the dizziness was "like spinning" or "uneven, like being on a boat."

"Uneven," Maria said, appreciating the distinction.

Finding the positive, Howard said. "If dizziness is the only new significant symptom, that's good."

Determining that her appetite was still strong, he added that if she had a loss of appetite, felt sluggish, or stayed up late worrying, with her mind racing for several nights on end, that would mean her yin was more compromised.

"Without yin," he reminded her, "yang burns out," and then the body cannot heal. "There's simply no energy to fight the cancer with."

"My homeopath prescribed two remedies for me," Maria continued. "The nosode is *Tuberculinum bovinum*, which helps with wasting diseases and the constitutional is . . ."

Howard interrupted to add, "Consumption is all about yin deficiency."

"Yes, we're all circling around the same fire, you, Dr. Dickey, Christine. And the second remedy is *lac delphinum*. It's prescribed for people who have a history of emotional secrets and who come from families where emotions weren't talked about."

Listening attentively, Howard said, "Raw emotions deplete yin. Processing of any intense and shocking emotion, particularly when you're stuck in them—when they're unresolved—depletes yin." He stopped, choosing his words carefully, "People can let things churn for a very, *very* long time. You need to resolve them, by letting the feelings come up and out," and then you can use the energy that once went into churning—or denial—for life and healing.

THURSDAY, JULY 1ST

Maria was the one taking *lac delphinum*, but the constitutional remedy seemed to be working on the whole family. In the morning, I was doing yoga on the living room floor. Satchi was sitting on the couch behind me meditating, a prayer shawl with fifteen thousand prayers stitched into it draped over his shoulders (it was made by our friend Nancy, a minister, who said a prayer for every stitch she knit). Maria was in the kitchen reading the newspaper and eating breakfast.

Suddenly, I heard Satchi crying and turned to see him curled up on the couch. I crawled over to him and asked, "Do you want cry alone, or do you want me to be with you?"

"I want you to hold me." He cried on and off for five minutes, and all the while his fingers moved along the smooth, round, sandalwood beads in his *mala*, or prayer necklace. I held him tight, with my hand on his back. I began to feel my own tears rising, but held them back, so as not to draw attention to myself when *he* needed me.

If Maria dies, I thought, Satchi and I will be alone, and I'll hold him like this when he cries for his mother.

The image tore through my body, like an electric shock. A few minutes later, Satchi sat up, looked me in the eyes, and smiled, the kind of transparency in his eyes that occurs after a powerful emotional release.

"You released a burden in your heart."

He nodded and said, "Yes, Dad."

An hour later, I walked Satchi the four blocks to Codornices Park, where he had soccer camp. He reached out and held my hand as we talked about soccer and which team we favored to win in the World Cup Quarter Finals. Nearly at camp (waiting for the right moment), I said, "Honey, what were you crying about this morning?"

"I worry about Mom," he said, "I want her to get better. It's taking so long."

"Yes. It is. Fighting cancer can be a very long process, but Mom is making slow and steady progress." Turning my attention to him, I added, "It must be so hard to worry about your mom. I'm glad you can tell me about your feelings. I'm always here to listen." Arriving before camp started, Satchi asked if I would kick the ball at him while he practiced being goalie.

Within the space of an hour, we had flowed in and out of talking about feelings several times. We were getting used to talking about emotions in a way similar to how the German national team plays soccer: quick, crisp passes that create space on the field and allow for unseen possibilities to emerge.

I'D SNAPPED AT Maria a few nights before. I had just come home from seeing clients, was tired, and needed to rest. Dishes from breakfast and lunch filled the sink, and Maria was writing emails, waiting for me to tidy up.

"I know you have cancer, but I wish you'd clean the dishes."

She burst into tears and said, "I wish I were dead so I didn't burden you so much."

Her words jolted me. I'd been feeling particularly unappreciated and resentful, but I thought I had done a good job of hiding those feelings from her. After all, how can a good husband tell his wife, who's fighting for her life, that he's resentful and angry that she can't do more for the family, and him? Her response snapped me out of my fantasy that I could make my feelings go away or hide them from someone who, after twenty-seven years, could nearly read my mind.

Cancer by its nature gives rise to impolite or, worse yet, taboo thoughts and feelings, the kind you believe you shouldn't have and definitely cannot share with your partner—like hating her for having cancer and changing your life, or wanting to run away to a less complicated life.

Fortunately, Satchi did not yet suffer from the same prohibition against sharing his mind. Maria told me that Satchi, in the middle of a conversation with her, had turned to her and said, almost matter-of-factly, "It would be easier if you were dead, Mom."

"Oh, my God! What did you say?" I asked.

"Well," Maria started, "I collected myself and said, 'I know. Part of you wishes I were dead, and I know another part of you wants me to live forever. Of course you'd have both feelings. You can love me and still be really angry at me for having cancer and sometimes ruining your life.'"

As proud as I was of my son for his honesty, I was even more proud of my wife for being able to hold love and hate side by side, without collapsing the two into one. She recognized that Satchi's words were a cover for important underlying feelings. I had had the same thought on occasion, but I feared that the words, if uttered, would cause irreparable damage. And yet, if I didn't share my conflict, she wouldn't have the opportunity to show me empathy for how a caretaker often wrestles with private thoughts of love and hate.

ROUND ELEVEN WENT more smoothly than any previous round. Maria had less exhaustion and fewer side effects, and felt encouraged that her plan to manage nausea by replacing pharmaceuticals with Tibetan herbs was working. Resting more deeply during the week, she felt steadier and experienced no dizziness and only very mild nausea. Remembering that Howard had told her to eat yams if she experienced mouth neuropathy ("They boost spleen, which is connected to the mouth"), she ate yams at the first sign of rubbery lips. The yams did the trick; the neuropathy dissipated.

THURSDAY, JULY 8TH

Nearly fifty years ago, D. W. Winnicott, a British pediatrician and psychoanalyst, wrote that the infant experiences the mother in two ways: as the environmental mother and the object mother.

"The environmental mother comprises the whole background world in which the infant exists," Joseph Lichtenberg wrote in *Psychoanalysis and Infant Research*. "The air the infant breathes, the warmth of a blanket, the beam of sunlight, the general emotional climate—all these are part of the environmental mother." The "object" mother, on the other hand, "is the one who responds to the infant's needs, the mother with whom the infant interacts. She is the mother who feeds, the mother who answers a cry, the mother whose face invites exploration, the mother whose action may jar."

For the previous six months, Maria and I had needed to rely on our friends and family to be our environmental mother during chemo weeks: to shop, to cook, to clean our dishes and do our laundry, to sit in the rocking chair while Maria napped, to answer our phones and pull our weeds, and to do so largely in the background, without expecting much interaction from us.

Like an infant, we were barely aware, much of the time, of the tremendous effort our environmental mother exerted to provide that kind of reliable and consistent care. For infants, that care gets stitched into their experience of the world; it just is. The same was true for us, and that care helped us to cope with the existential terror at the heart of learning that Maria had cancer. We had to circle the wagons, conserve our energy, and focus on survival. Had we also had to attend to all the tasks of running a household, it's likely we would've been overwhelmed, as many families are when they're not as fully supported as we were.

As Maria improved, I became less of a caregiver to her and more of a husband-partner. For long stretches of time, Maria needed me to be an environmental mother and bracket my own needs. Our most intense conflicts erupted when I bristled at the job description.

"Even caregivers have needs," I told Maria one night, taking Satchi's recent honesty as inspiration for my own. "I'm scared that my needs will always take a back seat to your cancer and that I'll live the rest of my life in your shadow. And then when you die, I'll be angry and resentful about giving up the best years of my life to take care of you."

I repeated some version of this fear three or four times just in case Maria didn't understand me the first time I said it.

Maria listened to everything I needed to say. The joke in my family is that Dad needs to say everything five times when he's upset. Then she said, "I'm so sorry. I love you so much. I don't want that to happen to you." My mind was clouded by my upset—and I could feel the reflex to push her away and keep complaining until I wore myself out and her down—but I could also feel her sadness and remorse, and that, more than her words, penetrated my heart. She continued, "You're the most important person in the world to me. Let's figure out how to create more space in our relationship for you."

With her persistence, I finally let myself soften. And Maria said, "I feel so much closer to you when you tell me about your anger and how you're suffering."

I was startled—and comforted—by Maria's equanimity, and told her so. It's hard to know precisely when the tide turned in our relationship. As an open-water swimmer, I know an ebb tide often gives way to a flood through a short period of still water, when nothing appears to be happening, even as the moon continues to exert its pull.

A FEW DAYS before, on the Fourth of July, Satchi and I had gone kayaking. We started off the beach at the Dolphin Club, the over-130-year-old swimming and boating club on San Francisco Bay that I belong to. We paddled out to the opening of Aquatic Park, a protected cove nestled between the Hyde Street Pier and Van Ness Avenue.

With the Golden Gate Bridge to our left and Alcatraz directly ahead, Satchi turned to me and said, "When people think they're going to die, they can freak out and say, Oh my God, I'm going to die, but when they *know* they're going to die, sometimes they can just accept it and be calm. That makes everything so much easier."

"Hmmm, that's really interesting, Satchi. Do you think you'll be able to accept death when it comes?"

"I think so, Dad."

"What will you miss when death comes?"

"I'll miss you and Mom and feel sad about leaving you both."

We kayaked in silence a good long while, back into Aquatic Park, under the Sea Scouts building, which sits atop pilings on the western edge of Aquatic Park, and then under the municipal pier for a quarter mile. While we were threading our way between boats gathering for the fireworks that night, Satchi asked, "How old were you, Dad, when you married Mom?"

"Well, I met Mom when she was nineteen and I was eighteen, and we got married when I was twenty-six."

Surprised, he responded, "Wow, you've known Mom a long time." Then he said, "I worry about Mom a lot." The wind had picked up, making it harder for us to make progress heading into it, so we turned back toward the Dolphin Club.

"What do you worry about?"

"That she will die because of the cancer."

"I'm so glad you're telling me. I worry about that sometimes, too. It's only natural, but you can see with your own eyes that Mom is getting stronger. No?"

"Yeah, I can."

Satchi was no longer holding on alone to the dread that his mommy would die. He was talking, and as he talked, he digested a little more of what is indigestible for a seven-year-old.

Talking to Maria that week, he said, "I'm angry with God for giving you cancer. It's really disrupted my life. I'm supposed to be getting all the attention, and you are instead." He added, with a twinkle in his eyes, "Shouldn't I get an extra month off this summer because of what I've been through?"

THURSDAY, JULY 15TH

I was sitting in the sauna at the Dolphin Club, looking out the window at Ghirardelli Square, which anchors Larkin at Beach Street, when an old swimming buddy who didn't know about Maria's illness asked how she was doing. I told him she had been diagnosed with cancer in January and was undergoing chemotherapy.

"Oh, I'm so sorry," he began. Even before he began his second sentence, I knew what he was about to say, and I wanted to stop him before he did—not for my sake, but his. He was about to feel terrible after I responded to his question.

"Oh, I'm so sorry," he said. "I hope they caught it early?"

There's no way to recover quickly from this question when the answer is "No, we didn't."

I'd had this very same conversation ten or twelve times over the six months since Maria's diagnosis. I understand the urge to say these hopeful words. I've said the very same words to friends when they have told me about a cancer diagnosis in their family. We want to believe that bad things won't happen to good people in our lives and that our friends will be spared undue pain, premature illness, and great calamity.

I remember a conversation I had with my friend Seth about a week after Maria was diagnosed. He'd just picked up my mother-in-law from the airport and was now sitting on the bed with me as I spoke to Bill Schmidt, the oncologist we enlisted to offer us a medical opinion about immunepheresis. I got off the phone, clearly overwhelmed, a little disorganized perhaps, and told Seth that I was having a hard time believing this was happening to Maria and me.

A long time Buddhist practitioner, he said, "We ask the question, Why is this happening to me? But really the question is, Why not me? Why should any of us be spared?"

Those words changed my life. They were the right words at the right moment. They penetrated my mind and rearranged any simplistic notion I had that Maria or I were any different than the people with whom we bump shoulders as we walk down the sidewalk. One day we all suffer an assault to our notion of what we believe we're entitled to in life.

Why not me? Those words helped me to find my rightful place in the universe and to accept that my privileged life, in this privileged country, is in fact an ordinary one, repeated over and over again everywhere on the planet—perhaps with a different set of external circumstances, but still guided internally by love, hope, fear, uncertainty, and faith.

"I REALLY AM a little frightened," began the voice mail from my mother that rocked my life in a new way.

She would often call in the middle of the day to hear my voice, but a trembling in her voice revealed a new level of confusion and fear.

"Can you come over to the house here? Someone is claiming to be my husband. And he's also Greek, obviously. But I'm afraid, so can you come over? Please come over. Okay? This is Mom. I don't want people taking me over with the house, with everything. I hope I'm wrong. Please come over. Van, please call me."

Her dementia had been slowly progressing for perhaps six years, but this was the first time she mistook her husband for an interloper.

Maria and I both called to see if we could walk her back from the edge of terror and help to contain Dad's distress, but to no avail. Mom was convinced the man in her home was not her husband, and Dad grew increasingly agitated as he tried to establish with his wife that he was indeed her husband of almost fifty-three years and that she was merely confused. There was little room to maneuver between their two interlocking fears, and my dad was not ready to accept the fact that his wife had slipped into an advanced stage of dementia. For him, that was unthinkable.

Maria and I went to bed that night, the night before her twelfth round of chemotherapy, anxious about her treatment and worried about my parents. Would my mother's paranoia remit? Would my father be able to accept her condition without losing his own bearings? Would I be able to juggle caring for my family and supporting my parents if my mother's dementia worsened?

The next day, I spent the morning alternating between the treatment room where Maria was receiving chemo, and an exam room across the hall, where I talked with Mom and Dad several times, and, separately, consulted with their family physician about medication to contain my mom's distressing perceptions.

Each time I returned to the treatment room, Maria would open her eyes and ask if I had managed to make any headway with Mom.

"Chemotherapy," Maria said, "doesn't seem all that bad compared to a terrified and fragile mind."

AFTER BRINGING MARIA home from her treatment, I drove to my parents' apartment, sat on the couch with Mom, and held her in the hopes of helping to calm her anxious mind. Good naturedly, Dad tried to remind her of who he was. But with each attempt, she grew more agitated, distrustful, and entrenched.

Dad and I walked into the bedroom to talk privately, but Mom followed us and said, "Why are you in here?"

"Mom, can you wait for us in the family room? I want to talk to Dad alone for a bit."

"He's not your father. I'm not leaving."

Now it was my turn to feel trapped. My anxiety spiked. I sat on their bed next to my father while Mom sat across from us in Pappou's, *her* father's, rocking chair, watching us carefully. Mom's icon of Jesus, sitting on the bedside table between her and us, felt like a fourth presence in the room.

I stroked Dad's back and said, "You've done an incredible job of taking care of Mom, and it must be so scary not to have her recognize you. You must be exhausted and lonely. It's so hard to be a caregiver. I can really relate to what you're going through."

"Why are you giving this man sympathy?" Mom said angrily. "He's threatening me. Why do you care about him and not me?"

Realizing I was on a tightrope, I said, "I can see how scared you both are, Mom. You don't know who this man is and you feel threatened."

She snapped back at me, "I don't feel threatened. I just want him out of the house. This is my house, not his."

I knew there was little more I could do under the circumstances. "I have to go home now, Mom. Maria had chemotherapy today and I have to take care of her. I'm so sorry I can't stay any longer."

As I opened the front door, I heard my mom calling after my dad, "Tell me, Manny, haven't I been a good wife all these years?" My heart sank that she would need to ask, after half a century.

Angrily, my dad said, in Greek, "You used to be."

Tears came to my eyes. But at least, for the moment, my mom knew she was his wife.

THURSDAY, JULY 22ND

"I'm tickled pink you're doing so great," Dr. Gullion told Maria as we left the consulting room.

He had just shared the results of Maria's third CT scan. There was no ambiguity: the news was unmistakably positive.

Dr. Gullion read the report line by line and translated its results. Maria had no tumors in her lungs or lymph nodes. The lesions in her liver had either decreased in size (although at a slower rate than earlier on) or remained stable, and there were no new liver metastases. The tumors in her pelvic area also remained stable.

"This is obviously good news," Dr. Gullion said. "To me, the most important piece is the liver. And the fact that the tumors are decreasing there . . . I know the chemo has beaten you up a little, but you're continuing to have shrinkage, and you're doing so much better than in January. On balance, this is worth it." By "this," he meant the FOLFIRI cocktail.

Excited by his report, Maria interrupted Dr. Gullion to correct the impression that she's felt beaten up. "I'm feeling more vulnerable emotionally, but I haven't felt beaten up physically. In fact, I feel better than I've felt in a year, and especially over the last two weeks, since I substituted the Tibetan herbs for the Decadron," the prechemo steroid.

Dr. Gullion then confirmed that Maria had no symptoms of hand-foot syndrome and fewer mouth sores and neuropathy.

Teasingly, Maria said, "Yes. Your memory is accurate. I've been eating yams and that has helped with the neuropathy in my mouth."

Intrigued by this new piece of information from the world of Chinese and Tibetan medicine, he repeated "Yams?" twice to make sure he heard her correctly. Little did he know that, while waiting for him in the lobby, Maria had taken out a whole cooked yam and started noshing on it, like an ice cream cone, one of her new favorite snacks.

Curious about the trajectory of Maria's treatment, I changed directions. "I'm assuming this question is not so easy to answer, but I wonder if you can tell over time, given the rate at which Maria's tumors are decreasing, how long the FOLFIRI will continue to yield results?"

"Your questions are never easy to answer." Then he smiled and added, "I was joking. That's a good question." I felt his affection for me, a husband who, like a chess player, tries to anticipate his opponent's—the cancer's—next ten moves. "The general pattern," he said, "is good response, followed by less good response, then resistance down the line. It's hard to know from a CT scan what's actually happening with a tumor. You can tell that a tumor has shrunk, but you can't tell what's inside it."

For instance, he explained, with Hodgkin's lymphoma, a tumor may shrink but never go away completely. It remains as scar tissue, and a CT scan would not be able to differentiate between active tumor and scar tissue. With colon cancer, the body does tend to get rid of dead cancer cells over time, leaving no scarring, but early on, as Maria was, you might not be able to tell the difference.

"What we're seeing on the scan may be scarring, debris, active cancer cells, or less active cancer cells," he said realistically. And a PET scan may not be a valid measure of cancer activity either. It could measure activity of a different kind, like, say, inflammation, where active white blood cells leave the impression of tumor activity. "In short," he said, "progress eventually levels off, and then it's hard to know precisely if the tumor has stopped shrinking or if it's become necrotic tissue."

"May Chen, Maria's other oncologist," I said, "recommended that if the liver lesions fail to respond to further chemotherapy there may be a role for chemoembolization."

"Yes. That and several other options, including invasive surgery, are options down the road," he said, "but we have to keep in mind that in addition to the liver lesions there are pelvic lesions. And we have to stabilize the pelvic lesions before we go after the liver lesions."

"We're trying to put out several brushfires at the same time," Maria later acknowledged.

"Yep," I replied. "Hope the wind doesn't whip up."

AN EMAIL FROM our Block Center friend whose husband had stage IV colon cancer awaited us when we returned home. It quickly let the air out of our excitement over Maria's good news. Her husband had learned in late May that after nine rounds of chemotherapy he had no visible signs of tumors in his body. From the email, we learned that, after a short-lived hiatus, the tumors in his liver, lungs, and rectum were growing again: over the last few weeks, his cancer had become resistant to oxaliplatin. The wind had picked up. We felt disheartened and grief stricken.

"YOUR DAD'S GONE crazy," my mom said on the phone. "He's moved us into a new apartment without asking me first. I want to go home."

Knowing that my parents hadn't actually moved at all, I called my mom's doctor, who told me to double my mom's medication and, if things escalated, to take her to the hospital for extensive testing. Even though he'd recently ruled out a severe bladder infection, a new one or a series of ministrokes could cause such spiraling delusions.

Later that afternoon, Mom walked out of their apartment alone, while my dad was dressing. She took the elevator down fifteen floors to the building lobby, where Dad, still in his socks, found her ten minutes later, loitering, and made her promise to stay put on a bench while he went to ask building security for help. When he returned two minutes later, she'd vanished again. Panicked, my dad called me and told me to come immediately. He was terrified that if we didn't find her and she wandered in front of a car and died, the police would put him in jail for negligence.

When I arrived, they were both upstairs in their apartment. My dad quickly recounted the whole story, hyperventilating and sweating as he talked. I worried that he was about to have a heart attack. The security guard on duty had found my mom wandering outside on the grounds of the condo complex, close to the swimming pool. Just then, my mom interrupted to add that my father had broken down and sobbed when he saw her.

"That made me happy," she said. "I didn't know he loved me that much."

"What were you looking for?" I asked.

"I went to look for my home and my husband," she said.

"And it looks like you found both," I said.

I sat on the couch between Mom and Dad, holding her hand and slowly stroking his back. She was as cool as a cucumber; it took half an hour for Dad to calm down.

BARELY FOUR HOURS later, Mom called to say that "that man" was in her house again, and if he didn't leave by ten o'clock, she'd call the police.

I could hear Dad beseeching her in the background. "This is my home, Stella. You're confused. We've been married for fifty-two years. Where do you expect me to go? It's late. I can't sleep on the street. I'll die from the cold."

Mom got increasingly agitated and defiant as "that man" pleaded with her; Dad got increasingly distressed as his wife repudiated their marriage. I tried to negotiate with her—"Could he perhaps sleep on the couch?" But Mom was adamant. "The man must leave. I will not allow anyone in my apartment. What will people think?"

Listening next to me, Maria got on the phone and said, "Don't worry, Stella. We won't tell anyone."

Mom said, "But *I* will know."

I felt powerless and began to worry for their safety. I hung up and consulted with a dispatcher in the police department, some friends, and Maria. The consensus was that my mom was no longer safe. She couldn't be in the apartment alone, and she wasn't allowing her caretaker to care for her.

I called my dad back and said, "The situation is getting worse, Dad. I'm coming over to take Mom to the hospital, and if she won't go with me, I'll have to call the police."

He seemed immediately relieved that the situation was now in my hands—and not his—and agreed with the plan, adding plaintively, "I can't do this anymore."

By the time I arrived, breathless and exhausted, Mom had regained her hold on reality. She recognized her husband, but made light of the events of the day and the week.

"There's no problem," she said, dismissively. "Everything is okay now."

I knew I needed to draw a line in the sand—(not only for their immediate safety but also because I would be leaving for Chicago in a day).

Sitting at their dining table—with pictures of my parents, my sister and me, and our families on the wall—I recounted the dangerous events of the last several days and made a plan with Dad to take Mom to the hospital if she cycled into confusion again and became defiant. If she wouldn't go with him, I said, "I think you need to call the police. They already know about the situation," and, in front of Mom, I handed him a piece of paper with the phone number for the police. He folded the paper carefully and put it in his wallet.

Mom felt shamed and angry, but I could also sense relief around the dining room table, as if we could all breathe again. Dad was no longer alone. He had a plan that he could fall back on if he started to lose his bearings. At the same time, Mom had scaffolding around her, which could catch her if her progressively tenuous grip on reality threatened to overwhelm them again. She herself had threatened to call the police only an hour earlier. They apologized for taking me away from my family late at night, and Dad, teary-eyed, depleted, and grateful, said, "I can't do this without you. I need you."

I looked at him and realized he and I were now connected in a way we'd never been before. For the moment, they were at peace, and I felt an incredibly tender love pass among the three of us. In its complexity, this moment was as intimate a moment as we'd ever shared.

SATURDAY, JULY 24TH

Ten minutes before the three of us boarded our flight, Dad called to say that Mom had a severe bladder infection. Irritated, he said he thought that her doctor had ruled out a bladder infection the week before. It had taken ten days for the doctor to learn that she had an infection.

In a game of point-the-finger, the doctor said the lab delayed the culture report, while the lab said they sent the report within two days of receiving the culture. We'll never know what really happened, but Dad was angry that we'd suffered so much and that the delay in diagnosing her infection could have endangered Mom's life.

Two years before, Mom had been hospitalized with what looked like a stroke. Suddenly, she couldn't speak or walk, and was confused. We rushed her to the emergency room and learned that in the elderly symptoms of a bladder infection often look like those of dementia or stroke. Then, as now, her doctors prescribed the antibiotic Cipro. It could take two to three days for the infection to be cleared. Until then, we wouldn't know if Mom's dementia had worsened.

TUESDAY, JULY 27TH

Once at the Block Center, Maria confided in me, "I'm afraid. I don't want to start another round of chemotherapy. I'm feeling as though there's no end in sight, and I'm just plain tired of it all."

I understood her tiredness. Each new round reminded her of how far she had come as well as how long the road is. I wondered if that's why Dr. Gullion asked Maria if the treatment was beating her up: that feeling must be common among cancer patients who do chemotherapy without an end in sight.

It would be easier to know if you were halfway done, or a third of the way done. We're programmed to be able to survive anything— so long as we know it's temporary.

As MARIA AND I waited in "Basil" for Jen, the physician's assistant, to arrive, I knelt next to her and placed my hands on her left shoulder, which had started to ache after her port was accessed. Maria cried softly as her shoulder responded to the warmth of my hands. "I don't wanna," she said softly. Jen walked in, noticed Maria's tears, and drew her chair forward to sit close to us.

"I'm feeling emotional today," Maria said.

"This is a good place to be when you're feeling emotional," Jen responded. "Has something happened to upset you here?"

"No, nothing's happened here. I woke up distressed," Maria said, feeling invited to share more. "Chemotherapy feels interminable, and the uncertainty is so hard. It's so hard not to know how things will turn out, not to have a guarantee. I don't know if I will live two years, or five years, or twenty years."

"Yes. This is a very, very hard process," Jen said, looking sad, too.

"And it's so much harder with a small child," Maria said. "I worry so much about Satchi and how this is affecting him. And what I fear the most is going downhill, and Satchi having to watch me waste away."

Maria then told her about a conversation we'd had with Satchi during a morning walk. "I accidentally tripped on his foot, and looking visibly shaken, he apologized to me, thinking he had done something wrong. When Van said, 'Are you worried that Mom is fragile and you can hurt her?' he responded by saying, 'She's the only mom I have.' I felt heartbroken."

PENNY BLOCK ARRIVED halfway through Maria's treatment. She was warm and loquacious, like her husband, and, though less of a physical presence at the Center, was every bit his equal with her incisiveness and integrative vision. "People get dispirited in the oncology world," she said. "We tend to forget the human spirit in medicine." Perhaps sensing that Maria needed no such overview, she zeroed in on what is most important today—Satchi—and asked, "How do you manage with a young child?"

"It's challenging. Satchi has held in his distress for a long time, but now he's talking about it more and more."

"Does Satchi know you have cancer?"

"Oh yes, almost from the day we found out."

"Good, because kids fill in the blanks when they don't have information about disease. The question is not whether to tell a child about disease but how you explain it to him in a way that is respectful of his emotional capacity."

"Van and I spend a lot of time talking about that. Recently, he's been worried that I might die suddenly."

"He needs to know that you're doing everything you can to improve your health," Penny said. "You can say, 'I'm not going to die any time soon.'" I find the clarity in her directness helpful and reassuring without being overly optimistic. Later, she added, "It's important to tell Satchi, 'You may not notice because it's gradual, but I'm feeling stronger.'"

"I'm not feeling particularly positive right now. I'm struggling with not knowing how long I'll live. And I wonder what to say to my child."

"Try this: 'I'm doing everything that we know about based on science to be around for many, many decades and to get old with you.'"

"I like that," Maria said, tearfully.

"The only difference between cancer patients and other people is that cancer patients no longer have the illusion of life's predictability or their own immortality. Illusions provide a cushion of comfort, so we'll need to help you find your own cushion of comfort that will allow you to meet each day with vitality instead of panic."

FRIDAY, JULY 30TH

As Maria rested in the hotel, Satchi and I built sand sculptures on the beach. First, we carved a complex of buildings, pyramids, and spirals into the sand, right at the high tide mark, and then we toiled in the hot sun to surround them with a series of moats and levees to protect our small city from the steadily rising tide. Satchi directed me where to shore up our defenses as the diminutive waves of Lake Michigan slowly and inexorably eroded our world.

"The waves will eventually wash it all away," Satchi said, "but we need to keep trying to delay the inevitable."

"The longer we delay the inevitable," I said, "the better the chance we have of figuring out how to save our city."

When we weren't saving our city, Satchi and I accompanied Maria to the Block Center. There, Satchi met the team of nurses and doctors who were helping us to build moats and levees around his mom. When Penny Block met Satchi, she told him that she wanted him to know that they were "all doing everything imaginable and possible" to help his mom be healthy. I could sense that he felt comforted knowing everyone he met here knew him and was on our team; we weren't building sandcastles alone.

SATCHI AND I threatened to make trouble in the infusion room, but couldn't find anything really bad to do. We fantasized about liberating patients from their IVs and secretly adding fish to the fish tank. Instead, we played checkers while Maria talked to another stage IV colon cancer mom.

As we left the Block Center, Maria said this woman learned that she had colon cancer four years ago, when her fourth child was only six weeks old.

"Oh, my God," Satchi said. "That is so young."

"HOLD ON," MY dad said. "I want to put your mother on." I had just plopped down on the bed in the Hotel Orrington, and in the few seconds it took for my mom to speak, I felt great dread.

"Hi, Van. I've put you all through hell, haven't I? Your dad has been wonderful. He's put up with all my confusion. I just wanted you to know that I'm back." She then complained to me that I haven't been as available as she would like: "You didn't come to me when I needed you."

"I know, Ma. I'm sorry I've disappointed you. I love you." I was relieved that she knew who her husband was; that was the most important thing. I also knew that she'd probably forget her disappointment in me.

ON OUR LAST day at the Block Center, Satchi sat on the infusion room couch and watched *I Love Lucy* reruns on our portable DVD player while Maria and I met with Keith Block. I could hear Lucy's and Ricky's voices wafting through the closed door as Dr. Block talked about the next steps in shoring up Maria's defenses against cancer. "I'm doing much better than I was when I was last here in May," she said.

"You look it," Dr. Block said. "Your color and energy have changed." Curious about how it is for Maria to bounce between two treatment centers, he asked how things are going with David Gullion.

"He's kind. I like him a lot, and he's very supportive of what you're doing here. And he has a beautiful infusion room overlooking Mount Tam."

Clearly interested, Dr. Block told us that Northwestern University had decided to reclaim the office building housing the Block Center. As a result, the Center would be moving at year's end to Skokie, the next town over, where rents were cheaper and space more available.

"The new space is large and lovely, but we will not be doing any pilgrimages around a mountain in Skokie," he joked. Reviewing the latest CT scan, he added, "The scans look good now, so let's review the status of other approaches that may help with long-term control."

Turning to our list of topics to discuss, Maria said, "Can you tell me about Anvirzel? You mentioned it four months ago, and I'm wondering if now is the time to introduce it."

By way of self-disclosure, Dr. Block explained that, though he sits on the advisory board of the company that produces Anvirzel, a patented oleander-based extract, he himself asked to do so after he realized its clinical potential.

"The preliminary data is favorable," he said. "Very impressive." He explained that Anvirzel works by inhibiting NF-kappa beta, a switch for inflammation that can promote malignancy and increase resistance to chemotherapy. There are also other mechanisms that can induce apoptosis (cell death) in human tumors but not normal cells.

"Do you mean that if I take Anvirzel, I might increase my chances of staying on FOLFIRI longer?"

"That's the idea," Dr. Block said, explaining that cancer cells have a specific protein—P-glycoprotein, or Pgp—in the cell membrane that acts as a pump. Just as fast as chemotherapy enters the cell, Pgp squirts the drugs back out, protecting the cell from apoptosis and rendering the anticancer drugs powerless. "It appears from preliminary research that Anvirzel may be able to block the activation of this self-protective mechanism in cancer cells."

In over my head with the science, I felt relieved when Maria, always practical, asked him for his opinion on a range of other supplements and treatment options we'd been collecting. He supported several of the supplements and added, "In conjunction with your full integrative program, I feel Anvirzel may offer some possibility of slowing or stabilizing your metastases. This will allow for more time and, hopefully, more options to become available."

I thought, "I hope his levees hold up better than the ones Satchi and I built on the beach last night."

MY MOM'S SYNAPTIC levees did not hold. I had a voicemail waiting for me when I returned to our hotel room.

"Van, call me," Mom said, in a desperate voice. When I called back and got her on the phone, she said, "I need to hear a familiar voice. I've never been so alone in all my life. Where is your dad?" I could then hear her raising her voice at the man who was in her house.

Dad took the phone and said, "Van, convince her that I'm your father."

"I don't think I can convince her, Dad. And trying to fight her delusions only makes her more irritable and defensive."

Weary, he said, "Maybe I should take her to the hospital and, if she won't go, call the police."

"I think that's a good idea. Do you still have the number that I gave you for the police."

"Yes, in my pocket."

"Whatever you do, I want you to know I think you're a good husband. But maybe it would be best to find an assisted living place where Mom could be comfortable and not so scared."

I could tell he was struggling with the inevitability that one day soon he would have to relinquish control over her life to someone else. It was only a matter of time before a fog of confusion would descend on his wife. The course of antibiotics was finished but she was still cycling in and out of frightening delusions—her dementia had gotten worse.

From my own experience, I understood why he would want to delay the inevitable, hoping for a long and stable hiatus the next time the fog lifted. It appeared unlikely that would happen, but I couldn't blame him for hoping. It can't be easy to make the decision to change the structure of your life as you have known it for fifty-two years— your wife by your side in your own home—even if that has become a terrible burden.

MARIA DECIDED TO use a wheelchair at O'Hare Airport. Once in the terminal, we waited in the Special Needs area for an electric cart to carry us to our gate. Sitting in the cart, I felt Satchi pull at my shirt.

"Dad, look, over there." The object of his interest did not register quickly, but I could tell he was troubled by something. "Dad, look, there, on the wall." He pointed more forcefully to an attention-getting, 4-by-6-foot ad on the wall across from where we were parked. I turned and saw the photo of a very good-looking African American man wearing a light blue pullover.

Next to his face, in bold print, the ad said, "This is personal." I still didn't know what the ad referred to and would have turned away had Satchi not been glued to the words. I could tell that he was reading, if not rereading, the text:

> *"My mother was the cornerstone of our family. When she was diagnosed with colon cancer, it was like the whole family got cancer. She died when she was only 56. Let my heartbreak be your wake-up call."*

These were the words of Terrence Howard, an actor and musician. The "ad" was a public service announcement.

My first response was anger. Shit, I thought, why did we have to be parked in front of that? Then I put my arm around Satchi and hugged him. I said, "Oh my, that must be so distressing to read. She died so young. How tragic." Satchi teared up, his eyes still rereading the text. I then quickly read the text under the picture:

Colorectal cancer is the second leading cancer killer in the U.S., but it is largely preventable. If you're 50 or older, please get screened. Screening finds precancerous polyps, so they can be removed before they turn into cancer. And screening finds colorectal cancer early, when treatment works best. If you're at increased risk—if you have a personal or family history of polyps or colorectal cancer, or you have inflammatory bowel disease—ask your doctor when to start screening.

Screening saves lives.

Just then, our cart pulled away. I don't know if Satchi had the time to read the entire text; I barely got through all the words myself. I kept my arm around him as we drove to our gate. Soon he was enthralled by the cart ride and the wonders of O'Hare Airport: the jumbo-size elevators we needed to use to change floors, the 72-foot-long Brachiosaurus dinosaur in Terminal One, and the ever-changing neon lights in the tunnel connecting concourses B and C.

"Wow, this is amazing," Satchi said. "Look at that!" The man driving the cart laughed, and I imagined he was seeing the airport he'd seen thousands of times before for the first time through Satchi's fresh new eyes.

I just wanted time to slow down—the tide was rising much too quickly for me.

eight

◆

ALL THINGS ARE POSSIBLE

SATURDAY, AUGUST 7TH

Hoping to support me as I think through end-of-life issues for my mom, Maria decided to read Atul Gawande's article in *The New Yorker*, "Letting Go: What Should Medicine Do When It Can't Save Your Life?" She read the first page and started to cry. She came looking for me in the kitchen.

"Have you read Gawande's article yet?"

"No, I'm not ready. I heard him on NPR this week and knew what to expect."

"I wished I'd known. The first page was just too much for me. I didn't know he was going to talk about incurable diseases, like cancer. He starts by telling the story of a woman who's thirty-nine weeks pregnant and learns that she has an incurable kind of lung cancer—and less than a year to live. She's thirty-six-years old and probably won't live to celebrate her child's first birthday."

"Oh no."

"I'm scared, Van. Satchi's birthday is in two days, and I don't know how many more I'll be around for."

I ASKED MY mother's doctor if, given the complexity of her medical situation, he could guess how long she might live. I worried he might think I wanted her to die; what I really wanted was to help my father start thinking about the endgame. Did my mom have five months? A year? Two years? Longer?

"I learned when your mom survived a diagnosis of liver cancer a couple of years back that I should never predict anything about her resiliency or longevity." We both laughed. He added, "She could survive for many years in this state of confusion."

I didn't want her to die, but I feared that she'd live for a long time—what a terrible paradox of feelings for a loved one. It was becoming painful to witness the daily suffering her mind's demise caused both her and my father. Moments of clarity when she recognized her husband were few, and even then, she couldn't understand why he came home only to apparently leave and abandon her again. It was tormenting when he was gone and confusing when he walked into the room unannounced. There was no oasis of peace anymore; she was living in constant fear.

My dad, sensitive to her anguish, had tried to explain where he went when he "went away." "I leave the house to find myself, and once I find myself, I come home." I loved this elegant, yet tidy explanation.

She said, "You're still trying to find yourself?" I laughed, and she got angry with me for laughing. I didn't try to explain how precious their exchange was.

Kindly, my dad then made up a story about his whereabouts, even though he hadn't left the house at all.

"When I left the house to search for myself, I went to the hospital and stayed in the waiting room. Do you remember, Stella? When you were in the hospital two years ago, I used to spend the night in the chair by your side. On some nights, when there was another patient in the room with you, the nurses wouldn't let me sleep next to you, and then I would have to sleep in the waiting room. Well, that's where I go. I drive to the hospital, park my car, and stay in the waiting room until I find what I've lost. Then I come home."

I was touched by my dad's story. She liked it, too. It made sense. She asked no follow-up questions, and remembered him for a full day and a half.

TWO DAYS LATER, my dad called the police. They'd been arguing all evening; she didn't want him to stay in her apartment. The firefighters arrived, joked with my mom, and took her to the emergency room for observation. After four hours in the hospital, the ER doctor gave her a new, stronger prescription for anxiety and a referral to a neurologist for further testing, and sent her home. They didn't think she was a danger to herself, so she didn't qualify for involuntary hospitalization.

Sitting on the couch with her the next morning, I asked, "How was that to have the firefighters take you to the hospital?"

Dressed in a blue blouse, with a necklace I had given her for Mother's Day around her neck, she said, "Those young men were very nice to me." She then turned toward my dad and said, in Greek, like an angry Medea, "God will make you pay for this."

After that, she believed the real husband made brief appearances but always left, and then the imposter husband returned to torment her.

"All these 'Mannys' are driving me crazy," Mom said. "Each one tells me he's my husband. I can't keep up with them."

If I were pressed to describe hell, it would be what my mother and father were going through. The person on whom you have depended your whole life for comfort and security either doesn't remember you (Mom) or has disappeared and left you (Dad), for some incomprehensible reason, at the mercy of others who are not familiar.

I recently heard a story about an elderly woman with dementia who went to live in a group home. Her husband would come to visit every day, but she no longer remembered him. Instead she met a nice man in the house and transferred her affections to him, not unlike Julie Christie's character in the poignantly beautiful 2006 movie about Alzheimer's disease, *Away from Her*.

That story makes me feel sad and hopeful at the same time. We can create angels for ourselves even in hell.

MARIA, SATCHI, AND I drove to Lake Tahoe for our yearly August pilgrimage to the Sierra Mountains. We'd delayed our trip by a day to see our friend Merlijn, who lived in Holland. Having last visited California two years before, she spent the night with us so we could bridge the years in the few short hours we had together. When I said good-bye to her, I believed I would see her again; I took our future reunion for granted. Maria and she embraced for a long time as Satchi and I waited in the car.

Exuberant about driving to the Sierras, Satchi made up a song from the backseat: "We're going on a vacation. We're going on a vacation. We're driving to the Sierras. We're driving to the Sierras." Noticing his mom crying, he stopped and asked, "Why are you crying, Mom?"

"Because I love Merlijn and saying good-bye is so sad when you don't know when you'll see someone again." I knew she meant, *If* you'll see someone again. Maria and Merlijn held their gaze as I slowly drove away from the curb. Satchi continued to sing his vacation song all the way to the freeway.

TUESDAY, AUGUST 10TH

It was the night before Satchi's birthday. We were sitting at the kitchen table, finishing dinner, when Maria started to tell Satchi about the day she went into labor. As Maria spoke, I realized that there were small details she remembered that I didn't, like what she ate for breakfast, and almost reflexively, I reached for the video camera. I wanted to make sure I had Maria's version of events.

I trained the video camera on Maria, added snippets of my own memory as she spoke, and zoomed in on Satchi as he mugged for the camera. When he tired of the details, I took him upstairs for a bath.

Later that night, as she stood by the dining room table and distributed her supplements into pillboxes, Maria dropped her glass of water, spilling some into the boxes. After twenty-two years of marriage, I knew that when she got distressed or overwhelmed she could become clumsy and drop things, or accidentally hurt herself. Visibly shaken, she got angry, started to cry, and stormed off to sit by herself. I cleaned up the water, then sat next to her on the couch and tried to console her. In three days she would start another round of chemotherapy, and I suspected she was anticipating that with some weariness, if not dread. She was inconsolable and didn't respond to my overtures; I began to sense that she was angry with me.

Crying again, she said, "It was so incredibly hard to have you videotape me. I just wanted to tell my kid his story. The video camera changed everything. I became aware that I was telling him his birth story and that, one day, I won't be here to tell it to him on his birthday."

My heart dropped. "Oh, my god, I am so sorry."

"And I began to think that maybe you wanted to videotape me so he would have a video to remember me by. It's just so damn painful to be reminded when I least expect it that I have cancer, and that I might die prematurely and not see my child grow up." Unknowingly, I had opened the cancer trapdoor.

"Had I known, I would not have videotaped you. I feel so bad."

I decided to wait until later to tell her that she was right. I did want to remember her experience of Satchi's birth in case she died without my knowing all the details.

THURSDAY, AUGUST 12TH

Maria handed Dr. Gullion a list of the Tibetan herbs she'd been taking. It read like a botanist's dream, for example, "Before bedtime: *Shiwuwei Chenxiang Wan,*" whose ingredients include *Aguila agallocha, Myristica fragrans, Melia composita,* and *Bambusa textilis.* Referring to the other supplements Maria took as directed by the Block Center, her acupuncturist, and her Tibetan doctor, he asked, "How do you keep all this straight?"

Maria laughed, and said, "That's why Van and I take such copious notes. I'm trying to keep everything straight."

"Any new developments from the Block Center?"

"I'm going to start taking Anvirzel," she said and then explained the potential benefits to taking oleander. Unfazed, as if he had been around long enough to hear about many promising drugs, including Anvirzel, Dr. Gullion wrote down "Anvirzel" on a piece of a paper.

"And how's that mystery gas?" he asked, referring to a rare physiological phenomenon that Maria had had for two months, gas in the bladder. He, as well as Dr. Nora and Maria's gynecologist, was baffled by how this symptom had endured even after her bladder and *Candida* infections had cleared. In rare instances, especially after radiation, a fistula can develop between an elimination organ, like the colon, and the urethra, but it's not usually seen with chemotherapy. And if there were, say, a fistula between the bladder and small intestine, Maria would have high fevers and be very sick.

"Still the same, maybe getting worse," Maria said.

"Odd. We can see funny things with Avastin," Dr. Gullion said, very careful to take any unexplained physiological change in Maria's body seriously. "When someone is on Avastin, we're very suspicious that that's the cause" of odd symptoms. And because Avastin can weaken cell membranes, you have to be careful to factor in Avastin's effect on the body, even if it makes no sense at first, he said.

He recommended that Maria see a urologist, picked up the phone, and called a colleague to ask for a referral.

"Good thing I have a PPO for my insurance," Maria said. "I can pick anyone I want."

"We're certainly taking advantage of that," I said.

Sensing our lightness, Dr. Gullion participated in our repartee, "Your insurance company is going to crack" under the weight of your demands.

Dr. Gullion then reviewed Maria's blood counts, reciting her numbers. "Your chemistries are all normal."

"And that's after thirteen rounds of chemotherapy," I interjected. Maria and I did a fist pump.

"And going on fourteen," Dr. Gullion added, and then in an auctioneer's voice, he said, "When will we sell?"

"We're going to hold out for a long time," I joked.

SUNDAY, AUGUST 15TH

August 15th is one of the most important religious holidays in Greece, marking the day the Virgin Mary ascended into heaven and took her place alongside the Son. Virtually the entire country shuts down for *Kimísis tis Theotókou*—literally, "the sleep of the Virgin

Mary." In an icon I remember from my youth, Mary, surrounded by the Apostles, has just fallen asleep, and above her, Christ holds her soul in his left arm, in the form of a swaddled baby. In villages all across Greece today, believers carry an icon of the sleeping Virgin Mary in a solemn procession throughout the village.

Twenty-seven years ago, Maria arrived in Athens on *Kímísis tis Theotókou* to spend two weeks traveling the Greek countryside with me. I picked her up from the airport, excited but nervous that she'd traveled halfway around the world to be with me, and brought her back to my father's childhood home, in a suburb of Athens. That first night, Maria and I made love under a wall-mounted altar that housed two icons, one of the Mother and one of the Son. A red glass votive lamp burned in front of the icons, bathing us in a soft, rosy hue.

"Do you remember that night?" I asked Maria, while we lay in bed those many years later. "I fell in love with you all over again."

"I do remember. That night, in your arms, I found my home."

"I know. Me too."

TUESDAY, AUGUST 24TH

I read an elegant study on the link between social rejection and inflammation that had just been published online in the *Proceedings of the National Academy of Sciences*. The study's authors had concluded that social rejection and the stress it causes trigger increases in the levels of two inflammatory markers. Over time, this social stress may promote susceptibility to diseases with an inflammatory component.

Though not a smoking gun, this study is the beginning of a long effort by science to prove what any schoolyard teacher knows by observation on the playground: it doesn't feel good when you want to play and are rejected by others. We may discover one day that persistently rejecting or nonresponsive relationships (including parenting) can lead to an increased vulnerability to certain inflammatory-based diseases later in life, such as heart disease, arthritis, diabetes, irritable bowel syndrome, fibromyalgia, Alzheimer's, and cancer.

Maria and I mulled these connections over as she prepared to take her second dose of oleander extract on Friday night. She took a small vial of dry Anvirzel out of the freezer, mixed in an exact amount of water to dilute its contents, shook it, and then used a syringe to squirt the liquid under her tongue.

After three minutes, she swallowed and said thoughtfully, "You know, I've been thinking about how my dad disinherited me and rejected us"—without telling Maria, her father had responded to her efforts to live independently by writing her out of his will—"and while I don't for a moment think that action caused my cancer, something got set into motion twenty-five years ago that has cast a shadow over my adult life, and maybe affected my health."

"I don't doubt that. Chronic stress can do that," I said.

"I know. When I teach clients about trauma, I explain how the body responds to a stressful event by first secreting hormones to alert the body to threat and then, when the threat has passed, turning off those hormones. But with chronic, low-level stress, the hormone-spigot never turns off. Like a leaky faucet, it continues to drip, causing long-term damage."

Maria didn't need to list the damage. I was familiar with it in my own work, especially with couples that never learn how to co-regulate conflict and stress. Over time, such ongoing stress can affect digestion, the immune system (inflammation is a protective response of the immune system), mood and emotions, sexuality, and the availability of energy for life.

MY MOTHER'S PSYCHOTROPIC drugs began to stabilize the worst of her delusions. She was beginning to accept that her husband was gone and that she was living in a new place with "the butler," as my dad refers to himself, the man who cooks and cleans and drives her around.

OVER THE WEEKEND, I briefed my dad on the options before him, from the least expensive, which was hiring an elder care aide to sit with mom for a few hours, several times a week, so he could leave the house on his own, to the most expensive, which was paying for an assisted living facility with a skilled nursing staff that could take care of Mom when she deteriorated further. I told him I thought he should hire an elder care manager, who could, like a general contractor, be responsible for our punch list, particularly since I could no longer provide that function.

A few days later, Dad called and said, "I called the doctor to ask him what would happen to Stella if I put her in a home. I wanted to know if she would ever come home again. He said, 'She'll die there, Manny.' Van, I'm not ready to do that yet. I want to do whatever it takes to keep her here with me." But then, he added, as though he knew he was only buying time, "Call and find an elder care manager. You can't do everything."

MONDAY, AUGUST 30TH

"I've gained seventeen pounds," Maria announced excitedly. She was now at her pre-pregnancy weight—and voluptuous.

"At this rate, you might have to go on a diet," I said.

"Get out of here."

Maria knew I thought she could stand to gain another ten pounds, and the Block Center Weight Gainer Shake—almond milk, frozen fruit, banana, whey powder, almond butter, MCT oil, and ice cream substitute—that she made once a day, would almost certainly get her there. In combination with a strenuous workout routine, her diet is adding the best kind of weight for a cancer patient: lean muscle. We both knew the stronger and healthier she was able to be, the better her chance of surviving setbacks in her treatment later on.

WAITING FOR DR. Gullion, I told Maria about a new study on how living in an environment rich with physical, mental, and social stimulation might itself curb cancer growth, at least in mice. The study, led by Matthew During at the Ohio State University Comprehensive Cancer Center (and published the month before in *Cell*), discovered that mice that lived in complex environments equipped with toys, hiding places, running wheels, and unlimited food and water had significantly smaller tumors than the mice in the control group, who had access to unlimited food and water, but no toys.

"That's amazing," Maria said. "What accounts for that?"

I didn't understand the complex biological mechanisms involved, so I paraphrased from two articles about the study I had tucked away in my notebook. The researchers discovered that an enriched environment activates a nervous-system pathway that allows the brain to tell fat cells to stop releasing leptin into the bloodstream. A hormone, leptin normally helps the body to regulate appetite, but it can also accelerate cancer growth.

"People tend to think that cancer survivors should avoid stress, but our data suggests that this is not completely true," During said in an interview. "We believe that our results suggest that people should be challenged socially and physically, perhaps engage in team sports or competitive activities involving larger social groups, in addition to increased physical activity. It means we shouldn't simply be avoiding stress but rather making our lives richer, more complex, more challenging, and a little stressful."

"I wonder if learning how to play the piano counts," Maria said.

"Only if you're a mouse," I started to say as Dr. Gullion walked into the consulting room.

ONCE IN THE infusion room, Maria handed me an article she'd cut out of our local newspaper that morning. The headline read, "Rules altered for cancer drug cocktails." The lead paragraph immediately captured my imagination: "A diagnosis of AIDS was a death sentence until the advent of drug cocktails in the 1990s, which helped patients suppress the disease indefinitely. Now researchers say a similar combination strategy may change the course of cancer."

I learned that biotechnology and pharmaceutical companies would soon be able to mix and match drugs still in development rather than wait for the FDA to approve individual drugs before they can be combined in a "drug cocktail." The streamlined approval process could shave five years off of the development of new cancer cocktails. In anticipation of the new FDA guidelines, companies were already testing new combinations of drugs in human trials; some were even working together to combine experimental drugs in which they each have a proprietary stake. In an age of increased interdependence, it would make sense that the only way to fight cancer is to blend your resources and plan for new synergies.

Integrative medicine is indeed the wave of the future; 2 + 2 + 2 might even work for pharmaceutical companies. I'm reminded of what the English poet and essayist Matthew Arnold once wrote, "The freethinking of one age is the common sense of the next."

TUESDAY, SEPTEMBER 7TH

A friend sent a note to Maria: "Remember that the *Course in Miracles* says, 'there is no order of difficulty in miracles.'" I went to my bedside table, took out the *Course*, which teaches that we can experience freedom and peace of mind if we become aware of God's inner guidance, and read, "The first thing to remember about miracles is that there is no order of difficulty among them. One is not harder or bigger than another. They are all the same."

That night I dreamed that Amma wanted to talk to me. I rushed to her room and entered breathless to find her laying on a daybed, an attendant at her feet. Sitting next to her, my heart sank when I saw that her face was pallid, sweating, and in pain.

Her voice spoke inside me. "The body is sick, but not my spirit. I have taken on the sickness, but it will go when the time is right. Don't worry, all things are possible."

MARIA EMERGED FROM round fifteen feeling strong and hopeful. "I think the Anvirzel must be making a difference," Maria said, "because I feel cooler and more present, as if my healthy cells had sunscreen on."

Though her tumor marker numbers had started to level off, indicating the FOLFIRI's initial success was starting to slow, one marker started to decrease at a slightly faster rate again. Maria and I celebrated the news. Perhaps the oleander had reversed the tumor's resistance to chemotherapy. We also knew that since oleander is a botanical, it takes longer to reach its full benefit than do most pharmaceuticals. We prayed that the Anvirzel Line would hold while the oleander amassed and launched its assault.

I WAS SUPPOSED to be on jury duty at Alameda County Superior Court. I take jury duty seriously, but under the circumstances I

couldn't imagine spending a day in court when my wife was starting her sixteenth round of chemotherapy. There was no category on
the jury summons for husbands of wives who have cancer, but, not
expecting to be excused, I called the courthouse anyway and told the
person in charge of juries that my wife had cancer and that I needed
to be with her during her chemotherapy.

"Absolutely, your job is to be with your wife," she said. Then
she added, "Don't you worry about anything. I'll take your name off
the jury list for a year, and if you still need a deferment call me again.
Good luck, and God be with you both."

WEDNESDAY, SEPTEMBER 15TH

My dad was rarely able to speak freely on the phone, since when
she was awake, Mom would pick up the phone to eavesdrop on
us. I would say, "Mom, are you on the line? If you are, please hang
up. I want to talk to the butler." Like a child, she complied for, say,
twenty seconds, and then picked up the phone again to listen. She
didn't know I could hear a click when she picked up the phone.

One night when she was asleep, we could finally talk. "It's like
living with a two-year old," he said. "I'm constantly on edge. I can't
leave her alone with herself, not even to toast a bagel. She could burn
the house down."

"How do you manage, Dad? How do you hold it all together?"

"I'm not managing well," he said. "Can you tell me again what
my options are if I have to find a place for her?"

I walked him through his long-term options. He didn't like any
of them. He couldn't afford a skilled nursing facility or a residential
care facility, and he didn't want to sell their condominium to live
with Stella in assisted living.

"Will Medicare pay for long-term care?" he asked.

"As I understand it, only for ninety days, and then only if Mom has been hospitalized first, for a minimum of three days, and she has a diagnosis that allows for rehabilitation, like if she fell and broke her hip."

He goes silent. "I thought we'd be able to depend on Medicare to pay for her care at this point in life."

"I know, Dad. The options aren't great. Maybe we're close to the point when we should go talk to an elder care manager about the next step, someone who really knows the ins and outs of Medicare and can act as a guide and advocate for us if we need to find a home for Mom."

"I'm not ready yet," he said. He changed the topic to ask about Maria; he knew she'd had chemotherapy that week. "You're taking care of Maria the way I'm taking care of Stella. You didn't expect your wife to have cancer."

"No, Dad, I didn't. But when we love people, we take care of them no matter what, even when it's hard."

"Yes. You're right."

"The big difference," I told him, with Maria listening in the same room, "is that Maria knows who I am and is incredibly kind to me."

Maria blew me a kiss.

nine

◆

CLOSING THE GAP

"It's too much. It's too much. It's *just too much*."

It was a late Friday afternoon. Satchi was outside playing with the neighborhood kids. And after a busy workweek, I had finally been able to get back to my writing. Then I heard Maria sighing loudly in the kitchen. I walked into the room, knelt down next to her chair, and put my hand on her thigh. That's when the floodgates opened.

Earlier in the afternoon, Maria had applied for Social Security disability benefits. The "claimant advocate" interviewing her wanted to know about all the doctors she had seen for cancer, starting with the family doctor who had diagnosed her anemia. She wanted to know about Maria's CT scans, pathology results, portacath surgery, and infusions in the hospital. She asked about her work history and income, and how many hours she worked prior to her diagnosis. And she wanted Satchi's Social Security number so that if Maria died, he could receive government benefits.

The very act of recalling the first nine months of her treatment—and the full weight of her diagnosis and disability—brought her to her knees emotionally.

"It's so hard to admit that I can't work anymore. I have always worked. Now I'm going on the dole." She started to sob uncontrollably.

"Hold on," I said. "You've contributed to Social Security your whole working life. You've earned whatever government support you receive. It's not a handout."

"I know, but 'people like us,' whatever that's supposed to mean, are not supposed to need government assistance. It's just not right; there are other people who need it more than us."

Before I had a chance to respond, Maria told me she'd learned that morning that one of our neighbors was recently diagnosed with breast cancer and had already had two surgeries. A meditation teacher, our neighbor specializes in working with cancer patients.

"It's not fair. Why would she get cancer? She has spent her whole life helping people deal with cancer. I know cancer is not about fairness, but it's just not fair."

I wanted to say something to make her feel better, but I knew she needed me to just sit with her and allow her to cry. I didn't need to *do* anything. Just then, I could hear Satchi laughing out front; it sounded like the three-year-old twins across the street were chasing him around the yard. I got comfortable on the floor, at Maria's feet, as wave after wave of upset washed over her—and me.

"Not only that, my body has been achy all day, and I'm feeling really weak. I'm not supposed to be feeling weak during my non-chemo week. Something is going on in my abdomen. I feel pressure there and weird sensations. I'm scared. I'm really scared."

Maria didn't need to tell me what scared her. Like most cancer patients, she feared the cancer had turned a corner on the treatment and was starting to spread. For most of us, a cramp in the stomach is just a tummy ache; for a cancer patient, the fear says it could be

another tumor. The fear lurks in the background and hijacks ordinary fatigue or physical discomfort.

"I know you're scared that the cancer is spreading, but remember that the tumor marker numbers are dropping, your recent blood
panel indicates that you're very healthy, and that Dr. Dickey said
your life force is stronger."

"I know. You're probably right. The cancer isn't spreading, but
something feels off to me. I just finished another course of antibiotics, but I haven't rebounded yet. Something is wrong."

Just then, Satchi came running inside. He noticed his mom crying and sat opposite the two of us.

"It's okay, Mom. Everything will be okay." He asked for a family hug and then ran off to immerse himself in Harry Potter. Maria
and I tabled our conversation until later. It was family time now;
cancer and its complications would have to wait their turn.

"CANCER DOESN'T KILL you; it's the side effects of the cancer
or the treatment for cancer that kills you. Do you remember when
Keith Block told us that?" Maria asked. "I'm beginning to understand what he means now."

Maria had just met with Dr. Gullion, a day in advance of round
seventeen. I was unable to accompany her to the appointment but
was home when our friend Gary drove her back to Berkeley and
gave me his handwritten notes from the meeting. At a glance, I saw
enough to wish I had been able to attend the appointment.

With Gary in the living room, Maria took me by the hand, led
me to our bedroom, and closed the door behind us.

"I need to talk to you in private," she said. "What do you want
first, the good news or the bad news?"

Not fully understanding the bad news, I chose the good. Her tumor marker numbers both had dropped, one minimally, but the other by more than 25 percent after having leveled off in early July. Its movement downward was, in our minds, confirmation that the Anvirzel had jumpstarted apoptosis again. And Maria's liver and stomach felt soft to the touch, Dr. Gullion said, another indication that her tumors were not growing or hardening or causing discomfort.

Turning to the bad news, Maria said, "It appears that the gas in my bladder is due to a fistula and not a urinary tract infection."

I had heard the term *fistula* before but wasn't sure what it meant. "What's a fistula?"

"Well, Dr. Gullion said it's an 'abnormal communication' between two organs that shouldn't be connected."

Where we once thought the gas might be a result of microorganisms producing gas in the bladder (hence, two rounds of antibiotics), it now appeared likely that a more complex process had been operating: the infections could be related to microorganisms and gas seeping *from* the gastrointestinal tract *into* the bladder, something that's not supposed to happen, but which is common enough to have a name, pneumaturia (air, or in the original Greek, breath or spirits) in the urine.

Since June, when the first signs of infection surfaced, the pneumaturia has come and gone—two days on, three days off, sometimes more, sometimes less.

Sitting on the bed, Maria, visibly rattled, said, "Dr. Gullion said that if I have a fistula, the surest way to deal with it is to divert the stream of material through my colon."

"What does that mean?"

"I would have to have a colostomy."

I was too shocked to say anything, and Maria began to cry. "I don't want to get a colostomy." My heart sank for her. If having to live with cancer weren't bad enough, she might soon have to deal with carrying a colostomy bag on her body for the rest of her life.

"Fuck," I said. "God, this cancer sucks."

I asked Maria what the treatment might be for a fistula before it got bad enough to require a colostomy.

"I don't know," she said. "I was so shaken I didn't ask a lot of questions. He said that he thought the Avastin could be causing a fistula. If that were the case, I might need to consider stopping the Avastin to allow my body to heal, but that would also put me at greater risk for the cancer growing. And if I didn't stop the Avastin, I run the risk of the fistula not healing, and then I would have to get a colostomy."

"Oh, my God," I said. "What a terrible dilemma!"

I began to wonder about the hidden costs of the treatment. Avastin, considered to be a wonder drug for strangling tumor growth and extending the survival of colon cancer patients, can also cause irreversible damage. I did not feel prepared to make decisions of the kind that might soon be before us. I wanted the evolution of this treatment to comply with *our* game plan.

MARIA HAD HAD her pump removed. The past three days had been uneventful, barely any nausea, and no side effects. Her appetite was strong and her sleep solid. She walked frequently and rested soundly.

She emailed Dr. Gullion to say she wanted to come up with a plan to treat the fistula as soon as possible; she didn't want to wait until her only option was a colostomy. She also emailed Howard to tell him about the prevailing hypothesis: that Avastin might have compromised the lining of the colon and created the conditions for an abnormal passageway with the bladder.

He responded, "In terms of Chinese medicine, the approach is to balance the relationship between metal (associated with colon & lungs) and water (associated with bladder & kidneys). My thinking also is that so long as your body is able to continue to put on weight and manage the various sources of inflammation, you may be more able to resolve the fistula."

I felt more hopeful after reading Howard's email. Perhaps the colon and the bladder should not be communicating, but they do have a relationship. And it is in relationship where there is the possibility for healing.

SATURDAY, SEPTEMBER 25TH

"I'd be surprised if the fistula opening is large," Howard said. We were sitting in his office in Oakland, the fingers of his right hand already gently undulating on Maria's wrist, listening for messages from within. "If it were, you'd have a fever and a severe infection." She might also have stool coming out of her urine, rather than just gas. One explanation for why Maria might have a pinprick-size breach in her colon, Howard suggested, is that the carcinoma is shrinking at a rate too fast for the body to replace the tissue occupied by the retreating tumor.

"That makes sense," Maria said, relieved to hear an explanation that suggests the fistula is, in a paradoxical though problematic way, a sign of progress in the treatment.

In response to a question from Howard about the role Avastin may be playing in the fistula mystery, Maria put two and two together: "Well, Avastin weakens membranes because it prevents them from growing new blood vessels. So if the primary tumor were shrinking, or pulling away from the lining of the colon wall, it would be hard for my body to keep pace with creating new blood vessels to fill the void."

"Yes, and I've been worried from the very beginning about the level of inflammation in your body," Howard said, explaining that he would expect inflammation in the tissue and stroma around the tumor even as Maria's overall inflammatory markers come down. "One of the reasons balanced yin is so important," he said, "is that it helps the body to reduce inflammation and to heal damaged tissue."

"My inflammation numbers are currently on the low end of what is normal, after being extremely high when I started being tested for them in late March."

"Perhaps you'd have a larger fistula and a really severe problem by now," I postulated, "if you hadn't gotten your inflammation under control so quickly."

"Most fistulas are discovered when there's already been a serious breach," Howard said. Referring to the on-again off-again nature of her pneumaturia (she hadn't had symptoms for thirty-six hours when she saw Howard), he added, "Your body's been teetering; let's get it to teeter back."

I liked the sound of that; we didn't have to wait for the inevitable to happen.

He recommended that Maria add aloe to her diet, saying it's considered by Chinese medicine to be a natural purgative and anti-inflammatory, and to help regenerate damaged epithelial tissues. When taken internally, aloe lines the walls of the stomach and intestines and helps to cleanse them of any residue (toxins and chemicals from our environment, and additives from our food) that has accumulated in the villi, the tiny fingerlike projections that massage and digest food throughout the alimentary canal. Aloe molecules also get absorbed into the bloodstream, where they find their way to damaged tissue and help repair it from the inside out.

"Everything else is looking good," Howard added. "You're strong. It doesn't make sense to do anything"—other than support the body—"unless the fistula worsens. If you were having trouble with other things, maybe we should be concerned. But all the things I gauge for yin energy are good, and you're picking up weight. Don't be too worried about the fistula; just trust your body. Remember, when the rice is strong, the weeds won't grow."

HOWARD STOOD UP to take Maria to the treatment room but paused next to his desk, where a large, framed portrait of his father hung on the wall behind him.

"In Chinese medicine, the lungs and the intestines are like husband and wife. A problem with one often means a problem with the other, so I've never stopped treating your lungs."

"You and your father have said before that my illness may have started in the lungs and may be very old and deep in my body."

"The lungs and large intestines are associated with metal. And metal is most affected by the mental state of grief. As you resolve lung issues, grief comes up."

"I think I've been stuck in grief for a long time," Maria said. "I think that's been a big part of my life and the fabric of my body."

"Yes, and it continues to be a part of all this. It's important to continue to let the emotion come up and to resolve it in the present."

I don't know if Howard meant to suggest that there could be a correlation (in the scientific sense of the word) between Maria's fistula and an inordinate amount of unresolved grief, but it made me wonder about the power of emotion to affect our bodies and our health. Could a lifetime of unresolved grief be one of the factors that contributes to switching on certain gene sequences that lead to lung and intestinal disorders, and maybe even cancer?

Time magazine's cover story from that week made an even bolder assertion: scientists had begun to trace adult health (including cancer, heart disease, obesity, depression, diabetes, and asthma) to the nine months before birth, when the wiring of the brain and the functioning of organs such as the heart, liver, and pancreas are permanently influenced.

"The kind and quantity of nutrition you received in the womb; the pollutants, drugs and infections you were exposed to during gestation; your mother's health, stress level and state of mind while she was pregnant with you—all these factors shaped you as a baby and a child and continue to affect you to this day." It may take years, or decades, before we know conclusively what factors predispose someone toward cancer (and which cancers, at that), but it's no longer unorthodox to say that one's health, like life itself, starts in the womb.

MY DAD AND I met in a café to discuss my mother's future. He had postponed this conversation for many weeks, but was spurred into action when his accountant told him that he could lose everything if he didn't have a well-thought-out plan in place for caring for Stella. He got off the phone with her and immediately called me.

Not unexpectedly, Mom refused to be left alone in her home while we met. She came with him to the café and catnapped in the front seat of the car while Dad and I, seated barely fifteen feet from her at an outside table, discussed their life together and his dwindling options. I could feel her presence over my shoulder and wondered what, from her point of view, it looked like to see her son and the butler huddled together talking.

"It's feels like yesterday that I first saw your mother on the *Queen Frederica*," Dad said, alluding to the ocean liner on which they met in 1957.

Stella, who was taking a cruise to Greece, had just arrived in the port city of Kalamata, when Manny, a cameraman working for Fox Movietone News in Athens, boarded the *Queen Frederica*. His call sheet: to film the noted Peruvian singer, Yma Sumac, who'd crossed the Atlantic on the same ship for a tour of European capitals. At a cocktail party that evening, Manny noticed a beautiful woman passing out See's chocolates and, when she bypassed the movie crew, remarked, in Greek, "*Emeís then tróme?*" (What, we don't get to eat?).

Stella, smiling, offered the charming, outspoken Greek man a chocolate. "Sweets for the sweet," she said. The couple had their first date the next day at the Parthenon. Four months later, after a whirlwind romance in Greece, they married.

"She's been a good wife and a good mother, but she's not the same anymore. I don't know how much longer I can take care of her."

The night before he couldn't get her feet over the bathtub to shower her. He wondered when she wouldn't be able to attend to her own personal hygiene anymore—weeks, months, perhaps longer if the momentum of her slide slowed. And yet he worried about the meaning of finding a residential placement for her.

"I can't afford a private facility for her for long, unless I sold our condominium, but if I did put her in a home, she may never come home again. She'll die there."

"Wherever we place her, Dad, it will be her last home."

He looked down for a long moment. "I never thought getting older would look like this." Another long pause, "What should we do next?"

"I think you should hire a professional elder care manager, someone whose job it is to guide families through the maze of finding the right placement for a loved one." I had prescreened several geriatric care managers and had found someone I thought would be a good fit. I popped open my laptop, pulled up her website, and showed him a picture of her. "You should call her."

He agreed and wrote her phone number down on his napkin and stuffed it into his wallet.

"I need the weekend to prepare."

THURSDAY, SEPTEMBER 30TH

On Sunday night, before the weekend ended and my father could call the elder care manager, Mom's knees buckled and she fell to the floor. Dad, wobbly and tired himself, panicked when he could not lift her. He kept trying, but she was dead weight. He called me just before midnight to see if I could come over to help lift her into the wheelchair and then onto the bed. Maria heard my cell phone ring, saw that it was from my parents, listened to the voice mail, and whispered the words I had long feared hearing in the middle of the night.

"Your dad just called. Your mother has fallen."

For a split second, I wanted to go back to sleep and pretend that I hadn't heard what Maria had just told me. Satchi and I had planned to wake up at 4:30 to drive to the ashram to participate in a predawn ceremony to celebrate Amma's birthday, something we've wanted to do for years, and I didn't want my mother's fall to disrupt my plans. I was resentful, and entertained the possibility of not returning his call. Let them deal with their own crisis, I thought.

Surrendering, I let go of my hopes and walked downstairs to call my father. "Your mother fell. She's been lying on the floor in the bathroom. I can't lift her. She's too heavy. Can you come over and lift her up?" She'd been on the floor for almost two hours before he called me.

"Well, let's think about this," I said. "I'll come over if you want me to, but if we get Mom back into bed, she won't be able to walk in the morning. Then we're right back in the same place eight hours from now. And it's possible there's something underlying her fall that needs attention sooner rather than later."

"Right."

"You won't be able to take care of her if she can't walk, Dad."

"Right. So what do we do?"

"Well, maybe we're at the point where we need to take her to the hospital so they can help us decide what to do next. Maybe she needs to be in a place where they can help her to walk again."

"Right. Do you think we should call the ambulance?"

"I think that's a good idea, Dad."

My dad was too jangled to call 911 and asked me to do so. After I called the emergency responders, I felt a terrible sadness, not because Mom had fallen and would be hospitalized, but because my father was no longer fighting the inevitable. He had come to terms with the endgame and was yielding to its painful and relentless logic.

In the morning, I called my dad and learned that my mom had been dehydrated the night before. That could have contributed to her fall, but the doctors were trying to rule out other more insidious reasons. He put Mom on the phone.

"Hi, Van. This is such a lovely place. I'm home."

Caught off guard, I said, "You mean the hospital is home?"

"Hospital?" she said, confused. "No, I'm home."

Dementia had taught me to change directions quickly. "Oh, Mom. I'm so glad you found your home. I'm going to come visit you later this morning."

By the time I got to the hospital, Mom thought she was in a nice hotel, the Alta Bates Hotel, not to be confused with Alta Bates Hospital.

"And the help is so kind," she said. "Did you know these nice people are not even on salary? They work for free. Everyone is so lovely here."

Everyone, it turns out, except her husband, whom she now recognized but was already fed up with. Neither of them had slept the night before, and she was testy and defiant. Before I had arrived, my mom had pulled her IV out of her arm and was now threatening to get up to walk around the hotel.

"Stella, sit down, let me call the nurse for you," my father said.

"Nurse? I don't need a nurse. You need a doctor."

Dad and I spoke to the nurses in charge and learned that the doctor was collecting information to determine if Mom needed to be placed in rehab to teach her how to walk again—the dementia, of course, couldn't be the subject for official rehabilitation. My dad knew that would be the best scenario; it would buy him time to meet with the elder care manager and, most importantly, Medicare would pay for the new "hotel."

I returned to Alta Bates again the next morning to see my parents before Maria and I left for a two-day Northern California vacation. The doctor had still not decided my mother's short-term fate—rehab or home—but Mom was comfortable and loquacious, and more lucid.

She told me a story I hadn't heard in twenty years, but whose outlines were vivid in my memory. When she was a teenager and living in an apartment with her father on 172nd Street in New York City (her mother had died five years earlier), she heard a knock and opened the front door to find a poor man who, she said, looked like Jesus Christ standing before her. He said that he was hungry and asked if she would feed him. Innocently, she invited him in and walked him to the kitchen in the back of the apartment.

"I cooked him bacon and eggs and sat with him as he ate. When he finished eating, he thanked me and said, 'God bless you, my child.'" He left and never returned.

Telling me the story again, my mother said, "That's when I first met Jesus. He's always with me."

I was relieved she still had that memory and prayed the dementia wouldn't steal it away. She wouldn't be who she was without her relationship to Jesus.

FRIDAY, OCTOBER 1ST

Maria hadn't had pneumaturia for eight days. Elated, she called Dr. Gullion to update him on the unexpected good news and to share her hypothesis for why this was.

For a period during the summer, she'd had excessive bloating and gas, which put pressure on the lining of her intestinal tract. "That pressure may have compromised an already weak area of my intestines."

After a second urinary tract infection, she'd started taking probiotics and pancreatin (a mixture of several digestive enzymes produced by the pancreas), and the gas decreased by 80 percent.

"With less gas pressure, I think my body's had a chance to begin to heal the fistula," she said on his voice mail. "I guess we'll know more in a few weeks when I get a pelvic CT scan, but for now, I'm *sans* gas." Once off the phone, she said to me, "I wish I had said no bubbly. That would have sounded better."

What she didn't mention to Dr. Gullion was that she'd also been receiving Reiki, the Japanese art of laying on hands, where one person transfers healing energy to another through the palms of their hands. "I believe the Reiki is making a difference, " Maria said, "though it's hard to know how much of my improvement owes to the enzymes and probiotics, the Reiki, or an open channel to Amma." Every night, I laid my hands over Maria's colon and bladder and invited the unseen healing energy of the universe into her body. Loved ones around the globe were also directing Reiki to her fistula.

SUNDAY, OCTOBER 3RD

At a hot springs retreat center, Maria and I met a Reiki master, a lithe man in his early thirties named Christopher Campbell. He walked into the dining hall where Maria and I were eating, meandered over to our table, as if drawn by an invisible thread, and struck up a conversation with Maria, who thanked him for leading a Reiki healing circle that we had attended earlier in the day.

When Maria disclosed that she had colon cancer, he told us that he works with cancer patients. "There are beings and guides in the spirit world who can heal cancer if they want," he said, his eyes penetrating, but kind. "They know how to do it. But there are also deeper underlying reasons why our bodies manifest cancer, and the healing may not occur on the physical level—in the body—but the spiritual."

Maria nodded her head in agreement. What he said next intrigued me. "Family members are connected through their health. In my experience, families pick the person best able to carry their ancestral secrets and pain. It becomes that person's inheritance to help bring the family's secrets into awareness." Of cancer, he added, "That ancestral inheritance can get expressed through a disease like cancer," which confers on a family "a tremendous opportunity to bring consciousness to itself and to release future generations from old emotional pain."

As he spoke, I couldn't help but think of *lac delphinum*—dolphin's milk—the homeopathic remedy Christine Ciavarella prescribed for Maria. "Often when one family member has cancer, secrets pop up throughout the family, as if the whole family were healing as one organism," he said. "When families participate in this liberating process together, the healing can happen on deeper levels."

"That's what I hope for my family, too," Maria said. "I'm working hard to free up my son from his ancestral inheritance."

TUESDAY, OCTOBER 12TH

"Life is tragic, Mom."

"Yes, honey, sometimes it is," Maria said.

Satchi had just finished reading the Harry Potter series. Three of his favorite characters, to whom he had grown deeply attached, had died in the service of fighting to save the wizarding world: Sirius Black, Albus Dumbledore, and the house elf Dobby.

"There are so many losses, Mom. It's just too much."

After Black and Dumbledore died, Satchi asked if anyone else would die. Maria assured him that no one else important did.

Then, in book seven, Dobby died. Satchi screamed at Maria, "You lied to me. You told me no one else important would die. You lied." Maria immediately recognized that behind his anger he was heartbroken, and that she'd failed to protect him from yet another devastating loss.

"I'm so sorry, Satchi. I forgot. I think I was so upset about Dobby's death when I read it that I just pushed it out of my mind. It's so painful to let yourself love a character—to get attached to them—and then to have them die."

Calming down, Satchi then said, "I can't make it if anything happens to you, Mom." Maria took him into her arms.

HOLDING BACK TEARS, my dad said, "I don't know why my brain is making me remember this now." We were sitting on my mom's hospital bed at Summit Hospital, on the skilled nursing floor to which she'd been discharged after her stay at Alta Bates. Medicare would pay for a week of rehab at a hospital, and then up to a month in a private facility.

My mother, unable to walk on her own, was seated in a chair next to her bed, looking affectionately at her husband as he told us the story of when he witnessed the miracle that changed his life. Holding my mom's hand, I wondered how much of my dad's story she understood with her mind—and how much with her heart.

It was August 15, 1955, the *Kimísis tis Theotókou*. My dad's boss had instructed him to travel to Tinos, a small island in the Cyclades, where one of the most revered religious shrines in Greece was located, the Church of Panagia Evangelistria (Our Lady of Good Tidings).

According to local lore, one night in 1822, a nun named Pelagia dreamt that an icon was buried in the village. She led her neighbors to the spot in her dreams, and they unearthed the remains of a Byzantine church—and an icon, the Panagia Evangelistria, depicting Mary kneeling in prayer. Church scholars believe the icon is the work of Saint Luke, and pilgrims to Tinos believe the icon can miraculously heal the wounded and the diseased.

Every year on August 15th, pilgrims line the half-mile road from the harbor to the church and wait for the icon to be carried from the crypt where it was found down to the sea. The sick sit in the middle of the road as four sailors, holding a bier on which the small icon is placed, pass the icon over their heads.

On this day, my father had met a family that had traveled to Tinos to pray to Panagia to heal their young son, who was crippled and mute. Ready with his Arriflex camera, my dad began to film the procession, panning from the church as the icon descended into the crowd of pilgrims.

"I was filming a close-up of the icon, when suddenly I heard screaming and shouting," my father said, his lips starting to quiver. "My assistant screamed at me to tilt the camera down to film what was happening below the icon. I tilted the camera and saw the six- or seven-year-old boy starting to stand and talk. His mother was screaming and his father was crying. Everyone was excited and gathered around the family." My dad himself grew excited. "It was a miracle, I tell you. That experience changed me. It gave me faith in God."

He sat quietly for a few moments, looking downward. I guessed that the emotion was too much for him, and he needed to recalibrate.

I reached out to touch his forearm and said, "That's so beautiful, Dad. I can see how that would have opened your heart."

I turned to look at my mother. She smiled at me, but looked vacant, as if she were lost in space. Dad changed the topic and started talking about Plato and Socrates. I was disappointed; I wanted to linger with him in the sweetness of the previous moment. A fifty-five-year-old miracle had given my dad faith, and now it brought the two of us closer together. And that was a blessing.

WITH THE HELP of our elder care manager, we transferred Mom to Winnetka House, a private senior living facility in El Cerrito. Her prescription was to get physical therapy to learn how to walk again.

When I arrived yesterday afternoon to visit, she and my dad were both napping, Dad in a chair next to Mom's bed. I watched them sleep until they woke five minutes later.

"Oh, it's you!" Mom said, delighted to see me, though still confused about where she was and how she got there. Transitions are difficult for people who are already confused. Because short-term memory is compromised, they can't remember how they got into novel situations. It's as though they find themselves plopped into a new scene without a narrative thread to organize the plot.

"I heard that Pappou just died," she said. "I wasn't there when he died, can you tell me about it?"

My dad said, "Stella, he died forty years ago."

Mom looked confused; time has collapsed for her. "Oh, Mom, he died a long time ago and you were there, but it must feel like yesterday. You loved him so much."

She started to cry. "He was my best friend. He took care of me. I miss him every day. He was everything to me. I must have blocked out his death. I don't remember anything about it."

Dad and I filled in the gaps for her: where she was when he passed, how he died, the jokes he told in the hospital the last night of his life. Dad said, "He had cancer, Stella, but didn't know. In those days, families didn't tell people when they had cancer."

"What was his funeral like, Van? Did you see him when he was dead?"

"Yes. I was nine years old when he died. You encouraged me to kiss his forehead when he was in the casket. You said I would feel better if I did. And you walked up with me and held my hand as I kissed him for the last time."

She struggled to find a memory that matched my story, but couldn't. "Oh, my, you kissed him? And I was with you?"

"Yes, Mom, and you kissed him too."

"Oh. Thank God," she said. Her relief was palpable. And then, "What did he look like, Van?"

"He looked calm, Mom. I think he must have felt very loved by all of us."

She let that sink in. Then, "Was I with him when he died?"

"No, he died alone in the hospital in the middle of the night." Once the words left my mouth, I wished I hadn't said them. In half an hour, my dad and I would be leaving her alone, in a strange place, with the evening—and nighttime—only a few hours off.

As Dad and I prepared to leave, Mom said, "Aren't I going home with you? I want to go home with you. Don't leave me here alone. I don't want to be left alone. Who else is here with me?" Her face looked tortured. I felt her fear and confusion. How would I be able to leave her alone? She began to argue with us. "I never left my father alone. How can you leave me alone?"

Dad froze, turned to me, and whispered, "She said the same thing last night."

Mom searched both our faces, looking increasingly desperate. I stepped in to the silence and explained, "You have to stay here for a while so they can help you get back on your feet again. You can't be at home if you can't walk. You could fall and get hurt."

"But I don't want to stay here," she said, protesting the power we had over her life. "I'm afraid. I don't know these people. I want you to bring me home."

Dad reassured her that she was safe. And I said, "Dad and I need to leave in three minutes." She calmed a little as the three minutes ticked by. We reassured her again and again that she was safe and that, though it was hard to have us leave, she would be all right. "Mom," I alerted her, "we're going to leave in two minutes." She looked at me with determination; I imagined she was counting backwards from three and preparing to rely on herself. In the meantime, she needed Dad and me to be her scaffolding. We told her that we would return, and that the plan was to get her up and walking again so we could bring her home, where she belonged.

"You have to work with the physical therapist to get strong. That's your job, Mom."

Once again, I reminded her of the passing of time. "We're leaving in one minute, Mom."

Even though my mother wasn't my child, in that moment she had become my child. She touched that place in me that is a father. "If I could, I would stay with you, Mom, but it's time for us to leave." We kissed her good-bye and walked out of her room. I did not look back and neither did my father. I couldn't bear to see the look on her face.

FRIDAY, OCTOBER 22ND

Dr. Gullion walked into the exam room wearing one of his signature heart pins and a strikingly colorful tie.

"Jerry Garcia Collection," he informed me.

He carved out time in his schedule to discuss the results of the latest CT scan and urine analysis. He wanted to make sure we had the benefit of his thoughts before Maria headed to the Block Center.

"Well, you have an infection again," he started. "Its strength is below the usual threshold to cause concern, but it's an unusual bug, one not often found in the bladder," *Citrobacter freundii*, a strain of bacteria resistant to the antibiotic Maria had taken twice in the last two months to fight bladder infections. It was likely this bug traveled through the fistula and taken up residence in the bladder. He prescribed a new antibiotic, adding that she should continue taking her "probiotics and all the other stuff."

He then pulled up the CT report from the radiologist on his computer and said, without sounding inordinately optimistic, "So it looks better. It didn't go away, but there is hope out there."

"Well, we're still working on it," Maria said, bravely.

"Each of the larger lesions in the liver has decreased in size," by millimeters and not centimeters, he said. "The report also says that most of the remaining lesions"—in the liver—"have decreased in size, and the pelvic masses have slightly decreased in size." Then, stepping back from the details, he connected the dots to Maria's treatment. "So basically, everything is shrinking in concert. You're making progress; you continue to feel well. Maybe the fistula has improved too. I guess the question for your doc at the Block Center would be, Is it enough to press on with what we're doing?"

Answering the question himself, he offered his assessment. "It seems like it would be. We tend not to change course in midstream when it's working. And we wouldn't go to oxaliplatin when the irinotecan is working. If the cancer saw a new drug it might respond also, that is, continue to shrink. But when something is working, you go as long as you can with it."

Looking at Maria, his voice softened, "You've had a lot of chemotherapy."

"Yeah," Maria said, recognizing how long the journey has been. "Should I expect the cancer to disappear after eighteen rounds?"

"Well, I think this is maybe what we have here: it's shrinking by a number of millimeters, not centimeters. You had quite a good response early on."

If you plotted the tumor marker numbers on a graph, he added, the slope would not be as steep now, compared to when you started. Maria and I already knew that; we've plotted her numbers from the beginning and have watched the slope level off, still above the normal range.

Not sure how to ask my next question, I start and fumble, "Is there a . . .? You said she's done a lot of chemotherapy. The question is, What's a lot?"

"You mean, what's the record?" Dr. Gullion clarified.

"That's one question . . ." I started, wanting another crack at asking the question more precisely. What I really meant was, "How long can a body endure this regimen?"

Dr. Gullion continued. "Twelve is standard for adjuvant therapy," for colon patients who have surgery first followed by chemotherapy. "When it's working, not infrequently we go out to twenty. I probably have patients who are in the twenty-eight-treatment range. Often we need to go to three-week intervals instead of two because of blood counts and toxicity. And many times we get about to some number—twelve, fifteen, something—and the cells become resistant, and we have to switch. That's a very common scenario, probably more common than making it to twenty-five treatments."

"So far, it looks very encouraging. And what's encouraging is that it's a tough road to hoe down there in the infusion room, but you're doing remarkably well." He turned avuncular, adding, "You are doing a lot of other things to support your well-being, and your will to live and your own inner strength have helped you a lot."

WE PASSED A cemetery while we were driving to the Block Center to start Maria's nineteenth round of chemotherapy. From the backseat of our rental car, Satchi said, "That's scary."

"What's scary?" Maria asked.

"Is that a cemetery?"

"Yes. What's scary about a cemetery, honey?"

"They creep me out," Satchi answered. "In all the books I read, creepy things happen in graveyards." Taking a contemplative turn, Satchi asked, "Mom, what happens when you die?"

"What do you think, dear?"

Satchi asked me to turn down the car radio so he could respond; a soprano was singing a beautiful aria on the classical music station. Before Satchi had a chance to respond, I interrupted and answered for myself, "I think we die and go to heaven, where all the souls that ever lived sing opera for the rest of infinity." Satchi and I started to sing arias, badly. Maria laughed.

After singing his aria, Satchi picked up from where he left off, no worse for the operatic detour.

"I think the body just rots, but the soul moves on; it goes back to God. If you believe in Jesus in life, it goes back to Jesus. If you believe in Amma, it goes to Amma."

"That's lovely, Satchi. I like that idea that we all return to the image of God that we believed in in life," Maria said.

"What about you, Mom? What do you believe?"

"Pretty much the same thing. What we spend our lives devoted to is what we become."

"Ooh, yeah," Satchi sang. "The two of us believe the same thing." Then, after a beat, "How 'bout you, Dad?"

"I like what you guys said. I'm on board with what the two of you think."

Satchi was excited that we all agreed about what happens when the body dies. "All right! We are all one!"

No sooner had we arrived at the Block Center than Dr. Nora walked into our room for Maria's prechemo consultation. Satchi, who was engrossed in Philip Pullman's *The Subtle Knife*, barely noticed her presence. "I don't know if you've been counting your treatments," she said to Maria. "This is your nineteenth."

"Yes, nineteen, I know," Maria said, as only a veteran of the infusion room can say.

"It's still doing its job," Dr. Nora said, starting off on a positive note. "And it's getting easier," Maria said.

The fundamentals covered (urinary tract infection, fistula, side effects, chemo-flow reports), Dr. Nora turned her attention to the CT report, the most important piece of business on our agenda.

"Dr. Gullion says to press on," I said.

"Yes. Press on. Everything is getting smaller," she said. "I know it would seem like, gosh, can we see more of a difference? But honestly, you're winning this battle, and nothing new is growing."

She quickly steered the conversation toward Maria's options for liver-directed therapies, the conversation Maria and I have been having with May Chen, who from our first meeting in mid-April encouraged us to attack the liver aggressively. In an email to Maria last Friday, Dr. Chen said that after reviewing her CT scan and tumor markers, she thought there could be "a potential role for hepatic chemoembolization to be used either in between chemo sessions or after you have finished this series of treatments."

Dr. Nora outlined Maria's options: surgery to remove portions of the liver, and radio frequency ablation or chemoembolization, which are targeted specifically at shrinking lesions in the liver, especially if they number one or two. If there are more, she explained, but only in one lobe, there was a new treatment called TheraSphere, in which little radioactive glass beads are directed into that lobe to cut off the blood supply to the tumors. "Typically, any of these global treatments are performed when everything else has quieted down in your body." She added, "You're getting there."

"Of all the options," she added, "I think chemoembolization is probably the best, or a resection. You can actually remove quite a bit of the liver or take out a whole lobe." She agreed that the time to perform one of these procedures was not too far off.

WITH CANCER, AS in life, it's important to learn how to appreciate increments of change. Maria had minor pneumaturia on days two and three again and, on the assumption that excessive gas put pressure on her fistula, adjusted her diet to exclude any gas-producing foods. By day four, she had no gas. Though impossible to know precisely what cause led to what effect, the slight dietary change seemed to yield immediate results.

When Maria updated Howard today on the fistula, he observed, "As the tumors shrink, the fistula will shrink. Everything is slowly moving in concert. But don't worry about the rate of change, as you get closer to the end, it gets tougher and tougher. The same is true with viral infections." As a body fights an infection, he explained, it makes headway fast at the front of the struggle, but then slows as the last vestiges of the infection take a final stand.

"As you get closer to containing the cancer," Howard said, "it's natural to feel you're losing momentum, but you have to remember that you *are* getting stronger."

Cell by cell. Fistula by fistula. Millimeter by millimeter.

ten

◆

ALONE WITH THE MOUNTAIN

When we returned from Chicago, I learned that Winnetka House, the facility my mom had entered for physical therapy two weeks earlier, had determined that she should be released into my father's care after twenty days, ten days ahead of schedule and before the full thirty days Medicare had initially approved for rehabilitation.

In a quickly called meeting, my dad and I sat across from the director of social services, or DSS, in a small, windowless, cramped room, a large desk between us, trying to make sense out of their decision. Dad looked tired and shocked as he lobbied for his wife.

"She can't come home. She's not the way she used to be. Sometimes she's a zombie. How am I supposed to support her? I'm eighty-two years old and not so good on my feet. I can't take care of her at home."

The DSS explained that the physical therapist and the rest of the Winnetka House team had determined that my mom would be competent to live independently with some assistance in a matter of days, and they could no longer keep her in a Medicare bed. If my dad couldn't take care of her at home, he would need to secure in-home support at his own expense.

I sat there feeling both frozen by her matter-of-factness and dumbfounded that the team of professionals entrusted with my mother's care couldn't justify additional days of rehabilitation to consolidate her progress while we made thoughtful arrangements for her post-discharge care.

"So, help me understand," I said, holding back my incredulity. "When you say my mom has made progress and is ready to be released, how do you measure progress? What precisely are you measuring?"

She explained that their orders were to help my mom walk again. Not bathe, not go to the bathroom, not dress—just walk. And, in fact, she was now able to walk with a walker.

"Walk?" Dad said. "She can't walk. She needs my help to get out of bed, and she gets tired after walking a few feet. If I'm not holding her, she'll fall. She has to stay here longer."

The DSS tried another pass at explaining what apparently should have been obvious to us, reminding us again that Medicare was only a short-term solution. Now that Mom was making progress toward walking, we would have to figure out how to support her at home or make other living arrangements for her.

I began to feel as though I were in conversation with a politician who had strict talking points. We knew the nursing home placement was a short-term solution; we only wanted to understand what the baseline was for measuring Mom's progress. I tried again, my voice starting to betray my anger.

"How do you measure whether she can walk? How far does she have to be able to walk—across the room, down the hall, 10 feet, 5 feet—for you to say she's competent? What's the baseline for progress?"

Leafing through a folder on her desk, she agreed that that information was relevant, but she didn't have it in front of her. The physical therapy staff established those goals upon her admission, she added, and measured my mom's progress against them. What she said next muddied the water: if my mom were not able to meet those goals, then Medicare would no longer pay for rehabilitation.

Now I felt confused. Had she made progress or hadn't she? I asked, "Okay, then how do you determine if she's not rehabilitatable? I get how you measure if someone can walk, say, 10 feet, unassisted, but how do you determine if someone's progress has tapered off or will pick up again? And why wouldn't you keep her a little longer to try to consolidate her progress if you thought it had slowed?"

I couldn't put my finger on why they'd want to move Mom out of her Medicare bed so quickly. After all, I thought, Medicare is the most highly profitable source of payment for a skilled nursing facility (SNF) *and* pays the highest rates for residents receiving rehabilitation.

My family had just entered the intersection between the Byzantine world of Medicare, which has formulas to measure everything that's measurable, and the mercenary world of elder care facilities in America. In practice, if not by design, once an individual needs long-term care, the current healthcare system inevitably drains all the assets a family has accumulated over a lifetime. And nursing homes, being a cog in the wheel of that system, participate in that transfer of wealth.

The director reiterated that we'd have to wait a few days until their staff meeting to learn their final assessment. But, she added, we could keep Mom on at Winnetka House in a program called Respite Care, which rents the patient a room on a temporary, per diem basis until the next elder care venue has been selected. Medicare wouldn't pay for this; Dad would have to pay out of pocket for the room.

Now the pieces began to fall into place. When I'd arrived an hour earlier, a marketing person had corralled me and said Mom could stay on at Winnetka House in one of their Respite Care rooms for anywhere between a $190 and $250 a day, depending on their assessment of how much assistance she would need.

At first the term *respite care* sounded kind, like a hot springs resort or a yoga retreat in the mountains—*I* needed respite care myself after a year of caregiving. But now I began to feel manipulated. I imagined they were trying to rush Mom out of a Medicare bed and into a private pay room, where they would continue to profit from her while keeping a higher paying Medicare bed available for another rehab patient.

Only later did I learn the true calculus of Medicare reimbursement. While I was right about the facility trying to optimize profits, I was wrong about exactly how that worked. The Medicare rate for rehab in the San Francisco Bay Area can be close to $800 per day at its highest reimbursement tier (there are fifty-three levels). But it drops substantially for unskilled categories of service. For someone like Mom, who, once she could walk down the hall, was deemed to be able to live with unskilled assistance (despite Dad's protestations), the reimbursement tier might be near the bottom of the pricing structure. If an SNF had to turn away another rehab patient it would "lose" money by keeping a low-tier patient in that bed, even if the confused and vulnerable elderly person might benefit from such continuity of care.

The nursing staff at Winnetka House had managed to make Mom feel safe and secure—and even, admirably, to help her take her first steps toward walking—but the business team had disrupted and scared the rest of our family in the process.

OUR ELDER CARE manager, Debra Johnson, visited Winnetka House, reviewed Mom's medical chart, and met with the physical therapist and charge nurse. Mom, they had determined, was no longer making measurable progress. Despite Debra's formidable instinct to protect her clients, there wasn't room to negotiate. On the expedited discharge day, Dad met with Winnetka House staff and was told he could transfer Mom into Respite Care for a $190 a day until he found another nursing home or long-term care facility or could take her home. He chose Respite Care. And for the first time all week, we rested, knowing we had a plan in place.

I told my friend Marla, "I can't wait for the chaos with my parents to settle so life can return to normal."

"You mean, so you can return to cancer?"

"It would be a relief to just have to deal with cancer," I said. "Cancer is easier."

MY DAD SCREAMED into the phone, "Van, they're telling me I have to sign a contract for Stella to stay longer, and I have to give them a big deposit, and they're saying she has to stay for a minimum of ten days."

His anger sparked my indignation. What on earth were these people trying to extract from my father? On three separate occasions, the staff at Winnetka House had told us Mom could extend her stay in Respite Care for a *per diem* amount. Now, on a Friday afternoon, *after* they moved her to a different room, they entered with a contract and told my dad he had to sign it in order to keep his wife there, or else she couldn't stay. And they told him she couldn't stay just for four or five days, as he'd planned, but for a minimum of ten days, or $1,900, with $500 up front as a down payment.

Moments before Dad called, the DSS and the marketing person had met with my dad alone in a private room. The marketing person explained the policy to my dad. Blindsided and feeling cornered, Dad argued back. He told them the new rules were "bullshit" and that his son, who knew Ivy League lawyers, would sue them. The marketing person said she would ask the executive director for an exception for my family. This was somewhat reminiscent of a used car salesman who leaves the room to triangulate with a backroom boss.

When my dad asked the DSS if she knew about this policy, she said she didn't. Apparently, the left hand at Winnetka House didn't know what the right hand was doing. My dad knew that either deceit or incompetence was at play. But they persisted: for Stella to stay, the terms were fixed. By the time Dad called me, he'd been worn down.

"What can I do, Van? I can't put Stella out on the street. I have to sign."

"Dad, don't sign anything. *Se pézoune*" (literally, They're playing you). "Put whoever is in the room on the phone. Let me talk to them." I knew before that person got on the phone that I wasn't in the mood to listen. I was going to give them a piece of my mind.

"What's going on?" I asked, sounding calm.

The marketing person said that my mother needed to stay for a minimum of ten days and that she had asked the executive director to make an exception for my family, but he couldn't make one.

"You have to be kidding," I started, ignoring the false hope of an exception. "I've never heard of such a requirement. You told me twice that my mom could stay for $190 a day. You told our elder care manager the same thing. You never once said there was a minimum stay."

"I'm sorry if I didn't tell you, but that *is* what we require."

"That doesn't wash," I said, my voice rising as I became progressively angrier. "I don't know about you, but when someone says you can stay here for a hundred dollars a day that means you have the choice of how many days you can stay. There's a difference between saying You can stay for a $190 a day and You can stay for a minimum of ten days for $1,900. You misled my father and me. That's unethical."

"I'm sorry. I never meant to mislead you and your parents."

"We're speaking the same language, but live in entirely different universes." She was silent now. "You really scared my father. He thinks you're going to put my mom out on the street if he doesn't sign your contract. That's wrong. You shouldn't be doing that with someone who's in his eighties and vulnerable. He trusted you. You told him one thing, then at the eleventh hour, on a Friday afternoon, when he has no options other than to keep his wife at Winnetka House over the weekend, you tell him he has to spend almost two thousand dollars to do so. How could you do that to him? You took advantage of him."

"I like your mom and your dad," she said, clearly fazed by my relentlessness and trying to impress upon me that it was never her intention to do harm.

I then threatened to file a complaint with the state and to advertise my experience. I told her I wanted to talk to the executive director. She took my number and got off the phone as quickly as possible.

"Don't sign anything, Dad. Just hold tight while I get legal advice."

I spent the next hour on the phone with Arleen Goodwin, co-founder of Senior Medi-Benefits, a nonprofit organization that helps the elderly sort out the complexities of Medicare, Medi-Cal, and long-term care. Then two other nursing facilities to see if they'd ever heard of such a bait-and-switch scheme (they hadn't) and to see if they had a available bed for my mother on short notice (they did not). And finally, I spoke with Deborah Espinola, a long-term care advocate at California Advocates for Nursing Home Reform, another nonprofit organization dedicated to improving the quality of life for long-term care patients and their families.

Nursing homes, I learned, routinely try to bilk older patients of their money—and often get away with it. Espinola said, "The good news is that your dad has someone to fight on his behalf; many elderly patients don't have anyone. And they get taken advantage of. My advice is to get everything in writing up front because nursing homes play fast and loose with their communications."

In the middle of my outreach, Dad called to say that they had reconsidered his situation and were now prepared to drop all their conditions. Mom could stay in her former room, in which she was comfortable and secure, for five days, not ten; the charge would be $190 a day; my dad would not have to make a down payment or sign a contract; and they would bill him later for the stay.

I called Goodwin back and asked why Winnetka House would do an about-face. "I think they must've been scared," she said.

Afterward I talked with my sister, Ariste, in England, where the elderly don't face such difficult decisions, since the national health system pays for long-term care for the elderly. I said, "They must have been scared to come up against such a crazy family."

"Hold on. Who's crazy? We're not crazy," she said, emphatically. I was grateful to her for her clarity; her indignation on the other side of the planet kept me on course. "Winnetka House put Dad in a crazy situation. *Your* response to *their* craziness was sane."

SUNDAY, NOVEMBER 7TH

Maria pointed to Dr. Gullion's tie as he walked through the door. "Another Jerry Garcia," he said, flipping his tie up with his finger.

"He was prolific," Maria said. "Then he died, and he was no longer prolific." Gallows humor is never too far from the surface in an oncologist's office.

Curious about Maria's Block Center visit, Dr. Gullion asked what Dr. Nora had had to say about Maria's fistula and the next step in her treatment.

"She said I'm winning the battle. That's always wonderful to hear. And she and Dr. Chen both suggested that before long there might be a role for chemoembolization." A little worried about the procedure, Maria asked Dr. Gullion to explain what it entailed and when it might fit into her treatment.

Starting slowly, Dr. Gullion explained that an interventional radiologist, using X-ray guidance, threads a thin catheter through the femoral artery, in the groin, and up into either the left or right hepatic artery, depending on the lobe of the liver with active tumors. The radiologist then injects chemotherapy and an embolic agent into the artery, delivering highly concentrated chemo directly to the tumor while cutting off its blood supply and starving the tumors.

"The tumors often get hit pretty well, shrink up, and undergo regression and calcification," Dr. Gullion said. With respect to side effects, "It can disrupt your liver function and your well-being for those days. It's a pretty major onslaught of phenomena. Your liver gets whammied. Your enzymes can go up, you can feel sick, and sometimes people have fevers and chills and other reactions." Just at the moment when I imagined Maria losing heart, he added, "But the liver has amazing regeneration capacities, and that improves, and you get better . . . So it's something to make a decision about carefully."

"It's not a little thing," Maria said.

"No, it's not like a little squirt of something," he added.

WITH FISTULA ON all our minds, Dr. Gullion checked the latest urine culture. We all eagerly awaited the results. If, as we suspected, Maria's fistula were improving, then the antibiotic she was taking to clear up the *Citrobacter freundii* should have wiped out the infection.

He smiled and, with not a small amount of amazement in his voice, said, "No growth. So gone. It looks like you may have had more of a smoldering chronic infection than we could've realized." Returning to his amazement, he said, "The no-growth is a miracle."

"Is that in the religious sense," I asked half-jokingly, "or the rhetorical sense—that it's a miracle?"

He laughed, "Well, frequently, we can never clear the urinary tract when there's a fistula. The infection keeps returning no matter what we do."

A man of measured hopefulness, he didn't go so far as to say that the fistula was healed (only a CT scan could confirm that scientifically), but the evidence was mounting. In the last week, Maria had begun to experience mild gas discomfort in her intestines. Most of us would not notice such a common phenomenon; Maria took it to mean that the gas was no longer escaping into her bladder. After uttering the word *miracle* he said guardedly, "Let's wait and see how you do over the next four days."

Maria and I filed out of the room after him, allowing ourselves to feel a rising tide of hopefulness: if her body was healthy enough, after more than nine months of chemotherapy, to heal a fistula, then perhaps her body was strong enough to contain cancer. An experiment in the improbable, I thought, as walked down the hall toward the infusion room.

WE TRANSFERRED MOM to an assisted living bed in Bellaken Garden and Skilled Nursing Center in Oakland, twenty minutes from Winnetka House. When I visited, she and Dad were slumped against each other in a leather love seat, sleeping, while a big-screen television blared in the corner of the glass-enclosed meeting room. The smell of meatloaf from the adjacent dining hall filled the air.

Mom startled when I kissed her, looked slowly toward Dad, then realized I was kneeling next to her. She sparkled and took my hands, as if we hadn't seen each other in months or years. There's a beauty in letting go of the passage of time; each reunion becomes an opportunity for delight. Dad pulled up a chair for himself as I scrunched in next to Mom on the love seat. She said my hands were cold; I said hers were warm.

"If we hold hands," I added, "mine will get warmer and yours will get colder."

She smiled and said, "That would be nice."

"How do you like your new place?" I asked.

"Oh, very much. The people are nice here. Everybody knows my name."

Within a few minutes, she fell asleep. The emotional toll of leaving Winnetka House and arriving at a new facility, with new faces, new surroundings, and new routines to integrate, must have depleted her already taxed system.

Dad introduced me to two members of the staff. "They were the ones who helped me two nights ago, the first day we were here. I called you that night. Remember?"

How could I not? When my dad rose to go home on that first night, my mom, pushing her walker, followed him to the elevator. She screamed for him not to leave her alone. Standing at the elevator door, he said, "No, Stella, you have to stay here. The doctor said you're not allowed to go home yet." The two nursing assistants held and comforted her as my dad walked into the elevator. Through the closing elevator doors, he could see his wife's tormented and crying face. When he got home, he called me.

"Do you understand?" he said, filled with emotion. "I've taken care of her for over fifty years. I've tried to make her happy and to protect her. I've done everything for her in the last five years. Everything. I can't do it anymore. *E karthía mou eínai spasméno"* (My heart is broken).

Before I left, I hugged Mom for a long time. I didn't want to go; I wanted to sit for the whole day and hold her hand. I walked outside, stood in front of the window, and watched as my father helped her up from the love seat, holding a thick cloth strap around her waist so she would not fall. It was lunchtime. My mother grasped the walker by the arms and shuffled across the television room to the dining hall, my dad by her side.

NAUSEA ASIDE, ROUND twenty brought both long-anticipated and unexpected good news. Maria didn't have any pneumaturia during chemo week. No bubbly at all. The fistula closed. No more abnormal communication between two organs that shouldn't be connected. In the five months since Maria first noticed the pneumaturia, she was able to control the inflammation enough that her body could repair the tissue on its own.

Though we didn't utter the word *miracle* to each other, we both developed a new respect for the miraculous capacity of the body to heal. For the first time in thirteen months, Maria had her period. Her body remembered its life-generative rhythm. In a body formerly ravaged by cancer, that *is* a miracle.

SATURDAY, NOVEMBER 20TH

"Theophanis, what're you doing here?"

Before I could respond, Dad said, "Stella, that's not Theophanis. Theophanis is your cousin. He died a long time ago. This is Van. He's our son."

Mom searched my face carefully. Her brain told her I was Theophanis, despite what her husband said.

Theophanis (or Teddy) died of a brain tumor when I was a young boy; he was in his early fifties. I remember playing hide-and-seek with my Long Island cousins in the basement of the funeral home in which Teddy was on view. We hid behind empty caskets and told scary stories while the adults congregated upstairs and talked in Greek about Teddy's short life and premature demise from *carcíno*—cancer. I have a special place in my heart for Theophanis, even though I don't remember him being alive.

"Dad," I whispered, "Mom thinks I'm Theophanis. It's okay. No need to try to convince her that I'm not."

I'm not sure if Mom overheard me, but she said, agitated, "If that's your son, Manny, then he has to be my son, and he's not. Don't confuse me."

I was startled by the coherence of her logic; both things could not be true. "It's okay, Stella. It doesn't matter who I am. What matters is that we love each other, and I love you."

"I love you, too."

I'd been preparing for the moment when she would no longer recognize me. The lack of recognition this time wasn't a passing and transitory phenomenon, as it had been in the past. I felt sadness, but also tenderness and awe. This remarkable woman was still my mother even if she didn't know it, and the love we felt transcended the limitations of the brain.

The next day Mom would have another birthday, perhaps her last. My dad would buy a cake and, in a ritual that connected him to

when he first met Stella on the *Queen Frederica*, offer See's chocolates to the other residents. We'd sing "Happy Birthday," and Mom
would soon forget it ever happened.

MARIA SCREAMED IN her sleep that night, as though she were
struggling with someone in her dreams. I shook her awake, and after
a few moments collecting herself, she asked, "If I do a powerful
kiai"—a karate yell—"will you attack me for it?"

"Of course not," I said. "You can have a powerful *kiai*."

Then I went back to sleep. In the morning, she told me that in
the dream forces were trying to disable her for being powerful, and
she was fighting for her life.

"In a way, I've felt this way for most of my life. I think the dream
was showing me how I disable myself as an adult by not bringing
myself forward, taking up my space, and staying connected and vulnerable at the same time. I've hidden out of sight and kept myself
concealed because I've been so frightened of being undermined and
blamed for being in my fullness. Fullness is scary." She quieted,
looked sad, put her hand on my chest, and said, "I'm afraid that
we've forged a relationship where I'm the fragile, sick, and frightened one, and you're the strong, able, and giving one. This doesn't
work for either of us. It's not healthy."

"I agree. It sometimes feels like that to me as well."

I could hear Satchi downstairs, talking to our cat. He got up
early, even on weekends, to sit in front of the heating vent, prayer
shawl around his shoulders, reading Harry Potter.

"Even if I only have a year left to live, I want to live differently.
I want to live more whole-heartedly and love more deeply," Maria
said. "I've always felt that I don't have what it takes to manifest the

life that I want to live. I'm working hard to change that." She caught me off guard with her next question, "Do you know the Priori Incantatem spell from Harry Potter?"

"Hmmm. I don't remember."

"Well, it's when a wizard's wand is forced to reveal the history of all the spells, or prior incantations, it has cast in reverse order. That's what's happening to me right now. I think the *lac delphinum* is revealing secrets in reverse order. I'm in the Priori Incantatem stage of my cancer treatment."

SUNDAY, NOVEMBER 28TH

"That Priori Incantatem is working through me," Maria said, waking from a restless sleep. "All the feelings I have stuffed into my liver are coming out now."

For three nights running, she called out in her sleep, sounding alternately scared then angry. The feeling of being threatened lingered for days. I, too, had unsettling dreams. In one, the security of my home was threatened; in another, my work; and in a third, my body—a bear attacked me as I left my house, and I, powerless and frozen with fear, witnessed my own mauling.

Amma's imminent arrival in town often precipitates an invitation from the Self to bring awareness to ongoing emotional and spiritual lessons. Perhaps I was being invited to explore what it would be like to lose everything precious to me: my work, my home, my own body. People with terminal illness face this challenge every day and must learn to do their part to fight on, knowing that there are forces at play larger than their own will to live.

Spiritual surrender is not an act of collapse or defeat, but a fierce acceptance of what is, while staying fully engaged and responsible

for changing that which we have the power to change. Once I surrendered in the dream to the bear mauling, I felt oddly at peace. Then
I could go on with my life.

MARIA WAS ON her knees next to Amma, waiting for Swami
Amritaswarupananda, one of Amma's senior swamis, to translate
our letter asking for guidance about her treatment. It was the second
day of Amma's public programs at her San Ramon ashram, and we
were fortunate to be afforded an opportunity to speak directly to
her, despite the crowd of thousands. Swamiji, as he's called, read our
letter silently several times and then asked Maria to explain what
oleander extract was—not a household botanical, I imagined, for
which he was used to supplying a Malayalam word.

"When we saw you in June," the letter began, updating Amma
on Maria's progress, "I had just completed my ninth round of chemotherapy; last week, I finished my twenty-first round."

Then we asked her for guidance on whether Maria's body and
immune system were strong enough to discontinue chemotherapy,
explaining that it was our hope that oleander extract could stabilize
and shrink cancer without chemotherapy. While Amma continued to
receive and bless the long lines of people who waited for her touch,
Swamiji read her the remainder of our letter, which ended with a
request to bless whatever liver-directed therapy the doctors would
eventually recommend.

Amma looked probingly at Maria and responded to our questions in a burst of Malayalam.

I was standing between Swamiji and Maria when he said,
"Amma says you should not stop doing chemotherapy. She says you
should strictly stick to your doctor's advice," punctuating the word

strictly. That pronouncement over, he then added, "Amma says that she will always keep you in her prayers and thoughts." He spoke with some hesitation, as though he worried we might dissect her words. "Amma also says that alternative medicine will not cure the disease; it can strengthen the body and the system. But in your case, to help the tumors to shrink, chemotherapy alone is effective."

I waited for more, something like "chemotherapy alone is effective, but once the tumors shrink then you can safely stop the chemo," but it wasn't forthcoming. I bent to share Amma's response with Maria, waited for the words to sink in, and then asked Maria if she had any follow-up questions. After a few moments, she responded, "No, I don't have any questions. I knew Amma would say I shouldn't stop the chemo. That's clear. She's right. Do *you* have any questions?"

I said I didn't, but already in the back of my mind I was wondering about the future: when and if the chemotherapy becomes ineffective, will Maria's body be strong enough to continue to contain the cancer? I knew Amma would not answer that question. Its premise existed in the future, and there was simply no way to answer a question whose time has not yet come. Right now Maria needed to continue to do chemotherapy. When the treatment or her medical condition changed, then we could ask another series of questions, and Amma could guide us through the next portion of the maze, but the future depends on the decisions we make now.

Maria and I walked away from Amma's side. Satchi, watching us closely, was waiting for us on the side of the temple. "What took you so long?" he asked, a little annoyed. "I was waiting forever." We walked out of the temple together and made our way to the dining hall. "Well, what did she say?"

"We asked her if I should stop doing chemotherapy," Maria said, "and trust that all the other things I'm doing will shrink my tumors. She said that I should not stop doing chemotherapy."

"Of course," he said with absolute certainty. "She's right."

Maria added, "She said chemotherapy alone will shrink my tumors."

"Amma knows what she's talking about," Satchi said.

THE GREAT RELIGIONS of the world say that God performs miracles through his creation. Any of us can be vehicles for these miracles, but in some beings, that channeling of divine grace is highly concentrated, like a laser beam. Throughout the ages, this divine grace has concentrated itself in a human body—Mohammed, Krishna, Buddha, Christ, to name but four—so that God can more directly and intimately affect the course of human lives.

On the second night of a three-day retreat with Amma, Shantamrita, one of Amma's American-born swamis, spoke about this divine mystery. It's natural for miracles to happen around one of these remarkable beings, he said. They only have to make a *sankalpa*, or divine resolve, and even if something is not written in the book of destiny, it will come to pass because of their intercession. He shared the story of one of Amma's devotees.

In 2004, while John was taking a shower, his aorta suddenly ruptured. Most people die of blood loss within minutes of such a cataclysmic event. John, however, called 911 and was rushed to the hospital. While in the ambulance, he received a call on his cell phone. The paramedics took the phone from his pocket, answered the call, and told his friend about the gravity of his situation. Just then, John died. "His heart and breathing stopped," the friend overheard them say. "He's Code Blue."

At the time she made the call, John's friend was in Chicago at a public program with Amma. Learning of her friend's death, she rushed to Amma, showed her John's photo, and told her what had just happened halfway across the country in Los Angeles. "By coincidence, I happened to be beside Amma," Shantamrita told everyone in the hall. "I remember how calm Amma was when she looked at John's photo. She looked at the photo for a long time, then closed her eyes and meditated."

Though he had been dead for thirty minutes, the ER doctors successfully defibrillated John's heart. Twelve hours of open-heart surgery ensued, during which he lost over twenty-five pints of blood, two and a half times the total blood in the human body. He didn't regain consciousness for another four days, and when he did, half his body remained paralyzed for another two weeks. His kidneys had failed during his paralysis, and he had to start dialysis.

With the audience listening breathlessly, Shantamrita shocked the crowd. "And he's probably right here in this hall somewhere." I couldn't see his face, too many people were standing to get a glimpse of him, but I could see him waving both hands to the crowd. "The hospital staff called him the Miracle Man," Shantamrita said. "They didn't know it was Amma's miracle, the miraculous healing power of a totally selfless being."

One among several thousand people in Amrita Hall, I began to cry. I've longed for Amma to make a *sankalpa* for Maria. The tears streamed as I sat staring at Amma on the stage, perhaps forty feet away from me. Her eyes were closed. She looked immovable, like Mount Kailash, Lord Shiva's home in the Himalayas. The room turned silent around me. I felt as though I were alone with the mountain. I prayed that it would be Amma's *sankalpa* that Maria live a long life.

eleven

◆

STARTING TO BOUNCE

WEDNESDAY, DECEMBER 8TH

From the moment I saw its title, I felt drawn to Siddhartha Mukherjee's new book, *The Emperor of All Maladies: A Biography of Cancer.*

There was something elegantly paradoxical about its title, as if the personification of cancer—as emperor—made it at once both more human but also less approachable: whoever heard of arguing with a Napoleon or a Genghis Khan? And yet this metaphor of unapproachable sovereignty is a hopeful one. Every despot has a weakness. It may take years to expose, but I keep reminding myself even Julius Caesar had his Ides of March.

I listened to an NPR interview with Mukherjee, an assistant professor at Columbia and an oncologist on staff at Columbia University Medical Center. The book, he told Terry Gross, the host of WHYY's *Fresh Air*, grew out of a question a patient with abdominal cancer posed to him, "I'm willing to go on, but before I go on, I need to know what it is I'm battling."

In a fundamental sense, Mukherjee said, he couldn't answer her question. "There are five thousand books on cancer, but I had no history" to relate to her.

He wrote *The Emperor of All Maladies* to explain what we know and what we don't know about cancer, and how that knowledge evolved over the last few centuries. The story of cancer, he said, is a tragic one, where optimism has often tipped into hubris, with doctors believing they had the ultimate answer, even if it drastically compromised their patients' quality of life without adding extra days to their survival. You "inspire confidence" in your patients, he reminded, "by being humble" and letting them know that when you no longer have the answers you'll reside in the not-knowing together.

Recent discoveries in the genetics of cancer, he told Gross, are driving the field of cancer research. Whereas researchers once thought cancer could be a virus, they now believe "cancer genes are often mutated versions of normal genes" and "are inlaid in our chromosomes," just waiting to be hijacked. The very genes that allow cells to proliferate, and to adapt and grow, once corrupted, can then be co-opted to attack the body. This discovery sent "a chill down the spine of cancer biologists," Mukherjee said, and has raised "deep philosophical questions about what it means to be human." It may very well be that it's our destiny as humans to have to contend with cancer; the longer we live, the more likely our genes will express some form of cancer. We're genetically (and metabolically) programmed to be vulnerable in this way.

Cancer researchers, he continued, are trying to develop drugs that target these specific genes—"the Achilles' heels of cancer cells"—without killing normal cells. One such example is Gleevec, a drug that's nontoxic to the body but which, "like an arrow, drives into the heart" of the protein that causes leukemia, a cancer of the blood. Gleevec doesn't kill cancer cells; it stuns them by turning off the gene that signals the cells to multiply, sending them into deep hibernation.

No such drug for colon cancer has yet been found.

In the meantime, according to Mukherjee, the activation of a patient's immune system does increase their chances of survival. And this is where Maria and I believed that integrative medicine has the most to offer contemporary oncology.

Round twenty-two of Maria's chemo was bookended by visits to her Tibetan doctor before and to her Chinese acupuncturist after. The integrative oncologist came in the middle. By all accounts, Maria's immune system was strong and, despite ten months of chemotherapy, holding steady. If cancer is the emperor of maladies, creative integrative oncology might be the emperor of treatments.

MARIA HAD CAUGHT a cold from me and Dr. Dickey was concerned that it would drop into her lungs and that chemotherapy, by compromising her immune system, would make the sinus infection worse. I sat across the room from Maria and Dr. Dickey, my own hacking cough, burning eyes, and penetrating sinus pain proof that I was still contagious. Several times Dr. Dickey commented on how bad I sounded and asked, "Did you catch from him or did you give to him?"

"From him," Maria said.

I felt terrible that I had infected my wife, despite taking extraordinary precautions not to do so, like using hand sanitizer compulsively throughout the day, even though I knew it didn't work against viruses. Dr. Dickey wondered if it were possible to postpone chemotherapy—scheduled for the next day—until she had a chance to clear Maria's infection. That would be the prudent course of action, she suggested.

Determined, Maria was not about to postpone her treatment. "What's our backup plan?"

Listening to Maria's pulses, Dr. Dickey said that with some very strong Tibetan herbs she could get rid of forty to sixty percent of the infection overnight, but Maria would have to start taking the pills right then and continue every four hours throughout the night. Dr. Dickey handed Maria a small brown pill, and within ten minutes, Maria began to feel better. I felt jealous and wished Dr. Dickey had some small brown pills for me.

"Reports are good," Dr. Dickey continued, referring to Maria's blood work and CT scan report. "Mass decreased in pelvic areas, and you don't seem so depressed."

"When I saw you last, I was worried about the fistula," Maria said.

"That's why I gave you anxiety pills."

"I love them. They've been so helpful."

"I was worried that if you are worried, it doesn't help you."

A few moments later, Maria added, "Since I saw you last, I had my period."

"Good. Getting period means the hormones are adjusting. Sometimes oncologists won't believe that you get a period when you're on chemo. That's why you have other supplements," Dr. Dickey said, to help normalize the body's rhythms. To emphasize the point, she shared a story about another one of her patients who had stage IV breast cancer. "She's doing chemo, but she's not losing hair. Her oncologists don't believe it. She's taking some Chinese herbs and Tibetan herbs. She didn't stop taking her antioxidant supplements, and she's not losing all her hair, it's just thinning a bit."

Nausea on her mind, Maria told Dr. Dickey that she's considered medicinal marijuana for her nausea.

"Let me try something different this time. It's a little tricky because you have the infection," Dr. Dickey said, "but I will give you a different tea for nausea," one with ginger, clove, and cardamom to settle the stomach.

"I'd rather not use the pot," Maria said.

"No," Dr. Dickey agreed. "Let's try the new herbs first. They're stronger than the old ones."

FIVE DOSES OF Tibetan herbs later, Maria showed up for chemotherapy. My sinus infection had worsened that night, while Maria's lifted. Now clearly contagious, I wasn't able to accompany Maria to the infusion room. Fortunately, our friend Kim, who was visiting from Australia, was able to spend the day with Maria, while Satchi (who also had a cold) and I stayed home to recover. We watched Harry Potter fight Lord Voldemort and the Death Eaters while Maria fought her own battles with the emperor of maladies. It was an epic day.

"You don't have the record yet," Dr. Gullion told Maria before the start of chemotherapy, "but you're getting close."

"I'm not sure that's the record I want," Maria answered, almost reflexively. "What I want is the record for longevity."

DRIVING HOME FROM Dr. Gullion's office after Maria got her pump disconnected, I said, "I can sense Mom slipping quickly. I really need your support, but I don't know if I can depend on you now, or if I should rely more heavily on my friends." Picking up steam, I said, "This is simply one of those times in my life when I need my partner, but I don't want to wait around for you to comfort me if you're not able to."

"I don't know, honey. I'm still not all back yet. I love you, but I can't answer you now." We drove home both feeling hurt and upset.

"It's so hard to have Van be disappointed and angry with me," Maria told Howard the next day when we arrived for Maria's postchemo rebalancing, glancing at me to make sure it was okay to proceed. Maria and I are comfortable enough in Howard's presence to have these conversations. "His emotions cut right through to my heart. I feel so open, but not always in a good way—not like I have a choice to be open, but more like I *have* to be open, or else."

"Yes. That's probably been your tendency for most of your life."

"I think that's how I survived," Maria said. "Nobody would tell me what was going on, so I tried to feel into everyone else at my own expense, and I became a sponge for those around me but lost sight of what *I* was feeling."

Over time this kind of vigilance to cues from the environment can lead to a pronounced deficiency in one's energy, he explained. And then the chronic pattern can move into the body and progress towards illness.

He challenged Maria to practice a new, healthier pattern based on choice.

"Any way you can develop your ability to decide for yourself when you want to be sensitive to other people and when you don't, that would be a worthwhile endeavor. Pay attention to moments when you slip into 'survival mode' and attune to what others are feeling." He added. "The key is to convince yourself emotionally that you're not in an emergency mode but are continuing to look out for yourself. Because feeling as though you don't know what you need to know may ultimately trigger a fight-or-flight response. And being in that mode twenty-four-seven depletes you in the very ways you're well on your way toward healing."

MONDAY, DECEMBER 13TH

About a month after moving into Bellaken Garden, her second care facility, my mom became unable to get out of bed even with assistance, or to walk or care for herself. We transferred her back to Alta Bates Hospital, where she had been admitted the night in early October that her knees buckled and she fell to the floor. She'd seemed stable, if not comfortable, at Bellaken Garden, but almost imperceptibly she had lost ten pounds and become severely dehydrated. On the day she was transferred she was nearly catatonic. She'd crossed an invisible threshold, and her precarious hold gave way. Because she'd been on an assisted living floor—and not in a skilled nursing unit—the medical staff hadn't noticed her worsening condition.

After her hospital stay, she would need to be placed on a skilled nursing floor to receive daily medical attention. However, all those beds at Bellaken Garden were occupied, so we had to find yet another home for Mom: Crown Bay Skilled Nursing and Rehabilitation Center in Alameda, half an hour from Dad's house.

The day Mom transferred to Crown Bay, Dad followed the ambulance, finally relieved that she would receive the right level of care. Sadly, his relief was short lived. When Mom arrived in her new home, her presentation shocked the director of nursing. In the twenty minutes or so it took to transfer her from the hospital, her temperature had spiked to 102 degrees. Her wrists displayed signs of cellulitis, a bacterial skin infection elderly patients often get in hospitals. And she appeared to be partially paralyzed on her left side from head to toe.

Angry and in disbelief, Debra, our elder care manager, called: "How could the hospital discharge Stella in such a debilitated condition?"

I hurried to Crown Bay, anxious that Mom might not survive the relocation. My heart sank when I saw her: her head listed to the left. Her face had caved in, and she could barely open her eyes. Her breathing was labored, and her words were indecipherable. Dr.

Emmon Collins, the facility's head geriatric doctor, said her presentation—fever, infection, and left-sided weakness—suggested a brain hemorrhage and wanted to admit her to a hospital. We could send her back to Alta Bates or admit her to Alameda Hospital, the hospital where Dr. Collins had privileges, only a mile from Crown Bay.

We chose his hospital. Kindly, he expressed regret that in one day my mom had had to endure the confusion of two hospitals, two ambulance transfers, and a new nursing home environment. That turmoil alone could take a toll on her very fragile body and mind.

Within hours, the hospital doctors ruled out a brain hemorrhage, thyroid or liver abnormalities, which could cause left-sided weakness, and a major stroke. Surprisingly, her symptoms pointed to yet another urinary tract infection, the third in as many months.

Once diagnosed, however, she rebounded quickly. Movement returned to her left side, and the physical therapist managed, without additional hands, to move her into a wheelchair. Yet the steady creep of dementia made it hard for her to swallow food or fluids, hence the ongoing risk of dehydration. It was only matter of time, we learned, before Mom would not be able to eat or drink, and then the end would be imminent.

TUESDAY, DECEMBER 14TH

"You've had as much treatment as any human has ever had from a chemotherapy standpoint, short of a bone marrow transplant," Michael Broffman said to Maria during our year-end consultation. "And to get through that—with your bone marrow basically intact, your energy intact, your appetite intact—to get through that as well as you have . . . that's a big deal."

We were sitting in the same small room at the Pine Street Clinic where we'd met Broffman ten months earlier to help us figure out how to manage the sumo medicine treatments soon to become the central feature of our life. At the time, Maria had just finished her first round of chemotherapy, was severely anemic, weighed ninety-five pounds, and had spent the better part of two months lying, exhausted, on the living room couch. She wasn't taking any supplements to support her immune system, could barely walk to the end of the block and back, and was eating a diet rich in fatty acids, which aggravate cell inflammation and perhaps embolden colon cancer.

We'd returned to Broffman, our first out-of-the-box consultant, to see if he'd be able to add even one small thing to the complex and interdependent treatment that had evolved with the Block Center, David Gullion, Howard Kong, Dickey Nyerongsha, and Christine Ciavarella. This team, and their expertise and prescriptions, were what Maria and I had come to call the *real* sumo medicine behind the sumo medicine. They were what was keeping Maria healthy and in the game long enough to benefit from the other treatments we hoped to introduce when the time and conditions were right: surgery or targeted liver-directed treatment; immunepheresis with Dr. Lentz, the German-based American oncologist who filtered decoys from the blood so that the immune system could directly engage cancer cells; new cancer technologies as they became available.

We knew Maria was approaching the upper limits of how much chemotherapy a human being could tolerate and hoped Broffman might have a game changer, some nontoxic supplement or treatment that could contain cancer without destroying healthy cells and compromising her immune system.

Wearing his trademark black-canvas tai chi shoes, Broffman observed, "Chemo is putting you in the driver's seat, and we want to take advantage of that because being on chemo is not sustainable—it's a temporary place—and we want that temporary place to last for a long period of time. The longer it lasts, the more we can add to your treatment and the better the chance of sustaining it."

Maria and I exchanged a hopeful glance when he said she was in the driver's seat.

"You basically have the disease on the run," he reiterated, "and have a low burden of disease. Now is the time to chart a long-term sustainable path to remission"—and beyond. "The overall strategy now," he continued, is to "reevaluate and recalculate the creative oncology approach to see if you're at the 'maximum threshold' of what's possible. Can we increase your supplements by a certain percentage? Would that be meaningful? I think that's the first thing, then based on that, we would start to add new things."

As he did in mid-February, Broffman recommended three categories of supplements: immune system boosters; those that stress cancer cells, including ones that disrupt glucose levels essential to cancer cell survival; and natural antiangiogenics, or substances that inhibit the growth of blood vessels, choking cancer cells off from their source of nutrients. He updated us on which supplements might be useful at this stage in Maria's treatment.

Among the products Broffman put in the first category, he singled out Zadaxin. "It's probably the strongest commercially available immune-stimulating drug on the market," he said. It stimulates the immune system by adding T cells and natural killer, or NK, cells to the body. Through a subcutaneous injection, Zadaxin floods the body with T cells "far in excess of anything your body can produce on a good day." The only problem with it, he said (in what would become a refrain), is that it's not approved for cancer treatment in the States, even though it's approved for use in over thirty countries.

"They've already done prospective gold standard, randomized, double-blind clinical trials," Broffman said, with a tinge of sarcasm in his voice. And it's been "peer-reviewed, published in lung cancer, primary liver cancer, and melanoma" journals. But you have to get a prescription to import it, even though the company that makes it is based in the Bay Area.

The amount of detail Broffman shared overwhelmed me. I knew we'd need days, if not weeks, to research and integrate the new material. As he spoke, though, I remembered an expression Dr. Block used when we first met in March: that in integrative oncology: $2 + 2 + 2 = 256$. Maria didn't need any one of these creative protocols to be a magic bullet. In the world of cancer treatment, it's very rare for a new treatment or medicine to be a game changer. What Maria needed was several more 2s to keep the balance tilted in her direction.

"WITH RESPECT TO paradigm-shifting treatments," Broffman continued, "I think AlloStim is in that category. Based on the theoretical work of a brilliant scientist named Polly Matzinger, AlloStim—and the world of drugs built on this platform—may well be the big shift in cancer treatment." They signal a shift away from chemotherapy and toward immunotherapies that enable a body's own immune system to track down and destroy cancer cells.

To help us understand the new paradigm, Broffman entertained us with Matzinger's story. A former Playboy bunny, jazz musician, and dog trainer, Matzinger was waitressing at a bar, when she overheard a couple of science professors from the nearby University of California, Davis, campus talking about their research. Without being asked, she interjected her two cents' worth into the conversation.

One of the professors recognized Matzinger's unusual intelligence and encouraged her to go back to school, which she did, eventually earning a PhD from the UC San Diego, continuing her postdoctoral work at Cambridge University, and working at the Basel Institute for Immunology. She's currently a section head in the National Institute of Allergy and Infectious Diseases at the National Institutes of Health in Maryland.

Clearly delighting in Matzinger's iconoclastic origins, Broffman continued to weave his story: colorful, if not eccentric, Matzinger used to sleep outside her Maryland home with her border collies.

"One night, Polly's outside with her dogs. It's quite dark. A fire is burning. The dogs, attentive, are sitting by the fire, and the sheep are just off the perimeter of the fire circle, in the dark." Polly is lost in reverie, imagining that the border collies are an extension of the sheep's immune system. "Looking at the dogs, she observes that they're constantly noticing things in the greater environment— a plane flying overhead, a car in the distance, random sounds. And yet the dogs don't respond to any of that. . . . But all of a sudden, there's a sound, and the dogs bolt. So her epiphany in that moment is that the traditional theory of the immune system—the theory that won the Nobel Prize—is wrong. The traditional theory says that the immune system is supposed to differentiate between you and not-you. But she realized that *that* was not true."

Broffman paused. "Then, she had this epiphany: it's not about difference, it's about *danger*."

Maria appreciated the distinction immediately. I could see it in her face, but Broffman picked up the narrative thread before Maria could interject.

"The immune system basically responds to danger. There are lots of different things happening in the body, very few of which are actually dangerous. You don't want to attack things that are just different. That doesn't make sense. But danger? Yes. So Matzinger built a platform on the concept of danger, and her work has become very interesting to various pharmaceutical companies because it's a whole new shift in concept. And AlloStim, the Israeli technology, is the leading edge of something that's now in the clinical setting."

"And that totally fits with cancer because it's not 'not-you,'" Maria said, "It's dangerous."

"Yes," Broffman said, "It's dangerous, but it's not different."

"It's me gone wrong."

"Yeah. And she's completely irreverent. The ol' boys club, Nobel Prize scientists, are beholden to the old theory, but she's not. She's just plowed through the orthodoxy. . . . Many scientists are working on it, but the Israelis have the leading version of it."

I thought of the Jewish prayer of longing for peace in the Promised Land, said at the end of every Passover Seder, "Next year in Jerusalem." I, too, wanted a temple restored: my wife's body and health.

"MOST MEDICAL RESEARCH is flat-out wrong." That, Broffman said, as we neared the end of our consultation, was the conclusion of the leading figure in medical statistics in the world, John Ioannidis, MD, the head of the Stanford Prevention Research Center.

His groundbreaking 2005 essay in the journal *PLOS Medicine*, provocatively titled "Why Most Published Research Findings are False," claimed that "most research findings are false for most research designs and for most fields" and "research findings may often be simply accurate measures of the prevailing bias."

In other words, medical researchers find what they set out to find, and then, once committed to a theory, continue to find evidence to support what they believe. "You can only advance your career by having findings that are favorable," Broffman said. "So if it's not favorable, you don't publish it, or if it's kind of favorable, you can massage it to make it look more favorable than it is."

In an article published in the *Journal of the American Medical Association*, also in 2005, Ioannidis examined the forty-nine most cited clinical-research studies of the previous thirteen years. Each had appeared in one of three major medical journals. Disturbingly, as David Freedman wrote in a 2010 profile of Ioannidis in *The Atlantic*,

> *Of the 49 articles, 45 claimed to have uncovered effective interventions. Thirty-four of these claims had been retested, and 14 of these, or 41 percent, had been convincingly shown to be wrong or significantly exaggerated. If between a third and a half of the most acclaimed research in medicine was proving untrustworthy, the scope and impact of the problem were undeniable.*

"It's damning to the whole scientific effort," Broffman said, "but even though his work has been widely accepted across the world, it hasn't actually resulted in any behavior change or policy shifts."

Elsewhere, Ioannidis has charged that as much as 90 percent of the published medical information that doctors rely on is flawed. Medical doctors continue to rely on studies that in many cases do not corroborate clinical practices.

"So where does this leave the average person?" Broffman asked. His answer: "Common sense. It puts a little more power in your hands."

I turned to Maria and commented, "You're more and more comfortable with that power. Aren't you?" I was aware that she was raised not to question authority—in fact, to defer to it—and that her cancer treatment had emboldened her to trust herself and ask for what she wanted, even if it caused consternation.

"Absolutely."

"It's disconcerting," Broffman interjected. "Because you want to imagine that science was a little more robust, a little bit more precise. But now you know that's not completely true."

"The further along I get into my treatment," Maria added, "the clearer it is that medical science doesn't have all the answers."

THURSDAY, DECEMBER 23RD

"The chemo is really primitive," Dr. Dickey said, during Maria's consultation on day two of round twenty-three, her last chemo of the year. "It's like, okay, there's this bad person in the village, so let's kill the whole village. That's why we need the herbs; they are more compassionate. They don't kill everybody."

"And I totally feel the difference," Maria said. Though increasingly tired and weary, she told Dr. Dickey that she felt better so far this round, more protected and steadier than she's felt in several months.

"Let's sort out the cancer from the innocent villagers a little more," Maria said.

"Exactly," Dr. Dickey said. "That's why I'm pushing a little bit now, because you're stronger. Before I couldn't push you. I had to be gentle."

In the margins of her notepad, Dr. Dickey sketched three circles and labeled them "cancer," "immune," and "herbs." With two arrows, she connected "herbs" to both "cancer" and "immune" system. "The chemo is attacking the cancer and attacking you, so you have to have protection from it." Sounding very much like Broffman and Block, she said the Tibetan herbs protected the body and supported the immune system, while attacking the cancer. "Even if I'm attacking the cancer, if you are too weak, the cancer will come again."

"When we met with Dr. Broffman last week, he said that right now I have the upper hand and that we should push all the formulas I'm taking."

"Yes," Dr. Dickey said. "Starting in January, I want to work hard with your blood and really build it up." She hands Maria several big black pills in a baggie. "These will improve your hemoglobin levels," she added, and increase resilience to the cancer. After my short experience with Dr. Dickey and Tibetan herbs, I had no reason not to believe her. And if a bitter tasting pill could increase Maria's hemoglobin level, that sure beat going to the hospital for half a day, at a cost of several thousand dollars, to get a blood transfusion.

"I'm so glad I found you," Maria said.

I wanted to say that, too, but I felt a little shy.

BARCELONA WAS THE site, in July of 2010, of the 12th World Congress on Gastrointestinal Cancer. Sponsored by the European Society for Medical Oncology, it was the premiere global event in the field. Over three thousand oncologists, cancer researchers, and oncology nurses from ninety-five countries met for four days to discuss the latest research from across the globe.

A similar meeting took place in the United States a year earlier. It had the same basic organizing committee and the same basic program. Less than a hundred people attended the U.S. Congress.

"Why is this?" asked John Marshall, MD, the chief of the Division of Hematology and Oncology and director of Clinical Research at Georgetown University Lombardi Comprehensive Cancer Center, in a Medscape News video blog he posted on July 13, 2010. "Why is the rest of the world flocking to these meetings, and we in the United States aren't really showing up at all?" While it's true, Marshall argued, that his European colleagues take more pharmaceutical money, allowing them to travel to Barcelona to participate in such workshops, restrictions on sponsored funding are only part of the reason Americans lag behind in participation.

"What I think we're seeing is a dumbing down of the U.S. oncology world. We've become very basic and very simple when the rest of the world is challenging and trying to move forward cancer medicine. We've become complacent and happy with what we've got, and we are clinging to what we've got." He added, "We've become so conservative, so careful about what we're doing, and we've lost sight of where we're headed."

Over the past five years, Europeans led all the major clinical research in GI cancers, Marshall said, particularly in colorectal, gastric, and pancreatic cancers. "You name it. They all have been done by European investigators and led by a very vibrant group of clinicians and translational researchers." Where Americans used to lead in innovation, he said, "The reality is our clinical research has not been very innovative" of late.

Some of that's due to complacency, but some, alarmingly, is due to deeply embedded beliefs and territorial positions about what is worthy of scientific investigation. "When our investigators from cooperative groups submit clinical trials to our regulatory bodies, there's a very conservative approach at our regulatory bodies, so that they're saying No, we can't do those kinds of clinical trials; that's too 'out there.'" Pessimistically, he concluded, "We're not really willing to push the envelope."

Sadly, the clinical trials that do get approved and funded disproportionately benefit large pharmaceutical companies. No one knows from where the next breakthrough in cancer will come, but novel, out-of-the-box creative ideas, like the immunotherapy drug AlloStim, have a harder time breaking through into the light of day.

Appreciating that the world of cancer research needs to find new treatment paradigms, Marshall asked, "How *are* we going to allow innovation in a medical world that so desperately needs new ways of thinking? Our European colleagues have figured this out, and they're leading the way. We've got to decide: are we just going to watch and consume what they produce, or are we going to get back in the game and play as leaders in the medical community?"

To HYDRATE OR not to hydrate? That is the question that my dad has to answer every four or five days now that my mom can no longer eat and drink enough to keep herself alive.

Were it not for the thousand milliliters of intravenous fluids that she received every night, Mom's organs would begin to collapse, one after the other, in a cascade ending in heart failure.

Five days after Mom arrived at Crown Bay, the skilled nursing facility that would be her last home, the nursing staff met with Dad and Debra to discuss end-of-life treatment choices. Based on their observations, the staff reached a consensus: my mom's quality of life had declined so precipitously that we should discontinue fluids and let the natural evolution of Stella's last days unfold without further intervention.

Dad and I spoke afterwards. We agreed with their assessment— Mom had declined dramatically—but disagreed with the prescription. We wanted to keep Mom hydrated to improve her chances of surviving until my sister and her family arrived from England, a few days before Christmas. The staff couldn't evaluate the importance of that factor; it was a family matter.

I spoke with Dr. Collins and convinced him to continue to order fluids until their arrival, a week later. At that point, we'd reevaluate whether to continue with the fluids or to allow Mom to die. And there was always the possibility that regular fluids might improve her condition, if only marginally, but enough to allow her to enjoy the company of her loved ones.

Four days into the new plan, Dad became suspicious. Stella slept for longer periods of time, was increasingly unresponsive when awake, and lost any interest in eating. Cracked and dry, her tongue had telltale signs of dehydration. Dad asked the station nurse if Mom had received fluids that night and was told that there was no order in place to do so.

Mom had fallen through the cracks at yet another nursing facility. Dr. Collins was as surprised as we were to learn this news—four days after he placed the order to hydrate—and again ordered his staff to reinstate the fluids. Tragically, in the absence of sustained hydration for those days, Mom's hold on life slipped even further. She appeared to be dying.

One morning she asked if she was dying. "Yes, Mom. You're dying," I told her. Then, I asked, "Does it feel like you're dying?"

"No," she said. Then she closed her eyes again. Something made her ask that question. I called my sister and told her that Mom might not last until her arrival, almost a week away.

With hydration, Mom rebounded slowly. At the suggestion of the activities director, Dad and I brought in a CD player and some of Mom's favorite music—Frank Sinatra, Greek *Zeibékiko*, Grigoris Bithikotsis, and big band music from the thirties and forties. On Sunday night, I returned to Crown Bay, sat next to Mom on her bed, and played *Zeibékiko* for her. With her eyes closed, she mumbled a few bars of music, but mostly did not stir, nor open her eyes. Eventually, I tired and started to nod off, saddened that her presence was so tenuous. I fought to stay awake and decided to play big band music for her—Glenn Miller, Tommy Dorsey, Benny Goodman, Artie Shaw.

Much to my surprise, she opened her eyes, recognized the music, and hummed along. "I love to dance," she said and then, in loose fragments, recounted going to dances in her youth with her cousins in Central Park. She'd dance late into the night. She took my hands, and we danced as she lay in bed. She led me in the Double Lindy, bouncing her hands up and down, gently tugging on my hands so I would follow her lead. She smiled. I could feel her moving her feet beneath her bed covers. We danced for almost an hour.

In between dancing, we talked about her youth in New York City, visiting her Aunt Malamou on Long Island, and about other long-dead family members she thought were still alive. At last, I told her I had to leave. She worried that I would miss my ride if I stayed and danced longer.

"I'm concerned," she said. "Will your cousins wait for you if you dance more?" I told her not to worry; my cousins would wait for me. The band played the last song, and we left the dance floor. I kissed her on the cheek, told her that my cousins and I were going to catch the A train back to Brooklyn, and thanked her for a lovely evening. She smiled and told me she felt close to me. I told her I would return in two days.

I left Crown Bay, moved that I'd just had a date with my mom on a dance floor somewhere in Central Park long before I was born.

I DROVE HOME and called my dad. "I think we need to continue with the fluids. She's still very much here and able to enjoy life."

Dad agreed, relieved to hear from me what he'd sensed as well: the nursing staff observed a bedridden, enfeebled old person who was near death. They didn't know Mom still longed for intimate contact and had the capacity to respond to overtures toward her. But we knew, and we were a united front.

Two days later, I returned at night again. Mom was delighted to see me. "You know how sometimes you feel comfortable with certain people and not comfortable with others? Well, I feel comfortable with you."

"I know. I can feel that when I'm with you," I said. A long pause, then, I added, "And I feel comfortable with you, too."

"Thank you." We both laughed.

What she said next surprised me, "I'd buy anything you told me."

"Well," I said, laughing. "How much money do you have to spend?"

"None," she said, smiling.

Mom and I were flirting. She was very much alive. She then asked me who I was.

"I'm your son."

"You're my son?" she said with amazement. "Is that so?" I didn't answer, but my eyes must have communicated my love for her. "How old are you?"

"I'm forty-eight."

"And how old am I?"

"You're ninety-one."

"I am? Oh my." She sat with that startling information for a long, poignant moment. I imagined how it would feel to be told you were ninety-one when you don't remember much of the last fifty or sixty years of your life. I felt a wave of tenderness toward her.

She asked me if I liked children. I told her that I did very much and that I had a son. She asked to see his picture. I produced one of Satchi, but she didn't recognize her grandchild.

"He's cute," she said. "He looks like you."

I asked her if she wanted to hear some jazz music. She brightened. I imagined she had some wisp of a memory of our date. She wanted to dance, so we held hands and she, still in bed, led me with her frail arms. Speaking over the music, she told me that she enjoyed being with me, whoever I was. I told her that I enjoyed being with her. I felt the blessing of being with her without needing to be anything to each other. We were mother and son and yet neither mother nor son. We were free.

When I got up to leave she asked if she could leave with me. "I wish you could, but you can't walk on your own, so it's very hard to take you anywhere."

She studied my face, probingly. "I can't walk?" she asked, looking surprised and forlorn.

My heart went out to her. "No, Stella. Not anymore. I'll have to come here to visit you again." I kissed her good-bye, then blew her a kiss from the foot of her bed, and said, "*Óneira glyká*" (sweet dreams).

FRIDAY, DECEMBER 24TH

"And thank God for Mom's cancer," Satchi added, surprising both Maria and me as we finished our dinner prayer. "It's given us many gifts."

Maria and I exchanged a quick look across the dinner table.

"What gifts, honey?" Maria asked.

"We have more fun now," he said. "There are more people in our lives; we always seem to have someone visiting now. And we spend more time together as a family."

"Agreed," Maria responded. "And we're trying to figure out whether I can take an extra week off from chemo between Christmas and New Year's."

Maria and I discussed how we needed a break from the unrelenting two-week cycle to enjoy the holidays without doctors, infusion rooms, and side effects. Listening, Satchi said, "I don't think you should take time off, Mom. You're making great progress with the cancer. Now's not the time to back off. You should keep fighting."

The next day, without much convincing, Dr. Gullion approved a three-week cycle. We were anxious, not knowing the latest tumor marker numbers, but he had no hesitation. "You deserve a holiday," he said and reported that tumor marker numbers sometimes bounce around at the low end of the assay, suggesting the tumors are learning how to resist the chemotherapy, creating a kind of stalemate: FOLFIRI would win one round while the tumors won another.

His assistant called after we got home. Both tumor marker numbers had decreased, the first time that had happened since early October. The CEA count, after having gone up for two cycles, went down by 22 percent.

"We're starting to bounce," Maria said, with a barely concealed hint of foreboding.

EARLIER THAT DAY, I'd overheard Maria and Satchi talking about the Buddhist practice of welcoming death into your awareness. "Some people practice living every day as though it were their last," Maria said. "They find that being aware of death allows them to live more fully."

"How does being aware of death help you to live more fully?" Satchi asked.

"Well, it's simple," Maria started. "You know how Dad has been letting go of Grammy for many years now, watching her decline, and grieving all the ways in which she can no longer give to him like she used to?" I could tell she'd decided to be concrete. "The more he lets go of her and doesn't expect her—or the situation—to be different, the more he's able to be present with her and enjoy the time they have together."

"I could never let go of you and Dad."

"You don't have to, honey," Maria said. "Dad is young, unlike Grandma. It's your time now to hold on to us both for as long as you want."

"I know about how to accept death," Satchi said. "You love someone with all your heart, and then when they die, you mourn."

twelve

◆

INVOKING GANESH

The day started joyously. My sister Ariste and her family came over early to start the Christmas dinner, English-style. The centerpiece was a turkey bathed in butter and then wrapped in bacon to seal in the juices—not your standard low-fat Northern California way to prepare a holiday bird, but my sister, her fiancé, Paul, and our niece live in Britain, and *they* were doing the cooking.

While the bird roasted, we all went to visit my mom at Crown Bay. Two weeks before I'd asked Mom what she wanted most in life. She said, "To have my whole family together in the room with me."

She got her wish. She was visibly moved and a little confused as her gaze drifted from one face to another, all of us looking at her, the center of attention, the emotional heart of our family for fifty years. At one point she said, "I don't know what to say."

The bird and gravy reached their perfection late in the afternoon; Maria ate salmon, yam, and steamed vegetables. Not having eaten pepper in over a year, she took a risk on a salad with a hint of pepper in the olive oil dressing. Three hours later, she felt sharp stabs of pain in the lining of her stomach. She lay on the couch to manage the pain, but it worsened steadily. And then the vomiting started. Stainless steel bowl in hand, Maria threw up her dinner and then, afterward, clear fluid.

Satchi asked why Christmas, which started so joyously, had to be ruined by his Mom getting sick. "Isn't cancer enough?" he complained. "And now this." He was crestfallen and no doubt scared.

Though he didn't need an answer, Maria responded. "I feel the same way. It doesn't feel fair to me either."

TUESDAY, DECEMBER 28TH

Maria continued to vomit for seventy-two hours. Though the frequency and vehemence tapered off within the first twenty-four hours, her body continued to reject even small sips of water. On Christmas night, she felt a burning pain that made its way from her stomach into the small intestine. Oddly, the burning never made its way into the colon but stopped midway through the small intestine. On Boxing Day, Maria lay curled up in bed, almost immobilized.

The on-call oncologist at Marin Specialty Care worried that Maria might have a partial obstruction in the colon and advised us to go to the emergency room if the vomiting worsened or the pain increased sharply. Though neither occurred, by Monday morning Maria was exhausted and counted the minutes until we could drive to Marin to see Dr. Gullion.

Almost immediately, Dr. Gullion learned that Maria hadn't had a bowel movement since Christmas. She was dehydrated and needed intravenous fluids. He sent her to Marin General Hospital for a pelvic X-ray to rule out a bowel obstruction. When the X-rays revealed no obvious obstruction, he wondered if perhaps a gastrointestinal bug of some kind was the culprit. Over the weekend, his medical practice had four patients, in three different counties, call in with similar symptoms.

Hydrated, Maria returned home with instructions to try a mild suppository for the constipation in the hope that her condition would improve. When the suppository didn't work, we returned to Dr. Gullion's office the next day for additional fluids, aware that if her condition didn't change by tomorrow morning, she'd have to be admitted to the hospital.

That night her discomfort reached a steady state: cycles of pain followed by relief, followed by pain again, exhaustion, green vomit. Maria began to wither. It was hard to know at that point if the ongoing abdominal pain was associated with whatever caused the vomiting in the first place or was caused by the vomiting itself, which placed unrelenting pressure on the muscles of her stomach and esophagus, as well as the rest of her digestive tract.

Sensing my panic, Maria said, "Don't worry, honey. I have leeway. I have to go deeper to find the rhythm of my gut, but I'll come out the other side." She was sitting in the chair in our bedroom, meditating on her gastrointestinal tract, a picture of Amma hanging on the wall behind her. She told me that she could sense that the pepper disturbance might have activated deeper underlying emotions in her gut—emotions related to what it felt like to be on chemotherapy for a year.

Her gut, she said, was irritated and angry, as if it were protesting the tsunami of poison that it's had to endure. With the exception of when we went to the Block Center in March, every chemo round has been a two-week cycle. This cycle, being a three-week one, was different, and by the end of week two, Maria didn't have to gear up for another treatment; she could finally let down and relax. Perhaps the extra week off, she speculated, allowed her gut to express pent up rage.

WEDNESDAY, DECEMBER 29TH

At four in the morning, I awoke to Maria's groans. The pain in her abdomen had been moving around, and despite four and a half liters of IV fluids and two suppositories, the dry spell continued. Two days earlier, Dr. Gullion had instructed Maria to start with a mild glycerin suppository and, if that didn't work, to escalate to Dulcolax, a much stronger softener.

"Now's the time to escalate," Maria said.

I ran out to the only twenty-four-hour pharmacy in Oakland and returned with our last option to avoid hospitalization. We lay in bed and waited an hour for the softener to work. Sleep overtook me. I dreamed of lying in bed and waiting for Maria to tell me the results of a pregnancy test.

Rousing me, Maria said, "It didn't work. We need to call Dr. Gullion."

The sun barely up, Dr. Gullion returned our call, asked for an update, and concluded, "I think it's time that you took Maria to the hospital."

"Do we have the time to try to see if an acupuncture visit might make a difference?"

"I think we're past that now. We've tried everything we can do on an outpatient basis. I'll call the emergency room at Marin General so they'll be ready for Maria."

As we prepared to leave, Maria started to see twinkling red, blue, and white lights floating in the air. Satchi and I, feeling playful, wondered if she could see the colors of the Jamaican flag—green, black, and yellow. She laughed. Then she started to see in triple vision. We picked up the pace of our preparation. Earlier in the morning, Maria had emailed Prana and told her about the blockage in her abdomen, the steadily building pain, and the likelihood of surgery.

"I'm in so much pain," she wrote. "Please pray for us and, if possible, ask Amma for her blessing."

I called Keith Block, with whom we had a phone consultation scheduled later in the morning, and apologized on his voicemail for the last-minute cancellation. We had been preparing for this meeting for three weeks, since our consultation with Broffman, and were disappointed about having to delay it.

Just as we were about to leave the house, Dr. Block returned my call. "Please don't worry about the cancellation. Tell Maria that my only concern is for her well-being."

He then explained that there are two types of obstructions, structural ones and functional ones. Tumors, lesions from prior surgeries, twists in the bowel—these are the main reasons for structural blockages. Functional obstructions are less clear cut, he said. Something can impair bowel functioning (a flu, bowel irritation, swelling, a new tumor), and then dehydration can cause what little stool is in the pipeline to harden. As it hardens, it can create a logjam and then quickly become as hard as cement. There may be nothing impairing the movement of the stool except the hardened stool itself.

Whatever the case, he assured, "This was just a bump in the road." Even if Maria needed surgery, it was a fairly straightforward procedure from which she'd recover quickly.

ONCE IN THE emergency room, Maria and I felt relieved to have additional support; three and a half days of waiting at home had worn us both out. Clark, Satchi's godfather, arrived to take Satchi for the day. The ER nurse gave Maria a barium sulfate "smoothie" to drink in preparation for a CT scan. It was the first "food" she'd had in almost ninety hours.

Later, after reviewing the CT scan, the ER doctor said Maria did indeed have a small bowel obstruction, and that Dr. Mohammed Ali Zakhireh, a surgeon, would arrive to discuss her treatment options. As we waited, Maria mused about how elegant the human body is.

"This is such a lovely example of how the body works. Since nothing can go out, nothing can come in. To protect itself, my body has established a state of equilibrium."

On some level, I knew Maria, though suffering, also deeply appreciated the physical theater unfolding in her body. "Our bodies are absolutely amazing," she added.

"And you are, too."

MARIA AND I almost didn't notice Dr. Zakhireh when he walked into the room. He didn't draw attention to himself. His manner was natural and unaffected, and there seemed to be a quiet spaciousness about him, as though he didn't need to get ahead of himself. We both felt comforted in his presence.

He didn't start with his diagnosis, as I expected, but a series of discriminating questions ending with whether Maria uses drugs.

"Just the prescription ones," she said, wryly.

"Good answer."

"It's been determined in some circles I'm considered a drug addict."

He lingered for a moment with Maria's humor and then returned to his line of thought. "You have a small bowel obstruction on the right side of your abdomen."

"Exactly where?" Maria asked, sounding like a curious child in science class. "How close is it to the entrance to the colon?" Touching her abdomen lightly, he showed her.

Fortunately, he added, Maria had no serious symptoms, such as fever, highly elevated white blood cell count indicating infection, or extreme bowel pain suggesting that the bowel was dying.

"These symptoms would force our hand and require immediate surgery. We can give your body a chance and see if it can resolve the obstruction on its own." He gave Maria a twenty-four to forty-eight hour time frame, perhaps longer if red flags didn't develop and the scans showed incremental progress.

The obstruction, he explained, would account for the vomiting. Everything upstream from the blockage—secretions from the stomach and the lining of the intestine, plus the water Maria had sipped—needed to go somewhere, and if not down, then it had to come up, creating a dynamic equilibrium. The stomach alone, he said, typically produces a liter to a liter-and-a-half of fluid a day. Immediately downstream from the blockage, he continued, it appeared that Maria's bowel had decompressed and collapsed, not an unusual consequence of prolonged intestinal inactivity, but reversible if the obstruction is caught early. Further along downstream, in the colon, there was still movement, he added. And, fortunately, the obstruction was far enough along in the small intestine that whatever had backed up above it would not likely overflow into the stomach. That was a blessing.

What he said next stirred my anxiety.

"We get worried when people without prior abdominal surgery have a small bowel obstruction because we don't know why they would have one. Typically, people get bowel obstructions as a result of adhesions from previous surgery. That's the most common reason. In your case, we'd suspect a lesion related to your metastatic colon cancer to be causing the obstruction. The question is, will it get better on its own or will it not?"

Maria asked, "Could be as simple as a garden hose that got kinked?"

"Yes, so the plan today is to put you on 'bowel rest' and to continue with IV fluids." He explained that the muscles of the intestines can get distended when there's an obstruction, and the more the distension, the more difficult it is for the intestines to contract and squeeze, stopping peristalsis. The goal of bowel rest is to try to decompress the stretched segment of the bowel so the muscle fibers can line up and begin to contract again. Continuing, he said, "It's impossible to predict whether bowel rest will work or not. I've seen some absolutely terrible bowel obstructions on X-rays that I've said, 'There's no way that's ever going to get better,' and they do. And I've seen some really simple ones, and they don't. There's no way to know."

If the obstruction persisted, Maria would need surgery, and that could delay her chemotherapy by weeks or longer, especially if Dr. Zakhireh had to resect the bowel and perform an anastamosis—joining two pieces of intestine back together. Freeing up a kink is pretty straightforward, but the surgical reunion requires longer healing. At a time when Maria was in the driver's seat, it would be a shame to have to spend down her hard-earned advantage on recovering from surgery rather than upping the cancer ante.

TREATMENT PLAN IN hand, I left the emergency room to call family members. When I returned, I was surprised to see a tube protruding from Maria's nose, even though Dr. Zakhireh had explained that a nasal-gastric tube would make Maria feel more comfortable. It would suck bile out of her stomach, relieving upstream pressure and hopefully helping the guts to unwind. Several skin-colored adhesives crisscrossed at the tip of her nose to keep the tube in place.

The nose tube looked like an elephant's trunk. Seeing my surprise, Maria said, "I know, I know. I look like Ganesh," referring to the Indian god who has the head of an elephant and the body of a man. Then, she added, "That's appropriate. Ganesh is the Remover of Obstacles, and boy, oh boy, do I have an obstacle I need removed!"

AT HOME THAT night I had an email waiting for me from India. Prana had taken our family photo up to Amma and explained the turn of events to her through a translator. Prana called afterwards: "Amma looked at your photo and made a sound that's so hard to describe, but it and her expression conveyed total compassion." I called Maria to read her the email. She was relieved that Amma had focused her attention directly on her situation and felt hopeful that her obstruction would resolve itself without surgery.

THURSDAY, DECEMBER 30TH

Maria's obstruction resolved itself overnight.

"What I see is better than what I could've imagined in twenty-four hours," Dr. Zakhireh told Maria.

The first sign of progress came in the middle of the night, in the form of gas, something we all either take for granted or prefer to keep to ourselves. But, as we learned, passing gas signals peristaltic life, the silent undulating rhythm that underlies digestion and elimination; without it, we would die. Before Maria went to bed last night, the nurse told her to call her if she went to the bathroom or passed gas, "even if you have just a little poof." Upon waking, she had her first successful poop. The rubric for getting better was very simple.

Despite not having rounds himself, Dr. Gullion arrived at the hospital to see Maria a little after seven in the morning. Maria, who was readying herself for her second walk of the day, invited him to join her as she circumambulated the triangle-shape fourth-floor surgery unit at Marin General.

From windows facing west, they could see Corte Madera Creek below and Mount Tamalpais bathed in the early morning light. Dr. Gullion explained that, after studying her X-rays, he didn't believe there was a tumor pressing up against the bowel from the outside. The obstructed area looked more diffuse, he said, more like what happens when you twist a long thin balloon and an adjacent part of the balloon expands. Once the air is let out of the expanded portion, it can take a while for the balloon to regain its normal shape and tone.

We may never know what stretched the balloon in the first place, but we're inclined to believe that a perfect storm of events that began with irritation ended with obstruction. A little later in the morning, Dr. Zakhireh confirmed the good news: the backup had started to move beyond the obstruction. He speculated that the barium "smoothie" Maria had drunk in preparation for the CT scan might have acted like Liquid Plumr, burrowing through the small intestine to the site of the obstruction, where it partially dissolved the blockage.

Maria and I celebrated by napping together in the hospital bed. After our nap, Maria said that just as people's bodies somehow remember the anniversary of a loved one's death, even if the person does not consciously remember the date, she believes her body is attuned to the one-year anniversary of cancer treatment.

"I spent part of the night breathing into my pelvic bowl," she said, "and I sense that my core—my abdomen—is letting down and releasing. Whatever else happened on the physical level—pepper burn, kinking, irritation, inflammation—on subtler levels I am also working out the kinks." She paused, took a deep breath, and continued, "I'll be fifty years old in two months. My body has endured a year of chemotherapy. I'm getting ready for the next act."

FRIDAY, DECEMBER 31ST

Satchi, Clark, and I started the day in a hot tub. Soaking in hot water, as the early morning light slanted in through the wood-slat fence, I was finally able to let myself feel how overextended and scared I had been that week. I knew Satchi shared these feelings.

"I don't know about you, Satchi, but I'm just catching up with myself. It was scary to see Mom vomiting and in pain. You, too?"

"Uh huh."

"There were moments when I worried that she was going to die. How about you?"

"Yeah."

"And then I didn't know what to feel when I saw her looking like Ganesh. I wanted to laugh, but I also felt queasy seeing a tube up her nose."

"Yeah. Me, too. At first, I stayed away from her when I saw her. I was scared."

"Yeah, but then I realized it was just Mom, no difference, just a funny tube making her look like an elephant."

SATURDAY, JANUARY 8TH, 2011

The CT scan of Maria's pelvic area did not provide definitive images of what caused her small bowel obstruction, but it did reveal disappointing news. For the first time since Maria started chemotherapy, one of the tumors in her liver had started to grow. Four millimeters is not a large amount by most standards (and another lesion adjacent to that one actually decreased by 26 percent—go figure), but in the rules-don't-apply world of metastatic cancer, it meant that one tumor had figured out how to resist the chemotherapy, and more were likely to follow. At what rate and where, no one could predict.

We'd been expecting the tide to turn but were still shaken by the news. The conversation initiated by Broffman about creative oncology options became that much more important. And Maria brought it to Dr. Gullion when they met to discuss her post-hospitalization recovery.

"Some of my getting sick is that my body was saying Enough already, I need a break from this chemo for a little bit of time."

Dr. Gullion agreed. "I think we should hold tight for a while longer and not give you chemotherapy for another week or two—because you need to recover. The last thing we want to happen is for you have some toxicity from the next round of chemotherapy that puts you back where you don't want to be: either not eating or bowels getting messed up again."

"Plan!" Maria said.

She then handed him an email we'd sent to Dr. Block two weeks earlier, in which we distilled Broffman's suggestions into an A list and B list of creative oncology options. "Hopefully, by the time I see you next week, we'll have more information on his thoughts and guidance about how to proceed."

Reading the lists, Dr. Gullion, perhaps somewhat surprised by the number of options, some of which he had previously expressed disapproval of, said simply, "A lot of alternatives."

Quick to sense a hint of disapproval, Maria said, "For the moment, I don't see these options taking the place of chemotherapy. We have to decide what's going to be the combination that provides the most powerful punch to my tumors."

"I certainly agree that just continuing the same FOLFIRI proto-col and maybe moving to an every three-week schedule is not really sustainable for too much longer. You're definitely having an accu-mulation of side effects. You've tolerated it remarkably well." The next sentence stood alone; it needed no explanation. "You've had a lot of irinotecan."

He stopped to let the acknowledgment settle in and then listed the many adjustments Maria had implemented to prevent overtox-icity. "But the writing's on the wall with your tumor marker num-bers," he added ominously, and much to our surprise, since he typi-cally refrained from dramatic pronouncements. "And now we have data from a CT scan to substantiate the bouncing numbers." Maria and he agreed to wait and see what Dr. Block would have to say about what new protocols to include in the treatment—and whether he would advise switching to FOLFOX—before deciding on the next step.

After her consultation and for most of the week, Maria felt dispirited. We didn't talk about it, but I could tell she felt deflated and worried, as I did, about what appeared to be a dwindling palette of chemotherapy options. She was tired of chemotherapy, but also didn't want to be at the end of the line with FOLFIRI, a familiar regi-men that had brought her back from the brink of death. It's hard to let go of old friends, even if they are poisonous.

"It's getting harder and harder to imagine doing chemother-apy again," Maria said, as we prepared for our phone consultation with Dr. Block. "I can see why people don't take extended time off or why they might choose not to return to chemotherapy after a long remission. Normal life is so appealing."

On the phone, Dr. Block wasted no time in reframing the meaning of the mixed response.

"Weird," he said, in response to learning that one tumor has grown and one adjacent to it has shrunk. He observed that there was a little more shrinkage than growth and added, "What I think is more significant than the growth increase is the size reduction." That, in combination with the recent drop in tumor marker numbers "suggests to me that we're heading in the right direction," he concluded.

"The problem might not be that FOLFIRI is ineffective," he said, catching both Maria and me off guard. We had thought about all the options except this one. "It may be that the current delivery of the FOLFIRI is no longer effective, given that you've had twenty-three rounds of it. Sometimes when a chemotherapy drug stops working, we can chronomodulate the drug and resensitize the cancer cells to the drugs again, and achieve an effective response."

Though I accepted the premise that chronomodulation could maximize cancer cell death while minimizing harm to normal cells, I was skeptical that it could reverse resistance.

"If a tumor's already become resistant to FOLFIRI," I asked, "are you saying it can change just through chronomodulation?"

"Through chronomodulation," he reiterated, "in conjunction with other treatments, like curcumin, melatonin, and Anvirzel. Research demonstrates the ability of these substances to counter resistance and potentially improve response. It's why using more than one intervention at a time—kind of like a full-court press— stands a better chance of working."

Acknowledging that it had worked well for Maria to alternate between the Block Center and David Gullion's practice, he wondered about the efficacy of continuing to do so now that she was at the limit of how FOLFIRI is traditionally delivered.

"These particular protocols are substantially different if they're chronomodulated. If I have a patient who's been on FOLFIRI and FOLFOX, and both protocols have failed the patient—and they've never received chrono—I treat them as if they've never received either protocol, because the drugs are that different when chronomodulated."

"As an experiment," he said, "if you could manage it, I would encourage you to come here for possibly three, or preferably four, treatments in a row. Not every other, but, literally, in a row. And then we'd retake scans in two months."

With the proposition finally on the table, he added, "After that, if we see the same pattern—one's growing, one's shrinking, or both are growing—then I would say it really is the FOLFIRI, and it's time to change to a FOLFOX regimen. If, on the other hand, you start to respond, then it really does raise some questions. Are you going to burn bridges on a protocol because of the way you're getting it, as opposed to getting it in a manner that may be more effective and potentially move you toward a remission?"

"Would the chronomodulation just be for the irinotecan?" Maria asked, reminding him that the last time we explored this option we learned about a study questioning the effectiveness of 5-FU chronomodulation for women.

"You can do it for the 5-FU *and* the irinotecan," Block said. Though Dr. Block couldn't see Maria's face, she looked surprised. "In response to that study," he continued, "I've worked with Dr. Hrushesky"—William Hrushesky, the dean of chronomodulation in the United States—"to modify the way we do chronotherapy so that it should be better suited to women's circadian rhythms." The adaptation requires a three-night, four-day regimen as opposed to the traditional two-night, three-day regimen.

Turning to why he hates to change course too early, he said that most patients in the United States can tolerate only limited rounds of oxaliplatin, the main drug in FOLFOX, before the side effects accumulate too quickly and one needs to abbreviate the treatment. "Our clinical impressions suggest that our chronomodulated patients tolerate oxaliplatin better than in most clinics and may be more likely to complete their full prescribed FOLFOX regimens."

When the treatment runs its course, "then we have to move downstream to another regimen," he concluded, without saying the obvious: and one stop closer to the end of the line for traditional chemotherapy.

Maria put her hand on my knee. We were sitting across from each in the living room, with the telephone in between us. I must have looked upset. She took my hand as Block continued to speak.

"And then the question is the same question," he said. "How fast would you stop responding or have to stop the protocol because of toxicity? And that's where there's huge relevance" to chronomodulation. "When I put all of this together"—the bulk of the tumors in your body are contained or shrinking, your tumor marker numbers are low, and you now have a mixed response—"I say something is going right. Can we make something go a little bit more right? If we're not getting anywhere, then I would switch to the FOLFOX."

I started to feel overwhelmed, much the way I felt when we first met him. "How the hell are we going to pull this off?" I thought.

It sounded like Dr. Block was framing the choice before us as one between chronomodulation, with the possibility of living longer, and business as usual, with a shorter life expectancy. I knew he was right, but I didn't want to hear it. I wasn't angry with him, so much as with an American oncology ethos so hostile to innovation that my wife had to travel almost two thousand miles to receive the treatment she wanted.

Maria and I glanced at each other. I could tell we were beginning to think the same thing, again: just do it.

BHARAT "BART" AGGARWAL, Dr. Block said, is one of the world's leading cancer scientists doing research on curcumin, the primary component of the Indian spice turmeric. He was also a distinguished professor of cancer medicine and the chief of Cytokine Research in the department of Experimental Therapeutics at the University of Texas MD Anderson Center.

Some years back, Aggarwal brought his curcumin research data to Razelle Kurzrock, then the chair of the department of Investigational Cancer Therapeutics at MD Anderson, one of the largest Phase I research departments in the country. It was Kurzrock's job to evaluate the data behind new laboratory discoveries and translate them into clinical trials.

"When Bart came to me," Kurzrock recounted, "he said, 'I want to show you some great results we've gotten in the lab with an exciting new agent.' But he wouldn't tell me what the agent was; he wanted me to see the data first." After reviewing the data, Kurzrock was impressed. She went on, "It was clear that this agent was just as potent at killing tumor cells in the lab as any experimental drug I'd seen from pharmaceutical companies."

According to Block, Aggarwal prescribed a very high dose of curcumin to a patient who had metastatic cancer but wasn't engaged in conventional therapy at the time. Surprisingly, the patient's cancer went into complete remission. At the request of the patient, Aggarwal cut the dose in half; the disease returned. And when Aggarwal put the patient back on the original dose, the disease disappeared again.

Block recommended that Maria increase her curcumin dose by 133 percent. He then turned his attention to Broffman's creative oncology options. While he tabled some, he praised quite a few others as worth investigating, including Zadaxin ("Would be on my list, except for high cost"), naltrexone ("I'd it give thumbs up"), and metformin ("There's growing interest and a low side effect profile"). And he promised to contact his Israeli colleagues to find out more about AlloStim.

When you add compounds to an already complex and individualized integrative plan, he explained, you don't always know which components are responsible for what happens therapeutically. "It's simply not possible to isolate all the factors in advance of treating real people." With that in mind, he advised Maria to add one compound at a time—or two at a time—every, say, several weeks to make sure she didn't have an adverse reaction to it.

"What we really need in this country," he added, linking the individual task ahead of us with the status of integrative medicine, "is a new and different center, not the National Center for Complementary and Alternative Medicine [at the National Institutes of Health] but a center that serves as an umbrella for all these different types of treatments and is able to put people on research studies so we can tell what's really happening with these compounds." In the absence of this umbrella, practitioners like him, and patients such as Maria, had to design experiments on their own.

His frustration with the structure of the medical and research community was not too far from the surface. "Take, for example, metformin," he added. Typically used to treat diabetes, it helps to control the amount of glucose in your blood by decreasing the amount absorbed from your food *and* the amount made by your liver. Block explained that while cancer cells hoard glucose forty to a hundred times more than a normal cell, metformin strangles sugar supply to cancer cells, wherever they are in the body, at the primary site or metastatic offshoots in, for instance, the liver.

"The only reason that metformin will never be a cancer drug is because, as a generic drug, it's like an orphan in the pharmaceutical world, with no company interested in backing it for clinical trials. That's the dilemma."

AFTER OUR CONSULTATION, Maria took an early nap. When she woke, she said, "I'm going to Chicago to do four more rounds of chemotherapy. I owe it to myself to make sure I give FOLFIRI every possible chance to shrink my tumors. The only way I can imagine doing chemotherapy again, now that I've tasted freedom for a month, is to try a kinder and gentler process. The thought of doing normal chemo turns my stomach."

We agreed that I would stay in Berkeley to work and would commute to Chicago as often as possible, perhaps every other weekend, or one week a month. When we told Satchi, he was as clear and determined as his mother. "I want to go to Chicago with Mom." We floated two possibilities for school: he could either be home-schooled or go to a public school in Chicago.

"I want to go to school in Chicago. I think that would be cool."

I hoped Arne Duncan, the current U.S. Secretary of Education, who was formerly the chief executive officer of the Chicago Public Schools, had made his elementary schools hospitable enough for a kid dropping in from Berkeley.

After Satchi went to bed, Maria and I drew a cluster diagram with all the tasks that we had to accomplish to determine if we could pull such a feat off in ten days. It was daunting.

The next morning Satchi hopped into our bed and told us about a dream. "Me and Mom are in a car, driving on the freeway. Our car swerves off the road. Really calmly, I ask Mom if we're going to die, and she says, really calmly, 'I don't know, honey.'"

Maria and I exchanged a parental glance. "Are you worried you and I will swerve off the road without Dad?"

"Yeah, a little. Dad's the guy who takes care of everything, and he's not coming with us to Chicago."

"It sounds like you and I are talking really calmly, but maybe we're scared on the inside not to have Dad with us?"

"Yeah. I'm kinda excited, but also scared."

"Me, too. But we make a pretty good team. With Dad helping from the background, we can handle anything."

LATER MARIA WROTE an email to Amma. She told Amma about FOLFIRI and FOLFOX, and the wear on her body and soul, and the hope of chronomodulated chemotherapy. She asked Amma if she should go to Chicago for treatment now and, if she should, for her blessing to help with side effects and with finding support so far away from home.

She ended her email poignantly: "In the last couple of months parts of me that have been cut off for more than twenty years are coming back to life. And now I WANT TO LIVE, to be able to enjoy life and love with Van and Satchi. But with this setback, with the liver lesion getting bigger, I'm afraid that I will spend the rest of my life struggling with cancer, getting worse, and dying."

The rawness penetrated my heart. I wanted my bride to live and love without struggle. I always had.

thirteen

◆

MELODIES ETERNALLY NEW

This little flute of a reed thou hast carried over hills and dales,
and hast breathed through it melodies eternally new.

— RABINDRANATH TAGORE

"IF I DIE, and you meet someone else that you're happy with, I want you to know that I would want you to be happy."

Maria had whispered those words to me late one July night in a hotel room outside of Evanston. We had just arrived in Chicago for our third visit to the Block Center amid a magnificent lightning storm. All of us lying in one family bed, Maria and I could hear Satchi breathing softly next to us.

"I want to tell you something that's been on my mind." Then she spoke into my ear. Instantly, the words evoked a complex *masala* of emotions and reactions—profound sadness, discomfort, denial, and guilt.

"I know you would. You love me so deeply." I paused, wanting to say more, but my words were eclipsed by the strength of my emotions. I lay in her arms, listening to the sounds of the storm, as the dark night pulsed with lightning. "You know you're the love of my life, and you'll always be my great love—my soul friend."

"We've both felt that way from the very beginning," Maria said. "Even during the dry spells, when we couldn't remember our love, I've known and taken comfort in it."

"Me, too." I opened my eyes. "Alongside that boy, the greatest gift in my life."

She kissed me lightly on the lips. I went to sleep in her arms.

CANCER CHANGED ALL of us. It would be fair to say that Maria became braver and more loving; I, more devoted and less resentful; and Satchi, more responsible and at peace with himself—though, to be honest, it's hard to separate normal human development from the influences of illness.

But there's more. We're changed in ways that are hard to put into words. In J. K. Rowling's *Harry Potter and the Order of the Phoenix*, Harry asks Luna Lovegood why only he and she can see thestrals, magical flying creatures, while their other friends cannot. Luna says, "The only people who can see them are those who've seen death."

The three of us, like any family with a terminal disease in their midst, were living with the presence of death. And that awareness allowed us to focus on what was important. It made us kinder, less rigid, and more grateful for the time we had together, knowing that what we had would one day come to an end.

A year before, Maria's cancer diagnosis had sent us reeling. Maria's doctors, our family, and friends—they helped us find our footing and gave us a new lease on life. And our lives returned to normal or, to be more precise, what passes for normal when you have cancer—chemotherapy, side effects, unexpected hospitalizations, traveling cross-country for treatments—all packed in around the edges of what's normal. We crave normal. Maria's first oncologist told her that once she started feeling better she could shift to a three-week chemo cycle and then travel to all those places she'd always wanted to see. In other words, I'll get you well enough that you can travel to, say, India to see the Taj Mahal before you die.

She meant well, but didn't understand my wife or my family. We learned to delight in opening our hearts to the normalcy of everyday life: eating together, cuddling, watching movies, talking about books, taking walks, being silly, fighting, making up. We stitched these precious, fleeting moments into our souls so that they became a part of who we are. Cancer could never take that away.

BEFORE HEADING TO Chicago, Maria made sure to consult with as many members of her sumo medicine team as were available.

"At a deep energetic level," Maria said, "I feel I have access to more healing, and I know that I need to be prepared to harness that energy when I head east. I can't do that without the full support of my team."

On Friday, she visited Howard, the every-other-week anchor in her treatment, who, along with Dr. Dickey, had helped her attune to the deeper healing energies in her body. Maria thanked him for his gentle persistence in drawing her attention to almost imperceptible states of mind that deplete life energy and interfere with healing. Maria became convinced that had she continued living the way she was living, without attending to the underlying currents in her body and soul that needed rest, the lesions would have started to grow sooner.

"There were no new lesions anywhere in my body this year," Maria told Howard. "That's not a coincidence. I think all the 'terrain work' I've done has kept metastases at bay."

By *terrain work* Maria meant the work to make her body stronger and less hospitable to cancer, as well as the more subtle work to replenish her yin so her body would have the reserves it needs to fight cancer.

In the past, Howard had had hesitations about the disruption long-distance travel can cause to patients who need to build their yin reserves. But he was optimistic about Maria's new adventure. "You've done remarkably well with transitions in the past. There's no reason to think you won't do equally well this time." His blessing meant the world to her.

MARIA AND SATCHI said good-bye to Stella for the last time. It was unlikely she would live long enough to see them return from Chicago.

In the preceding few days she'd started to clamp her mouth shut and turn her face away when Dad or a nurse offered her food. The day before she had eaten 10 percent of her food; that day, one bite. When I lifted the skin on her wrist to see if she was still hydrated, the skin no longer snapped back as it would on a well-hydrated body. She seemed to have entered that end-of-life cocoon where one's attention progressively withdraws from the external world and turns inward, as if responding to an inner call. She was peaceful and still and, in a way, beautiful.

At one point, I could see Satchi looking at me from across the room. I'd been stroking my mother's hair. I wondered what it looked like to him to see his father caressing his grandmother.

He walked over to the bed, stood next to me, and said, "This is Satchi, Grandma. I love you so much. I'm going to miss you."

Neither of us expected her to answer. I told Satchi that I believed she could hear us, even if she didn't respond. I examined Satchi's face as he examined his grandmother's. We've had conversations about what we believe happens at the time of death, and now Satchi was face-to-face with the first death of a loved one. He and I stayed suspended for some time in that moment of silent witnessing. Silently, I prayed that he and I would be spared a similar scene with *his* mother until he was a grown man.

My dad, who was anxious about Stella not responding or eating, asked me to call the doctor to see if there was anything the nursing staff should do to help her.

"I don't think there is, Dad. They're just trying to keep her comfortable now, but she won't bounce back. She's starting to leave us, and her body is closing down." I left ample time before the next thought so he could internalize the first. "She doesn't need to eat much anymore." And then, "Her body needs to focus on dying, not eating."

"Yes, you're right. She's dying." He hugged me.

I turned to join Maria, who'd been whispering to my mom. Three weeks ago Mom said to Maria, "If you die first, I'll die." Maria calmed her mind: "Don't worry, Stella. I promise you, I'm not going anytime soon. I have a lot of fight left in me." Maria and I sat opposite each other on Mom's bed and held her hands. Perhaps reflexively, Mom clutched our hands tighter and tugged them up toward her heart.

"We're both here now, Mom," I said.

"Stella, I want you to know that it's okay to move on to the next part of your journey, when you're ready. Van, Satchi, and I will be okay without you. We're taken care of. You don't have to worry about us at all."

From behind Maria's back, Satchi put his book down and said, "Grandma, this is Satchi. Don't worry; it's all going to be fine. Don't worry about anything." He returned to his book.

We sat in silence. I listened to Mom's shallow breathing. "I would love to be with you when you die, Mom. If you want me—or need me—to be here, you can let me know somehow. You can come to me in my dreams or send me a heart message, and I'll do my best to hear you."

"Stella, I know your son will hear you, and he'll come. He's an amazing and devoted man." Maria started to cry. "Stella, you've given me so many gifts in this lifetime, but giving me your son has been the best gift of all." Now I started to cry, too. "I know how much you've loved him because of how much love he's given me." Maria's hazel-green eyes, wide and glowing with feeling, found mine. An almost heartbreaking tenderness passed between us.

As we prepared to leave, Maria said playfully, "Stella, it would be fun to come back in another lifetime with you and do this all over again."

Satchi laughed and said, "Yeah, Grandma."

Maria kissed my mother's forehead. "Good-bye, Stella, I will always love you." The three of us then walked down the long hall at Crown Bay for the last time together.

"CONGRATULATIONS! TODAY IS your day. You're off to Chicago! You're off and away!" We'd woken before dawn that morning, and as we drove through Berkeley to the freeway, I jokingly quoted the opening lines from one of my favorite books.

"Do you remember that book, Satchi?"

"It sounds familiar, but I don't remember it."

"Dr. Seuss," I said.

"*Oh, the Places You'll Go!*" Maria added.

"Dad, I don't remember any of those childhood books. Mom's cancer has taken up so much space in my mind."

"We'll have to do something about that," I said, sounding a little too serious at 6:15 in the morning.

"Don't worry, Dad," Satchi said, rescuing me. "It's already starting to turn around."

At the airport, we waited for Maria's wheelchair escort to arrive and said good-bye to each other before the security checkpoint. Satchi, who'd only once been away from either of us for more than ten days (when he was an infant and I was in India for Amma's fiftieth birthday celebration), held on to me for a long time. I didn't want to let go either.

From behind a glass wall, I waited and watched them make their way through security. Then I climbed a stairwell to a viewing platform and, once they collected their belongings, waved to get their attention. The wheelchair escort pointed me out to Satchi as they paused just outside the long corridor that led to the departure gates. Every few yards, he turned, craned his head to locate me again, and waved. At some point, I could no longer see the details of his face but could still see his red shirt, and I waved to the shirt. The shirt got smaller and smaller, and then disappeared. For a moment, I felt relief to be alone and not feel responsible for any one's care; and then I felt bereft, as if two pieces of my heart had just been surgically removed.

Disoriented, I couldn't find my car in the parking lot, even though I had written down its location. I'd gone to the wrong floor. Driving north toward San Francisco, I decided to take an early morning swim in the bay and drove to the Dolphin Club. Handel's *Dixit Dominus*, a marvelously glorious baroque choral piece anticipating the Messiah's second coming, played on the radio. The music ushered in the sunrise.

I parked my car outside Ghirardelli Square, above Aquatic Park, and listened to the final movement:

Glory to the Father, and to the Son, and to the Holy Ghost
As it was in the beginning is now, and ever shall be
World without end. Amen.

I walked along the beach toward the club. High tide was just starting to ebb, and a thick fog blanketed the bay. Even at sunrise on a Sunday morning there were swimmers returning from the sacred waters. I walked through the still sleepy clubhouse to the locker room, changed into my swimsuit, and walked down to the water's edge. I put on my thermal cap and swim goggles, and stood silently, almost reverently, at the high-tide mark.

The water beckoned me.

I plunged into the 50-degree water and swam along the buoy line to the flag at the western end of Aquatic Park, and then north to the Municipal Pier. For a quarter mile, I hugged the gently curving pier and rounded it into the opening to the bay. From that vantage point, on most days, I could see the Golden Gate Bridge, Alcatraz, and the cityscape, but not that day; the fog was too thick.

You get used to not being able to see where you're heading when you swim long enough in San Francisco Bay. You come to trust your sense of things, and the current, and the good hand of God.

I swam back to shore and, though cold, decided to swim the buoy line to the flag a second time, and then back against a current that by now had grown much stronger. Finally, I stumbled onto the beach and up the stairs into the clubhouse, and then warmed my body in the sauna. My ritual complete, I felt hollowed out, like a little flute of a reed, ready once more for the next melody to pass from God's lips.

the

OSTINATO

fourteen

◆

MOUNTAINS ARE CALLING

JANUARY 17TH, 2011 TO JUNE 12TH, 2012

After Maria and Satchi boarded that plane seventeen months passed, during which the tumors continued to grow—despite chronomodulation, surgery, and more chemotherapy—to the point where they threatened to compromise the functioning of Maria's liver, if not her life.

The three of us had moved to the Midwest, to Kenilworth, Illinois, on Chicago's North Shore, ten minutes from the Block Center, where Maria received a novel chemotherapy protocol she couldn't get in the Bay Area. We'd come expecting to be there for two months; by June 2012 we'd been there for five.

At first the protocol worked—Maria's tumor marker numbers dropped significantly—but then, disappointingly, they reversed themselves, and a new tumor in the bladder announced itself with blood and clots in her urine. Maria took time off from chemotherapy to have the tumor removed, and when she returned to treatment five weeks later, she had one treatment without incident before having an allergic reaction to the oxaliplatin in FOLFOX—flushed face, quickened heart rate, high blood pressure, difficulty breathing. After a second, stronger reaction a month later, she was done with FOLFOX.

Subsequent CT scans revealed slight tumor growth in the liver and, for the first time, small lesions in the lungs and spine.

Within days we met with Riad Salem, a world-renowned interventional radiologist at Northwestern Memorial Hospital, to see if Maria qualified for radioembolization, an innovative and relatively new liver-directed radiation treatment sometimes referred to as TheraSphere, or SIRT—selective internal radiation therapy. After careful mapping of the liver to determine whether it was healthy enough to tolerate vascular radiation (it was), the radiology team, in a second procedure, injected half a teaspoon of radioactive glass pellets—one and half million pellets, each a third the width of a human hair—into the blood vessels of Maria's liver. Once there, they lodged themselves in the tumors and slowly released yttrium-90 radiation, trying to shrink the tumors from the inside out.

Three weeks later, we were waiting for the results. Because it can take up to four months to determine whether the yttrium-90 has shrunk tumors, and by how much, the doctors wanted Maria to continue with some form of systemic chemotherapy to contain the tumors elsewhere in her body. The march of the disease had been slow, but relentless.

"I keep thinking about your miracle cream dream, the one you had the night before I started chemotherapy," Maria said while eating a middle-of-the-night snack. "I'm so tired of chemotherapy. I'm open to gathering information about what the oncologists recommend now that FOLFIRI and FOLFOX have failed, but I don't know if I want to keep 'taking the cream.' Maybe it's time for me to leave the temple of chemotherapy."

Maria looked tired. She'd had ongoing pain, despite taking pain medication around the clock, and ascites—fluid in her abdomen—had distended her stomach, making it uncomfortable for her to eat large meals in one sitting or move around the house. We'd started to call our late-night assignations our heart-of-darkness talks. They helped us deal with the complicated emotions that come with the kinds of decisions we faced.

"Do you remember that story your friend Susan told us last year?"

"The one about the former priest in her cancer support group?"

"Yes, that one."

The man had reached the point in his illness where he decided to refuse any further traditional treatment. Instead, he decided to travel to visit friends and family, taking everything one day at a time. Within a year he was cancer-free. I remembered Susan adding, "Maybe if we can truly get in touch with our own unique path—and therefore with the stars—things will work out in the best possible way."

Maria continued, "Amma told me that chemotherapy alone can shrink my tumors, but that was a year and a half ago, and so much has changed since then. Lifetimes. Maybe, just maybe, my path leads in a different direction now."

"You've done more tours of duty than anyone I know," I said.

Then, reading from a book by Brother Lawrence, a seventeenth-century Carmelite monk whose conversations and letters I'd been sharing with Maria, I added, "'Resign yourself entirely to the providence of God: perhaps He stays only for that resignation and a perfect trust in Him to cure you.'"

"Maybe. Maybe not. With or without chemotherapy, I've always placed my trust in God. I know chemotherapy won't cure me. It may not even shrink the tumors anymore or contain the cancer. But I have to keep working on a plan in case I leave the temple."

I helped Maria walk from the kitchen to the couch in the first-floor living room—she couldn't climb the steps to the bedroom anymore. She then needed help to go from sitting on the edge of the bed to lying down. I held her knees with the crook of my left arm and, using my right hand to support her shoulder, gently lowered her body to the seat while lifting her knees up and on to the couch.

I turned to walk to my couch-bed, at a right angle to Maria's. She reached out to grab my hand, love radiating from her eyes. "I'm so grateful to you, my dear. Thank you so much. I love you more than I can put into words."

We held each other's gaze. After a day of caring for Satchi and her, I was tired and needed to sleep. But I had intimations that our time together was short.

I didn't want to part with my bride tonight.

HOW DID WE reach this pivotal moment in our lives? What happened in the year and a half since Maria and Satchi left Berkeley for the Midwest?

The very day Maria and Satchi boarded their plane for Chicago, it became clear that my mother's death was imminent. I went straight to Crown Bay after my swim, and my dad and I took turns holding a twenty-four-hour vigil by her bedside. Two days later, Stella died, with Manny by her side. Ariste, Paul, and Sabina flew in from England for the funeral, just a little over two weeks after they had returned home from California. Sadly, Maria had already started a new round of FOLFIRI, her twenty-fourth, and she and Satchi were unable to attend the funeral. I grieved the loss of my mother and the absence of my wife and child.

Though my dad's loss had been progressive, the final good-bye was heart-wrenching. He cried more in three days than I'd seen him cry in my whole life. In church and at the cemetery, he fell into my sister's arms. He dropped one last red rose onto Stella's casket as it was lowered into the earth. Two days later, while he sat watching, Ariste and Sabina went through Stella's clothes and belongings. At the end of it, Manny wasn't ready to part with anything. He knew he needed to go through them on his own one day, touching everything himself one last time before he could say good-bye.

A week later, on February 1st, Maria called to remind me that it was the first anniversary of when she started chemotherapy. She cried inconsolably. After one round of chronomodulated FOLFIRI, it was already clear to her that she could no longer endure receiving chemotherapy the traditional way. During her short trial, chrono-modulated FOLFIRI had proved to be easier on her spirit and body.

"We need to find a way for me to move here," she said. Maria's friend Tom, with whom she'd stayed close ever since their Princeton days, and his wife, Georgia, offered to rent an apartment for us. And I began a twice-monthly commute to Evanston to be with my family.

That spring Maria received twelve more rounds of chronomod-ulated FOLFIRI at the Block Center, making thirty-five rounds of chemo in all—the most that any of her oncologists had administered to a single patient in his or her practice. And while the chronomodu-lation gave her a chance between drugs to recover from side effects, its effectiveness began to wane. Scans indicated that, while the dis-ease appeared to be stable in the pelvic floor, it was continuing to creep in the liver and colon.

AND THUS BEGAN the second movement in Maria's cancer treatment cantata: the dream to remove the last vestiges of disease in her liver.

We returned to the Bay Area to consult with several different hepatic surgeons. One, Jeffrey Norton, the chief of Surgical Oncology at Stanford University Hospital and Clinics, shocked us when he said that he could do one surgery to remove all the visible tumors in Maria's body. *One* surgery, he emphasized when Maria and I started to cry— one to remove the tumor in her colon and all nine tumors in her liver.

"This surgery won't cure you," he added. "You can't stop terminal cancer dead in its tracks. But this is your best chance of setting back the clock. You're young and healthy. I wouldn't tell you I could do this surgery if I didn't think it would add years to your life."

A year and a half of chemotherapy had brought Maria to the verge of the improbable, a life without cancer. We were exuberant. "I've made it to base camp," Maria said. "Now I'm ready to scale the summit."

But then, the cantata hit a discord.

We met with the other members of Maria's surgery team to review new presurgery scans: Andrew Shelton, a GI surgical oncologist, and Jonathan Berek, the chair of Stanford's department of Obstetrics and Gynecology and the director of its Women's Cancer Center. The scans revealed what earlier scans at other hospitals had not detected, the tumors in Maria's sigmoid colon had spread to adjacent organs. The surgery would not be confined to the liver and the colon.

"With that much disease," Dr. Shelton said. "One surgery's not possible."

They advised an immediate surgery to remove the colon tumor and as many organs in the lower abdomen as needed to stabilize the disease. Maria might come home with a colostomy. Liver surgery, if at all possible, would have to wait.

With Dr. Norton, we'd cried tears of relief—with Drs. Berek and Shelton, heartbreak, disappointment, and disbelief.

THE SURGICAL TEAM, minus Dr. Norton, first removed Maria's uterus, ovaries, and fallopian tubes, and then two portions of her colon. The surgery left Maria with active disease lining the back of the bladder and running down along the peritoneal cavity. To have removed all the disease—and the bladder and cervix with it—would have increased the chances of death.

"It's unlikely Maria will ever be a candidate for liver surgery," Dr. Shelton said immediately after the surgery. "Not with active disease in her pelvic area." He paused, took a deep breath, and added, "I wished we could've taken out all the cancer."

Our friends Seth and Laurie, who had spent the day waiting with me, helped to anchor me as I listened, stunned, to my wife's prognosis: FOLFOX will prolong her life for a period of time, but it would not stop the tumor's eventual progression.

Later, I waited by Maria's bedside in the post-surgery holding area, dreading the questions I knew she'd ask when she awoke. When she opened her eyes, I squeezed her hand. She smiled and said, "I can tell the surgery was a success. I don't have a colostomy bag."

My heart broke for her. Because of the pain medication, she couldn't feel her abdomen and mistook the lack of sensation for the absence of a bag and the opening, or stoma, it was attached to. "Oh, my dear, you can't feel it, but you do have a bag. They couldn't reconnect the colon."

She immediately registered what that meant. She hesitated and, not wanting to hear my answer, asked, "Did they get all the cancer?"

"No. They left cancer in your pelvic floor." She listened silently, with eyes closed, as I told her what I knew. She asked no more questions.

The next day Amma called Maria in the hospital to find out how the surgery had gone and how she was doing. They discussed treatment options. And she told Maria she would continue to pray for her and keep her close to her heart.

We returned home from Stanford with our friend Laurie, who, when we first moved to San Francisco, had helped us to explore our early childhood experiences, and who now nursed Maria back to health during the first three weeks of her convalescent summer and fall. Having recently had major abdominal surgery herself, she understood the long healing process—physically and emotionally.

Together, she and I tried to help Maria use this time as an opportunity to repattern her own early childhood experience around feeling invisible and neglected. There were days when the burden of it all—and the thought of chemotherapy again—were too great to bear, and Maria would despair. As autumn crept forward, Howard suggested that Maria start writing in her journal again to release the pent-up anger associated with her slow recovery and limited medical options.

> *I don't have folks around much to talk to—so maybe these pages can absorb some of my feelings. I don't get to hate much, to put words to what I hate. Maybe I need to do that more. To get really clear and be vocal. Yes, it is OKAY to HATE. It is GOOD to know what you HATE. It is HEALTHY to know what I hate and to name it and to honor it. Hating gives protection. It gives me the chance to create space around myself.*

Once she'd given herself permission to indulge her feelings, she continued.

> *I HATE EVERYTHING!!! AND EVERYONE!!! I HATE LIFE! AND DEATH! I hate it all! And I want to kill it all!*

There is nothing else to say, just HATE, HATE, HATE! I hate hospitals! I hate doctors! I hate people being nice, even kind, when they are sticking you or cutting you or causing suffering! Even in the name of relieving it! I hate that that just is. I hate being weak, and tired. I hate crying all the time. I am so tired and bored of what I have been doing and how I have been living! I am so miserable! I want to feel good! I want to feel joy and happiness and capability— being so powerless SUCKS!!!

Turning to her medical options, she wrote,

I really, really HATE chemo. I REALLY REALLY HATE NAUSEA! I hope I never feel nauseous again in my life! It is the WORST thing on earth! Give me pain, but spare me nausea!

Nearly emotionally spent, she ended,

I'm just so hurt right now, feeling let down. I'm just so tired! It has been really really hard, this healing from surgery. I hate it so much. This pain, the tiredness, the goddamn stoma—I just want to shit naturally, and not to have to care about my digestion! I friggin' hate this thing. Not my body—but being left with this goddamn bag. I hate the goddamn bag. And everything around it! I hate it all. FUCK IT ALL!!! FUCK IT! And never to get free! FUCK IT. FUCK IT. FUCK IT!

But the worst part is feeling so goddamn powerless and incapable! I HATE that! I want to DO, to make, to dream, to create—without all this weakness!!! Just makes me crazy!!! I see no options—what do I do? What do I do? What can I do?

AND THEN A phone call from our old friend Lou ushered in the third movement in Maria's treatment cantata: trying to get to Bavaria for a miracle cure.

Lou called one night to tell us that Maria might be eligible to participate in a fully funded study for M. Rigdon Lentz's immunepheresis, the treatment he and Anne had encouraged Maria to try when (in January 2010) she was still chemotherapy naïve. Since then, both Keith Block and Michael Broffman had told us that Dr. Lentz was a brilliant scientist and that his compelling technology offered the genuine possibility of improving her condition without reliance on long-term chemotherapy. The main stumbling block to this treatment had been the cost: $65,000 per month. If Dr. Lentz accepted her into the study, that obstacle would be removed for an initial treatment.

A month later, we accepted Dr. Lentz's invitation to join the study with great delight, updated our passports, and bought three one-way tickets to Bavaria. Pretreatment scans in California revealed that the once-severable lesions in the right lobe of Maria's liver had started to coalesce. To our horror, Dr. Lentz called to say the liver lesions had grown too large. If Maria were to have a positive response with immunepheresis, the tumors could dissolve too quickly and lead to fatal blood clotting. Before coming to his clinic, Maria would need to start FOLFOX immediately, with the hope of shrinking the tumors by 50 percent. Only then would his treatment be safe.

Four rounds of FOLFOX later, Maria had new scans. We anticipated good news—her liver was softer to the touch, her white blood cell count was robust, and she'd gained nearly nine pounds since her lowest postsurgery weight. But in a now familiar ostinato, the scans revealed that the tumors in Maria's liver appeared to have stayed the same, if not consolidated further, and the tumors in her pelvic area had grown.

Dr. Gullion cancelled Maria's next FOLFOX cycle, saying, "I think it's time for you to consult with the Block Center and to look into clinical trials." He hung his head for a moment, and then added, "I am so sorry."

That was a Thursday afternoon. The following Monday morning we consulted with Dr. Block, and on Wednesday all three of us boarded a plane to Chicago. The new plan: Maria would do four more rounds of chronomodulated FOLFOX, with the addition of a drug not used for colon cancer but which tests on Maria's tumors indicated could slow her specific disease. I would work with my clients via Skype. And Satchi would transfer to a new school for the third time in a year.

Once again, our friends Tom and Georgia came to the rescue, introducing us to one of their best friends, John, who offered his home to us, ten minutes from the Block Center, for as long as we needed for Maria's treatment.

FIVE MONTHS LATER, we were still living with John, amicably and with deepening affection. The new protocol may have kept the liver lesions in check, but it didn't get Maria to the goal of 50 percent shrinkage. We still held out the possibility that the TheraSphere treatment might make a difference where chemotherapy had not. Maria's latest tumor marker number had decreased by over 50 percent in the month since early May—in the absence of chemotherapy. A graph of these numbers since late the previous year showed a steady downward trend, like the slope of a mountain range. Whether there was another peak beyond, or a plateau, or a long valley, we didn't yet know.

We had been disappointed too many times to speculate. When Maria had her first allergic reaction to oxaliplatin, she started to cry as soon as she could breathe freely again. I could see the worry pass across her face as she looked at me.

"I know what you're worried about."

"Every time I get close, close enough that I feel our trip to Germany is really going to happen, something new comes up."

Later that day, when we returned home from the Block Center, Maria said, "When I was first diagnosed, I knew I was too weak to fly to Germany for immunepheresis. But looking back, I'm incredibly disappointed—and angry—that no one encouraged me to try immunepheresis when I was healthier and the tumors were smaller. It just might have worked for me then."

"I wish we'd had Dr. Lentz looking at your scans all along. He might have told you to get on a plane earlier, like in early 2011."

"If I had to do it all over again, I'd definitely make sure that I had a radiologist and a surgeon and, maybe, Dr. Lentz looking over my scans from the very beginning."

From time to time, either Maria or I returned to this conversation, but it didn't lead anywhere. It was a dead end. We were there—in the present—waiting to see if radioembolization had worked. And Maria had the same complex mix of feelings about the timing of radioembolization: since it's much more effective with smaller liver tumors than with larger ones, like hers, it might have had dramatic results the previous spring, in conjunction with FOLFIRI.

"I wish we'd had better guidance about when to put chemo on hold to try some of these other approaches," Maria said. "Trying them at the eleventh hour is different than when you're relatively healthy and can risk the time off from chemotherapy."

Dr. Block had recommended one last drug for Maria: regorafenib, a drug awaiting FDA approval. On average, it can extend life by six weeks.

OUR GERMAN FRIEND Franziska wrote to say that Bavarians have a saying: "*Der Berg ruaft—i muass aufn Berg aufi!*" (The mountain is calling—I have to get up the mountain!).

With the help of an army of Sherpas, we had climbed many mountains. And were it not for these mountains—integrative medicine, chronomodulated chemotherapy, liver surgery, the hope of a cure in Bavaria—we would never have set out on this healing journey. Like Ithaka, the destination in Cavafy's poem of that name, these mountains had given us an unimaginable adventure, but they offered us nothing now. The TheraSphere treatment might shrink the tumors enough for Maria to travel to Bavaria. Maria might decide to try the newest miracle cream in the temple, regorafenib. But beyond mountains were more mountains, and none genuinely offered peace of mind, or true equanimity. Only a relationship to something deeper, something enduring—to God—could bring the quest to an end.

And this marked the cantata within the cantata of Maria's cancer treatment: continuing to climb whatever mountain was in front of us while recognizing that it was God, after all, the basso continuo, who had been calling all along from the heights. Whether Maria turned a corner on the disease or not, she was destined to return to her Beloved. That's what we're all destined for, however long the voyage.

IN A DREAM, I was standing atop a mountain. I was the last to make the ascent on this particular day, and other climbers were already preparing their descent.

"Hey, weren't you the first to the top yesterday?" one of them asked, having heard that I had also made the ascent the day before.

"Yes. That was yesterday. Today I'm much slower."

"Catch you at base camp."

One by one, the climbers left me. Alone at the top of the mountain, I feared that I might not be able to make the descent. I was too tired. I labored down from the peak feeling forsaken. Just then, I turned a corner to find the team of climbers waiting.

"We decided to wait for you," one of them said to me. "You need the help today."

I felt immense gratitude and relief. I needed these people, and they knew I needed them. I folded into their ranks and walked down the mountain protected on all sides.

Lying in bed, I told Maria my dream. She knew that asking for help had never been easy for me, but that the openheartedness of so many had created new, more trusting neural pathways alongside the old, less-trusting ones.

"Your people are going to help you down the mountain," she said. "I know it. The more you trust, the more God will provide."

SATCHI FINISHED THE fourth grade in Kenilworth. As we left his new school, not knowing if he'd return in the fall or be home in Berkeley, he told me he was sad. He let me put my arm around him.

"It seems as though this school, and these people, and this time in your life have been truly amazing for you, and healing."

"Mmm hmm!"

"I get it," I added. "Me, too."

We drove in silence. Then from the back seat, Satchi said, "You know, Dad, I love Berkeley and I love it here. Wherever we are in the fall, I'll feel sad. Because I love both places."

In the rearview mirror, I could see that he was crying. I had the same dilemma. I felt blessed that all the trillion chances in the universe had brought us to that place at that moment in our lives. And I knew we'd never be the same for it.

"When we let ourselves love so deeply, our hearts crack open," I said.

"Yeah, I know," he said, without a hint of sarcasm, as though I were stating the obvious.

"And when our hearts crack open, we can live and love more fully."

"I know," he repeated, though it wasn't clear who was leading and who following in the conversation.

Two days later, he left for Camp Kesem—*kesem* means "magic" in Hebrew—a five-day, five-night summer camp led by college students for children whose lives have been affected by a parent's cancer. The year before Satchi had come home from Camp Kesem having met kids who'd lost a parent to cancer. The experience made him wiser, more independent, and even kinder than he already was. He'd come home this time better prepared for when death would touch our little family.

"How are you doing?" I asked Maria as we drove to the Block Center.

"I'm in pain. But otherwise okay." A few moments later, she added, "I've slipped below base camp again. But life is good. I'm alive. I have my husband at my side. My child's at sleepaway camp. I'm living my life."

We turned the corner onto Wilmette Avenue, heading west toward Skokie. Maria said, "Hey, can I tell you about a dream I had last night? I was out on the water, surfing. I caught a wave before anyone else did. I was in the right place at the right time. I couldn't get to my feet, but I was on the wave and loving it. And I knew there'd be more. And I knew I'd catch them, too."

the

FINAL
MOVEMENT

fifteen

◆

FALLING THROUGH
IMPERMANENCE

"*Dum spiro spero.*" Maria woke up quoting Latin.

"Again?" I said.

"An expression from high school Latin. *Dum spiro spero.*"

"What does that mean?"

"Literally, 'while I breathe, I hope.' It's the state motto for South Carolina. When I was younger, I was told it had to do with Francis Marion, the 'Swamp Fox,' who resisted the British occupation of South Carolina, even after they defeated the Continental Army. But now it has more personal meaning. As long as I have my breath, I continue to hope." She hesitated, asked me to help her sit up, and then added, "And I'm hopeful that, after our vacation in Berkeley and seeing Dr. Dickey, we'll be able to return to Kenilworth."

Guiltily, I didn't share Maria's sense of hopefulness. My eyes told me that her decline was accelerating. She was too ill to participate in clinical trials and needed round-the-clock support. Two weeks earlier, when the three of us—Maria in a wheelchair—went to receive darshan from Amma in Chicago, I knew, not wanting to

317

know, that this family darshan would likely be our last, that Maria and Amma would not see each other again in this lifetime.

Despite protestation from ashram attendants, who could see Maria's fragility and wanted her to stay in her wheelchair to receive darshan, Maria insisted on getting to her knees before Amma. The effort alone—and the love, devotion, and dignity behind it—brought tears to my eyes. After our darshan, an attendant wheeled Maria backward, slowly, away from Amma, the two gazing into each other's eyes, as though acknowledging their farewell. The sadness on Amma's face mirrored the sadness in my heart. The moment was heartbreaking.

Afterward, I didn't share my private revelation with Maria. During a recent heart-of-darkness conversation, she had told me she wasn't ready to talk about dying.

"I have to keep my focus on living and being hopeful. I look forward to waking up every day and seeing you and Satchi. If I change direction, if I give up hope, I'm afraid I'll die. I'm sorry, but if you need to talk about my dying, you'll need to talk to someone else right now."

I respected Maria's wish, but bearing the loneliness of not being able to grieve *with her* was staggeringly painful. I worried that we'd waited too long to return to Berkeley, that she'd be too weak to be able to board a plane in eight days, and that she might not get to die at home, surrounded by family and friends. I wanted that for her, for me, for Satchi.

At the same time, I wanted to believe in the sheer force of her determination to live and her belief that, like those of the Swamp Fox, aggressive alternative tactics would arrest the spread of the cancer, allowing us to return to Kenilworth.

"I'll see you in two weeks," she told her beloved staff at the Block Center.

I could tell many of them wanted to believe her, too. "We'll see you in two weeks, sweetie. Enjoy California," they said.

MARIA WAS SLIPPING through my fingers, and I felt utterly powerless to do anything about it. I knew the moments we now shared
were the most precious God had given us. I prayed I was strong
enough to face what was before me. I prayed that my beloved would
confound everyone one more time.

MONDAY, JULY 23RD

The flight home was horrible. Maria was in constant pain. Mild
turbulence and the plane's low-level vibration, almost imperceptible to those of us who are healthy, made her body ache, especially her lower back and stomach, where the ascites had stretched
her muscles, weakening the integrity of her core. Midair, she and I
made a medical decision to increase her pain medication. That provided momentary relief. But the wear and tear of not being safe at
home in Kenilworth, which was a controlled environment, without
stimulation, took its toll. By the time she was wheeled to the waiting car at San Francisco International Airport, she broke down,
sobbing, like an inconsolable child who had kept a stiff upper lip
for too long.

Satchi looked irritated and embarrassed, as it took forty-five
minutes to settle Maria into the car at curbside. I think he was in
shock and scared; he hadn't seen his mother out in the world, where
her debility stood out in bold relief. Without the aid of pillows, I
had to pull clothing from our luggage and stuff flannel pajamas, soft
T-shirts, and a cotton chenille scarf under Maria's body. She didn't
have the strength to move her own body, so after positioning each
article of clothing, I had to readjust her torso to minimize torque
and pain. And when we got home, it took almost an hour to figure
out how to transport her into our house. Eventually, it took two
strong men carrying her in the wheelchair up twenty stairs to the

front door, a purple silk sari that Amma once wore wrapped around her torso to secure her to the wheelchair.

In Kenilworth, though Maria had barely been able to climb stairs when we made our California plans, we hadn't anticipated that she might be housebound once in Berkeley, unable to leave our home to visit Dr. Dickey or, if necessary, to get to the hospital unassisted. Once we were inside, we realized Maria couldn't climb the seven stairs to the second floor and our bedroom. We'd need to locate a hospital bed and commode and rearrange our home to care for her in the living room, where she could participate in the daily activities of our household and, through our west-facing picture windows, feel the late afternoon sun on her body.

Though our friends swooped in to care for us—and to find hospital equipment on a Sunday—by day's end, I felt shattered. I wished we'd never left Kenilworth, and I wondered how many days of Maria's life we'd squandered in the turmoil of the relocation.

THE NEXT MORNING, Satchi asked, "Can we talk about Mom, upstairs in my bedroom, alone?" I followed him upstairs, closed the door behind me, and sat on the rug next to his bed. Wasting no time, he said, "Is Mom going to die?"

I'd been preparing for this moment. Richard, one of my best friends from college, nearly lost his dad to illness when he was very young. His parents didn't tell him what was going on, though he could tell that something frightening was happening. His whole life, he's wished that as a child he'd known what was happening when he was in the middle of it all.

"I think you're asking because you can tell that something has shifted with Mom. Right?"

"Yeah."

"You can see with your own eyes that she is weaker and more fragile than she's ever been."

"Well, she doesn't seem as bad as when she had surgery at Stanford last year."

"Hmm. Good point. She couldn't walk without great effort then either. But there's a difference. Then she was weak from major surgery. Now she's weak from the cancer and all the treatments to stop the cancer. Does that make sense?"

"Yeah. But she's still going to make it. Isn't she?"

I stalled for a moment. "Well . . . Mom's doing a number of different treatments right now, including working with an ayurvedic doctor in India."

"The guy you and Mom have been Skyping with?"

"Yeah. He's an MD-PhD, and has helped a friend who has stage IV cancer become free of cancer."

"So, is the treatment working?"

"It's hard to know. The early signs are promising. Mom's special diet of goat milk and goat meat broth has helped the bloating in her stomach, and the hot oil treatments help with the pain. But if she doesn't get better, the cancer will continue to spread, and then we won't know how long she has to live."

"Like years or months?"

"Maybe even less."

Angered, Satchi asked indignantly, "Why can't science do more? After all we can fly to the moon. Why can't science cure cancer?"

"You'd think. I totally understand your anger. I've gone back and forth between feeling angry and helpless myself." I then explained how there are over two hundred different kinds of cancer, and since each one is unique, scientists have to figure out how to treat each one separately. "While they've figured out how to stop some cancers, they haven't figured out how to stop colon cancer yet."

"What about more chemo? Can't Mom do more chemotherapy?"

"Well, here's the thing. There are two main chemos for colon cancer, and Mom has already done both. They're no longer effective. There is an experimental drug, but Mom isn't strong enough to take it. Plus, she doesn't want to do chemo anymore. She just can't bring herself to put more poison in her body."

"I know. I don't want her to do any more either. It's cruel."

We sat in silence for a few moments. Then he pushed me away. "You can leave now. I want to be alone."

ON THE PLANE home I had read a breathtakingly flawless book of poems by Christian Wiman, *Every Riven Thing*. In one poem, he prays to God: "Make of my anguish / more than I can make." He must have been inside my anguish when he wrote those words.

WEDNESDAY, JULY 25TH

Dr. Dickey made a house call yesterday. Maria had been looking forward to seeing her, hoping the combination of aggressive Tibetan, Chinese, and ayurvedic medicine would become her new defensive shield. I feared they had become a kind of Maginot Line, instilling a false sense of security and soon to be outflanked. She had also come to love Dr. Dickey—they texted regularly about Maria's well-being while we were in Kenilworth—and felt a deep stirring to see her in person. If anybody understood her body *and* soul, Dr. Dickey did. And perhaps now Dr. Dickey would be able to sense some movement in her pulse that would offer new hope.

Sitting upright in her firm green sofa chair, my prayer shawl wrapped around her shoulders, Maria looked visibly comforted to be in Dr. Dickey's presence. They talked about her long healing journey and aspirations, and reviewed the treatment trifecta to make sure there were no contraindications to blending medicinal formulas from three different cultures. Dr. Dickey then read Maria's pulses, confirming that the ordeal to return home had nearly extinguished her thin life force. She provided neither hope nor discouragement, but encouraged her to use the time at home to be in touch with her internal guidance—and to pray to Amma. She hugged Maria goodbye, told her she loved her, and invited me, as she left the house, to come to her office the next day to pick up new formulas and Tibetan pain pills, and to talk in private.

That day, in her office, I asked the question foremost on my mind. "What's your sense of how long Maria has to live?"

She did not mince words. "Life force is very weak. Maybe two to three weeks."

"Do you think the new ayurvedic medicine and diet can help to reverse the ascites and stabilize the cancer?"

"Her life force is almost gone. The new medicine can support life force so she can be conscious longer. But the cancer is too strong now, and her body too weak."

Thankful to her for her honesty, I decided to use this opportunity to reorient myself toward Maria's last days. "Her Indian doctor said that morphine would sap her life force faster than some of the other drugs. Do you agree?"

"Yes. It's hard to be conscious with morphine. May not shorten life, but can weaken life force," drawing a distinction I knew Western medicine wasn't able to make.

As we ended, I asked, "Do you think I should tell Maria what you've told me about having two to three weeks left to live?"

She thought about her response for a moment and then said, "When Maria first came to see me, the cancer was strong, even then. I didn't think she would live long. She has strong will and determination. That has kept her alive for many years—and all the integrative medicine, which supported her body. I think if you tell Maria how much time, she will give up. Maybe she needs to keep fighting to stay alive."

FRIDAY, JULY 27TH

Ideally, we get to choose who we want to be with us when we die. In addition to me, Maria wanted two old friends: Prana and Laurie. Prana arrived directly from Toronto, the last stop on Amma's North American tour. Amma had told her that these were Maria's last days and Prana should go be with her, indefinitely. Laurie would arrive a week later.

In the first of many moments of clarity, Prana led me up to the bathroom—the only place we could speak privately—and, sitting on the tile floor, told me how very hard it was to be with Maria. In the hopes of finding an eleventh-hour cure, Maria had invested all her energy in following her ayurvedic doctor's instructions, which involved nearly round-the-clock interventions. She had become exacting in that pursuit.

"She's keeping us so busy with her physical care," Prana said, "there's no time for us just to attend to her, to be with the *person* who's dying of cancer. Amma sent me here to be with her, but there's no space for that. And now I'm worried that since she's so accustomed to fighting—she's been fighting for so long—she might not allow herself to accept death, and to use it as an opportunity to grow spiritually."

Prana's words resonated with me. Later, alone with Maria, I said, "Do you remember two years back when you told Prana that you wanted her, Laurie, and me to be your midwives when you died?"

"I do."

"Well, Amma has sent Prana to be with you now."

A framed picture of Amma adorned a makeshift altar in front of the television, now draped in a purple cloth. "Spiritual," by Charlie Haden and Pat Metheny, a favorite of Maria's, looped on the stereo in the background. Nag Champa incense burned on the altar.

"Prana's here, but you're keeping her so busy with all the details of your physical care that she's having a hard time really being with you. It seems as though you're keeping her at a distance, pushing her away. She has so much to offer, but she can't find a way to drop in with you, to reach you emotionally."

Tears started to glisten in the corners of her eyes. Her face softened. Her eyes invited me to continue.

"And I'm feeling scared, too, scared that Satchi and I won't have a chance to grieve with you. He and I will have a lifetime to grieve together, but I think he needs to grieve *with* you. You and I may be out of sync about our needs, but I'm worried that unless you take the lead and talk to Satchi about dying, he won't be able to bring the subject up with you."

I stopped to give Maria a chance to digest what I'd said, and then continued.

"And I'm worried that he's been avoiding contact with you. I can tell he's trying to figure out what's happening, but without clear guidance from you, he can't know what he knows deep down inside. He knows he's losing you, but we've also led him to believe that we'll be able to keep this fight up indefinitely. He must be so confused.

And unless you and I are in sync, and speak with one voice, I think
he won't be able to start to grieve with you."

Her face tightened. What I'd shared about Prana was easier to
hear. But now I was asking her to change direction and to surrender
the hope she'd been holding onto.

"Please don't deny him, or me, or yourself, the opportunity to
say all the things we need to say to each other."

"Okay, enough," she said, not angrily, but beseeching. "I want
to be left alone."

SUNDAY, JULY 29TH

It was *Tisha B'Av*, "the ninth of Av," the Hebrew day of fast that
commemorates the destruction of both the First Temple in Jerusalem
by the Babylonians in 586 BCE and the Second Temple, on the
very same day, by the Romans 655 years later. After the Romans
destroyed the First Temple, the Jews went into exile from Babylonia;
after the Second Temple, from the Holy Land. It has been called the
saddest day in Jewish history.

That morning, Maria called Satchi to her side. "Honey, I have
something I want to tell you." She then reached out to take his hand.
He raised his eyes to meet hers. I sat across the bed from Satchi and
watched mother and child. "I can't begin to tell you how much I love
you. I love you with every ounce of my being. You're the most precious and important person in the universe. You may not know this,
but I truly believe that you're the reason I've lived so long. Seeing
you every day and being with you has kept me alive. You are the best
medicine in the world."

She spoke simply and haltingly, but there was a majestic timbre
to her voice, as though it came from a deep, archetypal place within.
Time stood still. Satchi started to cry, slight trembles rippled through

his body. Prana and I looked at each other, communicating with our eyes the nobility of the moment and our astonishment at the power of Maria's presence. Maria then asked Satchi to lean forward so she could hug him. She caressed his head, and the two cried together.

"I love you so much, Mommy."

"My sweet child," she whispered, "you're the best thing that ever happened to me. I wanted to be your mommy more than anything else. And being your mom has been the best thing I've ever done. Every day I pray for more time so I can savor another day with you. You're an incredible person, so loving, so kind, so beautiful from within. I am so proud of you. I am so fortunate, so blessed, to be your mom. I want you to know that I will love you forever, for always and always. I will always be with you."

Satchi's face glowed. His mother's words had penetrated his heart. I imagined a golden cord reaching from her heart to his.

FOUR HOURS LATER, Maria called Satchi to her side again. This time, he decided to sit in my lap. He must have sensed that this conversation would be different, harder.

"I've been thinking, honey. You can tell that I'm not doing well. I'm weaker than I've ever been. It must be so hard for you to see me this way, to see me getting weaker and weaker. I've tried to protect you, but I want to let you know what's happening, because you need to know."

Maria paused. Her eyes darted to find mine. She was about to cross the Rubicon. She wasn't looking for reassurance, but recognition. I communicated a lifetime of love and devotion with my face.

"My sweet child, I'm not going to beat this cancer. I'm going to die."

The aftershocks were immediate. Satchi convulsed in my arms. I held him tight, as wave after wave of grief coursed through his body.

Then my own little heart lost its limits in grief, and we cried together as Maria and Prana looked on.

"What am I going to do without you, Mommy?"

"Oh, honey, you and Dad are an amazing team. You love each other so much. You'll grieve together, and you'll miss me, and you *will* find a way to move on together. And I will always be inside of you. Whenever you miss me, you just have to look inside and you'll find me in yourself. I'm a part of you, my love. I always will be. I will never be far from you. I will always be as close to you as your own heart."

Satchi leaned his head back onto my shoulder and cried into my ear. I could feel the heat of his body against mine. It felt good.

IN MY LATE twenties, I had carefully copied an eighth-century Buddhist verse for Maria and framed it along with a line drawing of a woman's body. It read, "Here in this body are the sacred rivers: here are the sun and moon, as well as all the pilgrimage places . . . I have not encountered another temple as blissful as my own body." Maria hung the framed picture in our bedroom, next to her wall mirror. Twenty-two years later, it still hangs there.

She can no longer see it, but I pass it several times a day, and remind myself that when the temple is destroyed, when the last breath leaves the body, this diaspora will return home.

MONDAY, JULY 30TH

For many years, a picture of a four- or five-year-old Maria adorned with angel wings sat atop our dresser. Under the picture, Maria had affixed a slip from a fortune cookie that said, "God is not done with you yet."

God is not done with Maria yet, or with me.

THEIR CONVERSATION LOOKED conspiratorial: she leaning in close to Maria, Maria casting quick glances in my direction, hushed voices. By the third time I looked up from my book at Maria and our friend Margo, who owes a jewelry store in Berkeley, I began to wonder what plan they were hatching. Just then, Maria called me over.

Even before she spoke, she started to cry. "I've been wanting to talk to you about getting me a diamond." Our thirty-year history washed over me in an instant. When we married in our mid-twenties, I couldn't afford diamonds. When I could, we'd long since decided that such material objects weren't important to us. But maybe something had changed. For Valentine's Day the year before, Maria had bought me a silver ring with a small diamond, and I loved receiving that symbol of her eternal love for me.

"I've always wanted a diamond, but I haven't wanted to ask. You've sacrificed so much for me while battling this illness. And the financial burdens have been so great. I've watched you suffer under the weight of it all. But I worry that maybe you don't love me, maybe you've never loved me in the kind of way that would make you want to buy me a diamond. And now I'm dying."

"Oh my God, Maria. I had no idea. I'm so sorry. I never knew you wanted a diamond." I took her hand and started to cry, as Margo looked on. "I wish I'd known. I feel so badly that you're not sure of my love for you. It's not for my lack of love. I've just been so overwhelmed with everything that I haven't even thought to buy you one."

"I know you've been consumed with taking care of me and making sure I get the best of everything. But I've wanted you to know to buy me one, without my having to tell you."

A small part of me felt defensive, but I knew what I said next had the power to heal a lifetime of longing to feel loved. I said truthfully, "I've totally screwed up, Maria. I want to get you a diamond. Really."

With a glimmer in her eye, she said, "Well, Margo and I have worked it all out already. She's going to bring a small teardrop diamond pendant over in the next day or two as a placeholder for a larger, round one, which she has to make."

"That's what you've been talking about?"

"Uh huh."

"You know," I joked, "You didn't have to go to such extremes to finally ask for a diamond."

Maria laughed. "I'm learning."

TUESDAY, JULY 31ST

The diamond teardrop arrived late in the afternoon. I opened its clasp and draped the chain around Maria's neck. She looked beautiful. She asked me to text a picture of her wearing it to Laurette Ferraresi, her psychologist at the Block Center. Maria, I learned, had spoken to Laurette many times over the years about wanting a diamond, but especially during the last months of her life. She didn't know how to broach the issue with me. And week after week she talked herself out of mentioning it.

Laurette called and asked to talk to Maria. The two delighted in Maria's accomplishment, and Maria and I laughed about how therapists should break confidentiality to tell thick husbands about diamonds.

WEDNESDAY, AUGUST 1ST

We began preparing for death. Hospice workers taught us how to turn and clean Maria's body, now that she was bedbound, and how to manage her pain more precisely. For as long as possible, Maria told RaeLynne, our hospice nurse, she didn't want the pain medication to interfere with her consciousness. She'd tried morphine after her surgery at Stanford and found that it deadened her awareness and sapped her life force.

"Anything but morphine," she told RaeLynne. "I want to be clear and present to my own death and to my family." We settled on several other drugs (oxycodone, which Maria had been taking since the surgery, and methadone) and agreed to hold off on the morphine until it was absolutely necessary—when Maria's desire to be pain free was greater than her desire to remain conscious.

At sunset all that week, Maria had spurts of energy during which she wanted to talk about her final wishes. She was sure of two things: She wanted her female friends to come to our home after she died to clean, anoint, and shroud her body—no funeral home viewing, no strangers touching her body—only her girlfriends, who have cared for her body and her soul. She had learned of this ritual of honoring the body of the deceased from her friend, Rabbi Diane Elliot, and asked that I contact Diane to make sure she could preside over the ritual.

And she wanted to be cremated, and for me to distribute her ashes among her loved ones and friends so they could spread them where they had spent time with her in nature.

Later, upon hearing this, Prana said, "It's a triumph for Maria to trust people with her ashes," an implicit recognition that, within days, Maria had relinquished control over every aspect of care for her body and surrendered to the ministrations of her loved ones.

THURSDAY, AUGUST 2ND

Maria continued to bless us with her presence. All week, hospice staff had told me that she could die any day. ("But she's a young woman," RaeLynne added, "and I've seen young women hold on for a day or two more.") Her body is barely functioning, but her life force and sense of humor keep her anchored here in the center of our life. Recently, as two friends bent over her bed, each attending to a different need, she said, "I've never seen as much cleavage as I have the last two weeks." Even Maria laughed at her own predicament.

The previous night, Prana and I stayed up with her for most of the night. She needed our companionship as she worked through layers of fear about leaving her body. When Maria fell asleep, Prana told me that, at the time of his death, her husband had suspected a recurrence of a childhood cancer. He knew something in his body was terribly wrong; he had written as much in his diary. After his death, Prana learned that cancer had indeed spread throughout his body. If he'd lived, she would likely have had to help him die, much as she is now helping Maria die.

"By sending me here, Amma is giving me the opportunity I didn't have to serve Phil."

By sunrise, Maria was radiating peace and joy—a truly remarkable transformation in the dark of the night.

She slept holding a picture of Amma close to her heart. Our home took on the feel of a sanctuary—a hushed reverence, a mindfulness, even a kind of joyful expectancy, as though we were preparing for a birth. Friends and family provided love and care and support so we could walk with Maria to edge of the known universe. The first shift of caregivers arrived before breakfast to cook meals, do laundry, run errands, and sit by Maria's side; the last cleaned up after dinner, leaving Prana and me alone with Maria. On most days, my dad arrived late in the morning, bringing bagels and lox and a Greek salad with garbanzo beans.

"How's Maria doing?" he asked every day as he walked through the kitchen door.

"Not so well, Dad. She's going to die soon."

"Ahh, shit," he said, and then took his seat at the kitchen table to talk about Stella and his double loss.

THE SECOND DIAMOND arrived. I opened the jewelry box and was ready to fasten it around Maria's neck when she forcefully said, "The words!" Prana furrowed her brow and looked at me, questioningly. I smiled. I knew exactly what Maria wanted. I got to my knees and took a deep breath.

"You will always be my bride. When I look at you, I still see that radiant girl that I fell in love with at Princeton. You remember when we fell into the snow at Princeton, and we looked into each other's eyes. Well, I knew then that I wanted you. And the wonder and awe I felt in that moment has never changed for me. Through everything, my love has only gotten stronger. It's eternal. Nothing can ever stop it from flowing toward you. It feels like a rushing river."

I stopped. Those Princeton eyes had tears in them again. I could tell she needed me to say *all* the words. I allowed the river to carry me downstream.

"I have loved you with every ounce of my being. I wish I had laid diamonds at your feet, my dear. That still wouldn't measure what we've had in this lifetime. But if you will marry me again, my bride, I'd want to offer you this small diamond. It would give me great pleasure and joy if you would have me again. It would seal our love forever. Please have me."

Too weak to talk, she devoured me with her eyes. Utter delight. Then, she said, "Now!"

I unclasped the teardrop diamond and adorned her frail chest with her first diamond from her husband.

FRIDAY, AUGUST 3RD

With each breath, Maria whispered Amma's name. Some say it's a blessing to die with one of God's names on your lips.

Our time together in the previous twenty-four hours had been stunningly, exquisitely, beautifully heart opening. Laurie arrived late the night before. We slept very little. The urgency of the moment imbued us with energy. I was receiving so many gifts from Maria, even in her death.

SATURDAY, AUGUST 4TH

Maria's life force persisted.

She was still with us, aware and present when not in a deep place of birthing her Self. Diane told us that it can be very hard for the soul to separate from the body when the body has fought so hard to stay alive—and enjoyed life so much. In the middle of the night, Maria turned to Laurie and said, "I want to go home." To me, the next morning, she said, "I don't know if it's worth it anymore." By "it," she meant staying in the body. And yet, the body continued, tenaciously, to hold on.

Every half day or so, Maria signaled to us that she was dying, and we would call Satchi from his room or the playground or a friend's house, congregate at her side, and meditate on her in and out breath, waiting for the last expiration. By the third or fourth time, when she didn't die, I began to feel the exhaustion at the heart of this process, not unlike a pregnant woman at forty-two weeks who loves her unborn child but just wants to birth the damn baby.

Satchi and I talked about how hard it is to hold such complex feelings as wanting your mom/wife to live and yet knowing you'll feel relief when she passes and you can start to live more freely again, without cancer as the focal point. He was relieved to know that what we were feeling was normal, and expressible, even if heartbreaking.

After our conversation, I showed him a letter I'd found the day before as I went through Maria's secret closet drawer. She'd written it before her surgery at Stanford the year before, fearing she might die during surgery. It included her last words to him. He read it quickly, almost hungrily, and stashed it in his own secret desk drawer.

SUNDAY, AUGUST 5TH

I dreamed I had returned to my childhood home in New Jersey. The white fence that surrounded the property on three sides no longer existed. I stood on the front lawn, disoriented, and looked for the familiar boundary. There was something attractive, almost irresistible, about its absence, but the freedom it promised was also frightening. I'd spent my childhood confined by that fence, and now it was gone. I stood there immobilized as I contemplated a life without my familiar white fence.

I awoke from my dream and walked downstairs for my middle-of-the-night shift to learn that a skunk had sprayed our cat, Chaipaw. In Native American tradition, skunks represent respect for boundaries. You test a boundary, and you can get sprayed. Ever in tune with Maria, Chaipaw was now also testing boundaries.

In the previous twenty-four hours Maria's breathing had exhibited the Cheyne-Stokes pattern, which announces the final stages of life in the body: a short few breaths followed by a long, silent apnea. As death approaches, the apnea phase lasts longer and longer. For most of the night, the pause had lasted for ten seconds; now it was up to fifteen seconds. It can last for up to fifty seconds.

In some patients, but not all, a gasping for air follows the apnea. My mom gasped for several hours at the end of her life. The sound broke my heart, though the hospice worker assured me she was in no pain.

That night, Tom, one of Maria's closest friends from college, would arrive from New York City. Maria had asked for him to come the week before, but he was out of the country. She'd cried and grieved his absence when she learned she wouldn't see him again. I decided not to tell Maria that he was arriving until the last moment. I didn't want her to prolong her already pronounced labor. But perhaps the veil was thin, and she already sensed his imminent arrival.

Boundaries are dissolving for all of us.

MONDAY, AUGUST 6TH

Maria awoke suddenly and said, "Food." Then, "More food, always."

We gave her goat milk rice pudding with ginger. For years, she and I had tried religiously to feed her more of the right food, in the hopes of reviving her body and fighting cancer. Feeding her that day, I realized I'd harbored an unconscious fantasy that she would rebound from the brink of death, start to eat more food, and then recover fully. My heart broke as I shed one more level of attachment to Maria getting healthy.

After three tiny spoons of rice pudding, Maria told Laurie that benevolent beings had come to her and were instructing her to faint. "But I'm afraid to faint," she said, each word spoken deliberately and slowly. Her brain is closing down from lack of oxygen, and finding words, a higher left-brain function, is hard in the absence of oxygen.

"Letting go of the body can feel like fainting," Laurie explained. "When you transition from one state to another, you can lose your ground momentarily." She asked if Maria could let herself give way to the fainting, adding that one of her teachers once told her, "When you feel faint, simply allow yourself to fall backwards into the hands of love."

Maria's eyes were closed. Secretions coated her long lashes, making it hard to keep her eyes open. But she nodded.

In a soothing, loving voice, Laurie continued, "You have everything you need internally to let go. You have trusted falling into the arms of your loved ones many times in your adult life. You just have to trust one more time when you're ready."

Maria's lucidity lasted for half an hour longer. I applied warm compresses to her eyelids to soften the yellow discharge. She opened her eyes.

I said, "You're so amazingly lucid and clear, Maria."

She demurred. "I feel confused," she whispered, and then she seemed to go away again. I imagined her returning to her benevolent friends and deepening her dialogue with them about letting go and falling into the hands of love.

TOM WOULD ARRIVE in two hours. Once he had boarded the plane in New York, since it appeared Maria was still strong, I told her Tom was on his way.

"Good," she said.

TUESDAY, AUGUST 7TH

Maria's reunion with Tom was glorious. Unable to speak, she held his hand and gazed into his face, beaming love, delight, and relief. She quickly slid back into sleep. Then Prana and I pointed out to

Tom the jewelry she had carefully selected to wear. Next to her diamond necklace, she wore the necklace Satchi had had made for her, emeralds, interspersed among green tourmaline beads, and one ruby to symbolize his love. On one ear, she wore a blue sapphire earring, also from Satchi, and on the other, an emerald earring Tom had given her at Princeton, when they were dating. Tom and I, on either side of her bed—he holding one of her hands, and I the other— talked deep into the night.

"What, where, when?" Maria asked when she awoke.

Prana and I oriented her, reminding her that Tom and Laurie had to leave: Tom that day, as planned, but Laurie the next, unexpectedly, to return home for medical tests. Though Maria and I were previously unaware of any problems, in an unimaginable twist of fate, Laurie had just learned from her doctor that she had breast cancer and needed to return immediately to discuss treatment options.

"And Satchi's birthday is in two days," I added. "I've been worried about the possibility of your dying on Satchi's birthday. I know it's been on your mind, too." She nodded. "We've had to cancel Satchi's birthday party. Is there anything you can do to affect the timing of your passing?"

With authority and finality, she said, "I'm in control of nothing."

I sensed that she was repeating something she'd been told in her journeys inward. It felt like a pronouncement, like wisdom. Perhaps the benevolent friends had told her this.

Later she said, "I want to talk to my momma." I called Jane, who'd just been with us for a week, and mother and daughter videochatted, though Maria largely just smiled and communicated with her eyes. Jane told us about a very good friend of hers whose mother died on her birthday.

"My friend says it's the best gift her mother could ever have given her."

I was grateful for the reframing. It opened up the possibility that if Maria's "birth" day overlapped with Satchi's birthday, he could write his own script about its meaning. It need not be a tragic convergence, a life sentence to hold his birthday hostage every year.

Prana and I have become curious about Maria's birth, wondering if the way she entered the world might shed any light on how she's leaving it: carefully, making sure every last detail is lined up before committing. I asked Jane what she remembered of Maria's birth.

"It was unremarkable," she said. "My labor wasn't very long. In those days, of course, everyone was drugged, so I didn't feel any pain. Though, now that I think of it, Maria arrived ten days after her due date. She came into the world with her own timing."

"Just as we suspected," I said. "In my beginning is my end."

Maria began to tire. She and Jane held each other's gaze for a long time. Tom, Laurie, Prana, Satchi, and I sat in silence.

"I love you, honey," Jane said. "I have always loved you."

"I love you, Momma." Then, "I love you too much."

"You can never love too much," Jane answered tenderly. "Surely Amma has taught you that."

WEDNESDAY, AUGUST 8TH

"The more I get to know Maria," RaeLynne said, when I told her Maria was awake for much of the night, conscious and communicating, "the more I realize I don't know her, and what she's capable of."

Maria's confounded our hospice team; they had said she was not likely to survive for twenty-four more hours every day since the previous Friday. More strikingly, they were impressed by how conscious and alert she continued to be, monitoring her care and initiating conversations about her life, death, and wishes.

When a nurse walked in that morning, Maria was in the middle of a conversation with Prana and me. In barely audible and halting words, she recounted how, when she was seven years old, she felt truly connected to herself.

"After that, there was pressure to become someone other than *my* self. I lost that innocent connection to who I was." She paused for a long time, looking at both of us, her right eye stuck shut. "People expected me to be a certain way. To become someone I wasn't. That took me away from myself. I've spent my life trying to get back in touch with *my* self. With who I am. Now I need your help to complete that. I want to die being exactly who I am."

"What can we do to help you?" Prana asked.

"I'm not sure."

"Just by telling us, you're well on your way," I said and kissed her on the forehead, amazed at how she continued to grow even as the body deteriorated—at how she was using death to blossom.

THURSDAY, AUGUST 9TH

It was almost midnight. I'd been watching the clock for hours. In fifteen minutes, Maria would have survived Satchi's tenth birthday. She'd held his hand that morning, with obvious joy in her eyes, and sang him a fragile, abridged version of "Happy Birthday"—what she could still remember of the song. The joy of the moment was painful to watch.

Afterward, Prana and I felt conflicted about whether to take Satchi out to dinner to celebrate. We had not yet left the house together, and Maria had gotten used to our continual presence. She looked distressed whenever I broached the issue. RaeLynne encouraged us to go, saying it was important for us to take our space apart from Maria. She added, "Sometimes people need their loved ones to leave the house so they can die." It had not entered my mind that perhaps *our* presence might also make it harder for Maria to die. She had become attached to the idea that we would be with her, by her bedside, when she died. For all of us, this was no ordinary dinner.

Prana spoke to Maria in private and offered to stay. Torn between her own need and her wish to overcome her need, and to give Satchi his birthday wish, Maria said, "No, I want to share them with you, it's just that *I* want to go, too."

When we prepared to leave, Maria protested, even though two friends, Robyn and Joan, sat by her side and held her hands. She sobbed and called out after me. My heart broke. I turned my back and snuck out of the house. I could hear her anguished cries as I left.

SATURDAY, AUGUST 11TH

As the days turn into weeks, we're getting to live intimately with the beautiful poetics of impermanence and dying. Every moment spent with Maria's body and mind reminds me that we're all slowly, imperceptibly heading toward our own reunion with the vast stillness from which we all arise and take human birth. A wrinkle around the eyes, a strand of gray hair, an ache in the knees, a forgotten word: all signal that nothing stays the same, that we are slouching toward death. Everything points in that direction, even, poignantly, our children's birthdays, which we celebrate with great joy. Death is our constant companion.

I sat next to Maria as she slept, watching her thin heartbeat pulse next to her rising and falling throat. Her blood pressure was so weak the hospice nurses hadn't been able to measure it, though her heart rate had remained steady over the previous two weeks, sixty beats per minute, give or take. Cheyne-Stokes had come and gone, and returned again, and left once more.

Recently, Maria had told Prana and me she wanted to die. It was the middle of the night—again—and the "Sri Lalitha Sahasranamam" (The Thousand Names of the Divine Mother) was playing in the background, just loud enough to register in awareness but without demanding attention. Maria asked us to take her arms and hands— she couldn't move them on her own—and to gently allow them to float down to her sides, as though they were wings opening her heart to surrender. We floated her arms as instructed. Her breathing slowed. Peace crossed her face.

"You're falling back into love," Prana observed. "Trusting."

In the morning, Maria said she wasn't ready to die. "I want to live for two or three more days."

Exhausted, spent, feeling powerless, I grew angry. Taking Prana aside, I said, "I can't take this anymore. I just want her to die. What does she mean, two or three more days? Hasn't she had enough?" The strength of my reaction startled me. I continued to rant, listing all the ways I've felt frustrated and thwarted by my wife's need to be in control. Prana listened. She knows us better than anyone. She has heard and seen it all. I looked across the room at Maria's broken body, her eyes glued shut. My breathing slowed.

"Oh, my God," I said. A weight lifted from my soul. "I thought I'd already come to terms with our history. But I have to surrender it all completely for Maria to die. She's giving me more time so we can sew up loose threads in our marriage."

I WAS COUNTING Maria's breaths: sometimes eight short breaths in a minute; sometimes fifteen long, grounded ones. A bit of quick math yields anywhere between twelve and twenty-two thousand breaths in the day. During periods of apnea, I'd waited anxiously for the next breath. That had changed. Now I sat and enjoyed the stillness in her face and the peace that came between breaths. There was no effort in between. It was the anticipation of the next one that churned the mind.

How would I want to spend the last ten thousand breaths of my life?

Earlier Maria had awoken and said, "Familiar beings are inviting me through the door. I don't want to go through the door."

"What door?" I asked.

She didn't answer.

"You don't want to die?" I asked.

"Yeah."

"You want to live?"

"Yeah."

We sat in silence. I wondered what was on the other side of that door. I wondered if her benevolent friends were inviting her to enter again, and how much choice she had to delay. I said, "I can understand why you want to live. You have so much that keeps you here: Satchi, me, your family, your friends, all your dreams."

"Yeah."

"And yet you're lying on a bed. You can't move. Life is going on around you and you're in so much pain. And the pain keeps getting worse, every day. And that's not going to change. You're alive, but what a terrible price to pay."

"Yeah."

"Oh, Maria. My heart breaks for you. What a terrible dilemma. I wish it were otherwise."

Silence.

Long pause. Then Maria said, "I love you so much."

"I love you, too. I always have and always will, forever. I love
you so much I want to you to be free from this body. I want to you
be one with Amma's love and light."

"Yeah."

I don't know what I would choose: Amma's peace or one more
moment of embodiment. I pray that I never have to face such a
choice. But if it meant another moment with my child or my beloved,
I might choose to fight a battle that can't be won.

LATER, IN MARIA'S presence, I narrated the conversation to Prana.
Several people had described how frightening it could be for children
when a dying parent crosses a certain pain threshold—when they're
in constant, unremitting pain.

"Wouldn't it be beautiful to show Satchi that you could choose
to die with acceptance?" Prana said to her. "You've fought so
bravely. Now you can show him how to face every transition in life
by embracing what's to come next wholeheartedly." Prana stopped,
put her hand on Maria's shoulder, and continued, "You've already
given him this gift. You've shown him well. You've been an incredible mother."

Maria's face softened. She opened her mouth. No words.

Then, Prana added, "He has everything he needs inside already.
He's self-confident that he can face life and trust himself. Maybe it
could be scary for him to see you continue to suffer and feel more
and more pain."

I could tell Maria was listening intently.

"It could be a gift to leave your body before you suffer more—
when you can take life and death as one great adventure, without
any fear or hesitation. That would be an amazing gift to receive for
the rest of his life."

THERE WAS NO waste to this time. Every moment is precious. Every precious moment is fleeting. We fall through impermanence into love.

SUNDAY, AUGUST 12TH

Maria's eyes darted up to the ceiling and then to the left, over my shoulder. She labored to speak. "There . . . are . . . friendly . . . beings . . . in . . . the . . . room."

"Really? Are they here now?"

"Yeah."

"Can you tell us about them? Are they helpers?"

"Yeah." Long pause. "They're helpers." Long pause again. Then, "They are innocent. They are innocent friends."

Prana and I smiled at each other.

"Innocent friends. How beautiful," I said.

"Yeah. Innocent. They . . . are . . . innocent."

MARIA STRAINED TO open her eyes. "I want to hasten my death."

"Do you know how to do that?" I asked.

"Uh-uh."

Pause. Silence.

"Dying is taking a lot of effort," I said.

"Yeah." Short pause. "Too much." Long pause. "It's not worth it anymore."

"DO YOU REMEMBER the conversation we had this morning? You told me you wanted to hasten your death. Do you want to keep talking about that?"

"Yeah."

I didn't know where to enter the conversation; I didn't want to steer it in the wrong direction. I waited, listening for guidance. Then,

"Do you remember telling me about your innocent friends, the ones who are helping you?"

"Yeah."

"Are they still hanging around?"

"Uh huh."

"Can you talk to them about how to hasten your death?"

"Uh huh."

Pause. Long silence. I didn't want to disturb whatever dialogue might be happening between her and her innocent friends. Then, "Are they able to help you?"

"Uh huh."

Silence. I sat and prayed to the innocent friends for guidance about what to say next. Then, connecting the dots, I said, "Do you remember the other day you told me about a door?"

"Yeah."

"Can you ask your helpers if going through that door is something that would hasten your death?"

"Uh huh."

Long pause, as though Maria were preoccupied.

"Is going through that door something you can choose to do?"

Quietly, to me, Prana said, "I wonder if the door is already open and it's just a matter of walking through or if you have to be ready for the door to open."

I asked Maria, "Is the door a doorway that you step through, or do you have to open it first?"

Maria looked agitated. I had asked too many questions. We waited a long time. Then I said, "Are the helpers inviting you to go through the door again?"

Prana added, "Are you ready to go through the door?"

"Uh huh."

I LOOKED UP and noticed a very small mouse on the windowsill across the room. It was nibbling on a crumb. Prana walked over to the mouse, caught it in her hands as it climbed the curtains, and tried to free it through the open window. It jumped onto the floor and hid behind our red sofa chair. I brought Chaipaw into the living room to catch it. Within seconds, he was victorious and brought the mouse into the kitchen, where he played hockey puck with it, tossing it up in the air and batting it with his paws.

The tiny mouse escaped and hid under a plastic storage cart. Chaipaw thrust his paw under the cart, realized the folly of that strategy, and then jumped on top of it and waited. Thinking the danger gone, the mouse made a dash for the kitchen door. Chaipaw pounced and continued the torture. The mouse, exhausted and injured, surrendered. And Chaipaw lost interest and left the kitchen, sauntering outside. The mouse lay twitching on the floor.

I wondered why death had to be so cruel, why the mouse's demise had to be drawn out. I felt sorry for it and wanted to kill it to take it out of its misery. But I didn't have the heart. A friend put it in the compost. I prayed it would die soon.

MONDAY, AUGUST 13TH

We switched to liquid morphine. RaeLynne showed us how to tilt Maria's head so the morphine would travel along the crease between her cheek and gum, and, caught by gravity, drip down her throat. Her body had stiffened, and positioning her head and neck took a firmness and manipulation with which I was not comfortable. I imagined hurting her in the service of trying to forestall more pain. I had to suppress my feelings to do the things I had to do for her. I knew I would wake up months down the road and be haunted by images of the destruction of Maria's temple, a temple I have loved and worshipped in.

AS WE READIED Maria for bed, she said, almost inaudibly, "I just want to die . . . I just want to die . . . I just want to die." Then, "It's . . . not . . . worth . . . it . . . anymore."

Prana and I were too exhausted to keep watch at Maria's side. I asked a friend, Edith, to spend the night with her. I went to bed feeling guilty; the spirit was willing—I wanted to be with her that night—but the flesh was weak.

I checked on Maria in the middle of the night. Long stretches of apnea, followed by gasping. Jaw open. Cold hands. I kissed her on the forehead and returned to bed.

PRANA AND I turned Maria's body in the morning to see if her absorbent chux pad was wet. It wasn't. Her body had stopped draining. Then I tilted her head backward, moving it out of its natural curve and, using a syringe, slowly squirted morphine into the side of her mouth. She did not respond. The night before it would've been unthinkable to move her neck in that direction. The pain would've been excruciating. Now, I couldn't tell if I'd hurt her or not, and not knowing tormented me.

"Oh, my dear. Please forgive me. I can't tell anymore if I'm hurting you. I don't want to cause you any pain. I love you so much. If I'm hurting you, will you please forgive me?" I didn't expect a response.

She nodded twice.

AFTER A LATE breakfast, Satchi rose from the table and walked into the living room. I heard him pick up his eight-note kalimba, an African musical instrument his mother had given him for Christmas one year. He plucked a hauntingly beautiful song on the kalimba's metal bars. Prana and I, sitting in the kitchen, paused our conversation to listen.

We don't know exactly when Maria died, during Satchi's song or shortly thereafter, alone, when we were all out of the room. But I walked into the living room ten minutes later, at 11:08 a.m., and felt a wave of unearthly peace and stillness and joy wash over me. I knew Maria had begun to take flight of her body before I saw her. My intuition told me she had passed through the doorway into the heart of her beloved Divine Mother as her son serenaded her.

I closed her partially open eyes and tried to close her jaw, which had dropped and stiffened, but it would not yield to pressure. Satchi and Prana had gone outside and, when I called, came running to Maria's side. Out of breath, Satchi looked at me and knew without words that his mother had died. Spontaneously, Prana and I looked across Maria's body and smiled at each other. A celebratory air charged the space between us. Maria was victorious.

"You did it," Prana said triumphantly. "You were finally able to pass through the doorway."

I added, "I'm so relieved, my dear. You worked so hard. Now you're free."

Satchi had started to cry. Prana's and my joy gave way to the sadness Satchi was already expressing. Victory turned into disbelief and sadness. Satchi folded into my arms. Prana touched Maria's arm. Just as suddenly, again, our emotions shifted, and we felt the need to adorn her body. Satchi and Prana walked around the room, plucked white and yellow-pink rose petals from floral arrangements and reverently placed them one by one around Maria's still body, saving the white ones for her head. They placed a photo of Amma on her belly, a yellow orchid, resembling a butterfly in flight on her throat, and a pink lily at the top of her head. It appeared to reach upward with outstretched arms. I nestled Maria's wooden holding cross into the palm of her left hand, now lying on her chest, and prayed that God's infinite gifts would continue to grace my bride.

TUESDAY, AUGUST 14TH

Later on the day she died, thirteen of Maria's girlfriends gathered to perform the ritual cleansing. Led by Diane, they carried Maria's body from the living room up to our bedroom on her favorite surfboard, a Becker longboard. An hour later, they invited Satchi and me upstairs. They had cleansed and prayed over her body and wrapped her in a shroud her friend Carolyn had sewn especially for her. They left her face uncovered so Satchi and I could see it one last time, and placed flowers around her shrouded body, agapanthus, iris, and hydrangea—all in purple, Maria's favorite color—sprinkled among burnt orange, red, and yellow blossoms. Satchi and I placed flowers at her head.

Her friends then left Satchi, Prana, and me alone with Maria's body. I lay down next to her and held her close. Satchi, standing, and Prana looked on. I caressed Maria's face and noticed that her jaw, which had been open all day, was, miraculously, closed, and her lips formed into a smile. My hands explored her face, her chest, her belly, slowly, one last time. I felt unimaginable sadness at how much pain her body had endured, and reverence for the lifetime of service it provided to her and me and Satchi. I adored this now broken, dead body.

Out loud, I said, "It's been so long since I've been able to touch you without causing you discomfort. You're so beautiful, my dear, even in death."

I kissed her face. Satchi and I said good-bye. We left the bedroom and curled up downstairs on the couch as Maria's girlfriends finished their ritual.

When I saw Maria next, her face and smile were shrouded.

postscript

◆

FULFILLMENT

M Y SISTER-IN-LAW, ANNE, asked me if I wanted to say anything. Family members and out-of-town friends had congregated the night before Maria's memorial service, a month after Maria's death. I had not planned to speak, but before I could say No thank you, Anne, I found myself standing in front of forty people.

I began tentatively.

"I have nothing prepared, and I didn't plan on speaking tonight. But I've been so full of the most poignant moments of missing Maria and appreciating the life we had together. I wish we had thirty more years, because part of what our life together was about was learning how to love. I don't think we knew how to love when we were in our twenties. We worked each other very hard to learn, as our most intimate friends know.

"In the last few years, I finally felt like we had gotten to a point where we knew how to love. I didn't love her as a wife anymore, and I don't think she loved me as a husband. I think we were just devoted to each other and to something much deeper than the roles we were supposed to play for each other. And I feel robbed, in this moment, of being able to enjoy that with *her*. . . .

"I know there'll be others—friends, loved ones, who knows who'll walk into my life—but I wish it were Maria. And I wish I could continue to bring to fulfillment the love we learned together for the rest of our lives.

"I'm aware as I stand next to this guy"—I tousled Satchi's hair— "that he got to be a part of us learning. He also got to be a part of us bringing what we had learned to life, because we learned how to be so very kind to each other, even when we were disappointed in each other. And I hope that love and kindness comes into fulfillment in his life much sooner than it did in mine.

"I'm so grateful to Maria. She's the greatest teacher I've ever had. I'll never meet anyone else like her, because I'll never be twenty, thirty, or forty again. I can't do that again. It'll be different.

"And this is the last thing I'll say. A friend from Princeton sent me a note recently to say she bumped into me on campus right after I had a reunion with Maria as a junior, back in 1983.

"She wrote, 'Someone caught your eye, and you smiled and said, "There she is." I said, "Who?" You pointed me to a woman who was walking away from us, so all I could see was her back, with brown hair down to her shoulder blades. You said, "Maria." I asked, "Who's Maria?" And you had this beautiful smile and said, "She's the one."'

"I don't remember that conversation, but I trust my friend. She's a journalist. I know she got it right. So even when I was twenty-one at the time, I guess I knew she was the one for the first thirty years of my intimate life.

"And I miss her like crazy."

acknowledgments

A NNE BLESSING WAS the first person to encourage me to write about our cancer experience and a voice throughout to remind me that I was up to the task of writing a book while caring for her sister. Anne Cushman read the manuscript at various points in its evolution and provided invaluable advice about crafting a story. Alan Rinzler, my developmental editor, found the book within the longer manuscript and ably set the course for the work before you. Serina Garst, generous of her time, helped me navigate the maze of legal and intellectual property issues. Several people read all or parts of this manuscript and offered useful advice: Carolyn West, who inspired me to trust my writing voice; my father, Manny Metaxas; Charlotte Gyllenhaal; Linda Polsby; and my proofreader, Becca Freed.

The final version of this book owes much to several people: Prana Carpenter, who not only did an intelligent job of whittling it to the bone but also offered invaluable counsel about matters of the heart. Leslie Tilley, my copyeditor, who saw meaningful distinctions where none existed in my mind. Kimberly Glider, my jacket designer, who brought my jacket concept to fruition. And Megan Jones, whose simple and elegant interior layout captured the delicacy of our lives during this period.

It would be impossible to thank everyone who supported my family and me during the time I worked on this book. The truth is, we simply could not have survived the last few years without the magnanimous outpouring of support—financial, practical, emotional, spiritual—from family and devoted friends and neighbors in Berkeley and Kenilworth, and even strangers who heard about our ordeal and were moved to help.

In particular, I want to thank my mother-in-law and step-father-in-law, Jane and Hunter deButts, who gave generously, repeatedly, enabling us to stay afloat financially, and our friends John Adams, Tom Scherer, Georgia Nugent, and Shannon Hackett, who made it possible for us to have sanctuary when we were far from home.

My son, Satchi Grayson Metaxas, made great sacrifices while I worked on this book and graciously blessed its publication. He inspired me every day.

Maria Grayson-Metaxas, my wife, gave everything, and now nothing remains but love.

Amma, my constant companion, continues to shower me with grace.

Made in the USA
Las Vegas, NV
14 February 2021